VIRUS ALERT

Virus Alert

Security, Governmentality, and the AIDS Pandemic

STEFAN ELBE

 Columbia University Press *New York*

Columbia University Press
Publishers Since 1893
New York   Chichester, West Sussex

Library of Congress Cataloging-in-Publication Data
Elbe, Stefan, 1975–
Virus alert : security, governmentality, and the AIDS pandemic / Stefan Elbe.
p. cm.
Includes bibliographical references and index.
ISBN 978-0-231-14868-9 (cloth : alk. paper)
ISBN 978-0-231-52005-8 (e-book)
1. Security, International.   2. National security.
3. AIDS (Disease)—Political aspects. I. Title.
JZ6005.E43 2009
355'.033—dc22
2009000323

∞

Columbia University Press books are printed on permanent and durable acid-free paper.
Printed in the United States of America
c 10 9 8 7 6 5 4 3 2 1

References to Internet Web sites (URLs) were accurate at the time of writing.
Neither the author nor Columbia University Press is responsible for URLs
that may have expired or changed since the manuscript was prepared.

To Aris

In fact we have a triangle: sovereignty, discipline and governmental management, which has population as its main target and apparatuses of security as its essential mechanism.

—MICHEL FOUCAULT

CONTENTS

ACKNOWLEDGMENTS

Over the past couple of years many people have provided valuable comments on the wider research project that formed the basis of this book. In particular I would like to thank Tanja Aalberts, Chris Alden, Andreas Antoniades, Claudia Aradau, Tarak Barkawi, Tony Barnett, Roxanne Bazergan, Mats and Dominique Berdal, J. Peter Burgess, David Campbell, Malcolm Chalmers, Christopher Coker, Martin Coward, Mick Dillon, Jenny Edkins, Stuart Elden, Harley Feldbaum, Earl Gammon, James Hentz, Jens Hilscher, Yanzhong Huang, Jef Huysmans, Elke Krahmann, Ulf Kristoffersson, Philippe Le Billon, Luis Lobo-Guerrero, Colin McInnes, Antonio Missiroli, Rens van Munster, Andrea Oelsner, Robert Ostergard Jr., Sarah Percy, Karen Lund Petersen, Fabio Petito, Andrew Price-Smith, Julian Reid, Hakan Seckinelgin, Martin Shaw, Monica Singhal, Nadine Voelkner, Alex de Waal, Alan Whiteside, and Maja Zehfuss. I have benefited immensely from further feedback received at the International Institute for Strategic Studies in London, the International Peace Research Institute in Oslo, the Geneva Center for Security Policy, the Goodenough Trust, the 21st Century Trust, and several conventions of the International Studies Association. I would also like to thank the graduate students who attended my courses on international security and the global politics of disease at the University of Sussex. I feel particularly indebted to the anonymous reviewers of this manuscript and to my editor, Anne Routon, all of whom went far beyond the call of duty and who helped to improve the manuscript immeasurably. My deepest gratitude, finally, goes to Louiza Odysseos. Without her, it would not have been possible to finish this book, and it is she who ultimately makes the endeavor worthwhile.

Part of the research conducted for this book was supported through a grant made available by the British Academy (BARDA-47928).

A different version of chapter 4 has appeared under the title "Should HIV/AIDS Be Securitized? The Ethical Dilemmas of Linking HIV/AIDS and Security," *International Studies Quarterly* 50, no. 1 (2006): 119–144.

VIRUS ALERT

1 / VIRUSES, HEALTH, AND INTERNATIONAL SECURITY

Viruses are back on the international agenda—and not just as a matter of low politics. Infectious disease actually became the subject of international diplomacy as early as 1851, when delegates of the first International Sanitary Conference gathered in Paris to consider joint responses to the cholera epidemics that had overrun the European continent in the first half of the nineteenth century. During the twentieth century, though, the pertinence of controlling potentially pandemic microbes was gradually overshadowed by the more pressing concerns of avoiding the specter of renewed wars and the ever-present potential for a nuclear confrontation. The twentieth century's deep addiction to war, coupled with its important advances in medicine, reinforced the view in the West that that the world was moving in a direction that would eventually see infectious diseases controlled—a view that was quintessentially exemplified by the confident declaration made in 1948 by U.S. Secretary of State George Marshall that the conquest of all infectious diseases was imminent (Garrett 1994; Patocka 1996; Whitman 2000:1).

Over the course of the past decade that confidence has been profoundly shaken. At the outset of the twenty-first century there is once again considerable international anxiety about a host of potentially lethal "rogue" viruses circulating upon the planet—ranging from relatively new ones such as the highly pathogenic H5N1 strand of avian influenza and the corona virus responsible for severe acute respiratory syndrome (SARS), to the globally much more widespread human immunodeficiency virus (HIV) that causes AIDS. Other infectious diseases such as tuberculosis, malaria, and cholera have made devastating comebacks. If we add to this mix a string of rarer but nevertheless disconcerting microbes such as Ebola, West Nile virus, hantavirus, and the Nipah virus, then we could say that the world is currently experiencing an "epidemic of epidemics" (Whitman 2000:2). The optimism of the twentieth century—misplaced in considering viruses to be geographically containable and evolutionarily stationary—has given way to a renewed sense of unease (Garrett 1996:67).

Nowhere is this growing international anxiety more evident than in the choice of several international organizations, governments, and nongovernmental organizations to begin formulating the response to these infectious diseases in the language of security—thereby abandoning the decades-old convention of equating security with the absence of armed conflict between states (Fidler 2003; McInnes and Lee 2006). Infectious diseases are increasingly being debated and discussed as pressing existential threats that require urgent and extraordinary international policy responses; they are, in short, becoming "securitized" (Buzan, Wæver, and de Wilde 1998). The antecedents of this securitization can be traced back to 1989, when the U.S. National Institutes of Health and Rockefeller University cosponsored an influential conference on "emerging viruses" that was attended by more than two hundred participants, including many distinguished scientists and public health experts (King 2002:766). The Institute of Medicine of the National Academy of Sciences followed in 1992 with a widely read report titled *Emerging Infections: Microbial Threats to Health in the United States*, which warned:

> As the human immunodeficiency virus (HIV) pandemic surely should have taught us, in the context of infectious diseases, there is nowhere in the world from which we are remote and no one from whom we are disconnected. Consequently, some infectious diseases that now affect people in other parts of the world represent potential threats to the United States because of global interdependence, modern transportation, trade, and changing social and cultural patterns. (Lederberg, Shope, and Oaks 1992:v)

Evidence that these concerns were also beginning to register at the highest levels of the U.S. government emerged in 1995, when its interagency Working Group on Emerging and Re-emerging Infectious

Diseases (part of the U.S. National Science and Technology Council, Committee on International Science, Engineering, and Technology [CISET]) similarly cautioned about the growing "threat." Globalization, understood broadly as the compression of space and time, seemed to be creating new avenues for infectious diseases to spread quickly, as well as fostering new breeding grounds for them to emerge—be it through progressive environmental degradation or the growth of mega-cities. Add to this the rampant rise in the rate of cross-border travel in goods and people, and the United States seemed vulnerable to a pandemic outbreak of infectious disease, even if such an outbreak initially occurred outside its borders. By 1996 acceptance of these arguments had reached a sufficient level among senior officials in the United States that President Clinton issued a presidential decision directive explicitly calling for a more focused U.S. policy on infectious diseases with the aims of establishing a worldwide infectious disease surveillance and response system and expanding certain federal agency mandates to better protect the lives of American citizens.

As part of this new effort, the U.S. National Intelligence Council produced an influential national intelligence estimate titled *The Global Infectious Disease Threat and Its Implications for the United States.* The findings of the report, declassified in January 2000, confirmed many of these fears by pointing out that since 1973 at least thirty previously unknown disease agents have been identified (including some for which there is no cure, such as HIV, Ebola, hepatitis C, and the Nipah virus). It also found that during the same period at least twenty older infectious diseases have reemerged, frequently in drug-resistant form—most notably tuberculosis (TB), malaria, and cholera. According to the report,

> new and reemerging infectious diseases will pose a rising global health threat and will complicate US and global security over the next 20 years. These diseases will endanger US citizens at home and abroad, threaten US armed forces deployed overseas, and exacerbate social and political instability in key countries and regions in which the United States has significant interests. (NIC 2000a)

These findings were subsequently expanded upon by a number of influential think tanks, including the Center for Strategic and International Studies and the Chemical and Biological Arms Control Institute (Ban 2001; CBACI 2000). Such arguments were also given considerable scholarly grounding in the influential and pioneering work of Andrew Price-Smith, whose book-length study *The Health of Nations* concluded that "public health problems interact synergistically to threaten national security and national interests both through direct and indirect processes" (2001:139). The securitization of infectious diseases was now beginning to reach a much wider audience.

Within the broader securitization of infectious diseases, HIV/AIDS has been repeatedly singled out. As early as 1990 a few pioneering analysts at the U.S. Central Intelligence Agency had already begun to systematically analyze the likely impact of the AIDS pandemic on the political stability of foreign countries and U.S. interests abroad. To be allocated the time and resources necessary for examining this issue was a unique and unprecedented opportunity, as a similar request made only three years earlier, in 1987, had been turned down on the grounds that this was not an appropriate area in which to deploy CIA resources and that any impact on U.S. interests abroad would likely be benign (Gellman 2000). In 1991 the agency nevertheless produced a classified interagency intelligence memorandum (91-10005) projecting—remarkably accurately in retrospect—some 45 million HIV infections by 2000, but the report was still largely met with indifference as a critical mass of policymakers willing to embrace this new security dimension of HIV/AIDS did not yet exist (Gellman 2000). Nor had the situation changed much by 1994, when the Center for Strategic and International Studies produced another analysis of the wider social implications of the AIDS pandemic, including its security ramifications (CSIS 1994).

Yet by the end of the decade these arguments about HIV/AIDS and security began to be harnessed in a much more concerted manner by those with a specific interest in the international politics of HIV/AIDS— in part as a way of raising the profile and increasing the resources devoted to fighting the pandemic. The past few years have thus witnessed a deliberate attempt by policymakers to move beyond the health and development frameworks that had been widely used to address HIV/AIDS and to reposition the disease as a much more urgent matter of international security. By early May 2000 the Clinton administration even made the unprecedented gesture of designating HIV/AIDS a threat to the national security of the United States. Reports by nongovernmental organizations such as the Civil-Military Alliance to Combat HIV/AIDS (Yeager and Kingma 2001; Yeager and Ruscavage 2000) and the International Crisis Group (ICG 2001, 2004) further corroborated this relationship, as did a series of articles in prominent security and international relations journals (Eberstadt 2002; Elbe 2002; Ostergard 2002; Singer 2002).

How have the links between HIV/AIDS and security been drawn in these analyses? There has been considerable contestation among three different security frameworks utilized for analyzing the AIDS pandemic: *national security* (CSIS 2002; Harker 2001; Heinecken 2001a, 2001b; NIC 2000a; Price-Smith 2001a, 2002; Ostergard 2002, 2005; Sarin 2003; Yeager and Kingma 2001), *human security* (Elbe 2006a; Fourie and Schoenteich 2001; Kristoffersson 2000; Leen 2004; Pharao and Schoenteich 2003; Piot 2001), and *international security* (Bazergan 2001, 2003; Elbe 2003; GAO 2001; McInnes 2006; Price-Smith 1998; Prins 2004; Singer 2002; Tripodi and Patel 2002). One of the arguments linking HIV/AIDS and national security holds that the social, economic, and political stability of communities (and even entire states) could be undermined in the long run by a large disease burden. It is also argued that armed forces are particularly susceptible to HIV/AIDS, with controversial estimates indicating prevalence rates in some African armed forces ranging between 40 and 60 percent—raising concerns about combat effectiveness. With regard to human security, studies argue that HIV is a lethal virus and thus represents a direct threat to the human security of those who become infected, especially those without access to life-prolonging medicines. Beyond this direct mortality, HIV/AIDS is seen to have an important impact on other areas of human security because the effects of HIV/AIDS are not confined to individual human tragedies but have an abundance of wider political, economic, and social ramifications around the globe that will need to be carefully considered and addressed (Barnett and Whiteside 2002, 2006; Bloom and Godwin 1997; Garrett 1994; Godwin 1998; Holden 2003; Kalipeni 2004; Kauffman and Lindauer 2004; Kempe 1999; Linge and Porter 1997; Whiteside and Sunder 2000). In terms of international security it has been argued further that HIV/AIDS can also have a detrimental impact on great powers such as India, China, and Russia, that it could lead to wider pockets of instability in regions of sub-Saharan Africa with high prevalence rates, and that it is having important ramifications for international peace-keeping operations, which, because they are partially staffed by members of some of the armed forces with high prevalence rates, could serve as a vector of the illness where and when they are deployed.

These arguments have not fallen on deaf ears. Speaking before a Senate intelligence panel, George Tenet (2003), the former director of the Central Intelligence Agency, openly discussed the threat posed by HIV/AIDS alongside other pressing security issues ranging from terrorism and Iraq to North Korea. "The national security dimension of the virus is plain," he insisted. "It can undermine economic growth, exacerbate social tensions, diminish military preparedness, create huge social welfare costs, and further weaken already beleaguered states." In a historically unprecedented gesture, the threat of HIV/AIDS to international peace and security has even been the subject of six separate United Nations Security Council meetings held since January 2000 (meetings 4087, 4172, 4259, 4339, 4859, and 5228), rendering the AIDS pandemic the latest in a long line of wider social issues to become securitized. "Many of us," James Wolfensohn (2000), president of the World Bank, pointed out at the first of these historic meetings, "used to think of AIDS as a health issue. We were wrong. . . . We face a major development crisis, and more than that, a security crisis." The message of these meetings was clear: in the years ahead governments around the world would have to make it a political priority to reverse the scale and devastating effects of this pandemic. Unimaginable only a decade ago, HIV/AIDS is now widely recognized as an issue of international security.

By their very nature infectious diseases such as HIV/AIDS lend themselves particularly well to being portrayed as security issues. As David Campbell observes, viral discourses "have notions of insecurity in the form of systemic instability and vulnerability at their heart" (2008:15). Consisting merely of a piece of nucleic acid wrapped in a thin coat of protein, the human immunodeficiency virus that causes AIDS is imperceptible to the human eye and exists at the very margins of our conceptions of life. Human beings could be exposed to the virus at any time without knowing it, and die years later as a result. In this respect viruses are frequently portrayed as "silent" and "invisible" killers, and perhaps nothing is more frightening to many people than a lethal danger they have no way of detecting. Even the famous microbiologist Louis Pasteur, who pioneered the germ theory of disease, is said to have eventually developed an obsessive fear of microbes, refusing to shake hands with people, carefully wiping his plate before eating, and on more than one occasion even examining food served to him at a dinner party with his portable microscope! As in other areas of life, uncertainty tends to breed anxiety. Many viruses (including HIV) are also inherently parasitic; since they are unable to independently replicate their own existence, their only chance of survival consists of infecting the cells of a host organism in order to replicate. Evolutionary pressures thus favor viruses that are most adept at infecting (although not necessarily killing) other organisms—including human beings. "Viruses," Thomas Abraham notes, "evoke the same kinds of emotions in us as the great white shark or the giant carnivores from the age of the dinosaurs: a mixture of awe and terror at a form of life that is so basic, yet so perfectly suited to its ultimate purpose of preying on other forms of life" (2005:6). This innate and all too human fear of viruses also makes infectious diseases—including HIV/AIDS—particularly susceptible to being portrayed as security threats within contemporary policy debates.

Beyond these debates, the recent insertion of HIV/AIDS into deliberations about international security also raises three wider questions for the study of international relations—one empirical, one conceptual, and one political (Vieira 2007; Youde 2005). First, what social scientific evidence exists to justify this inclusion of HIV/AIDS on the international security agenda, and how robust is the empirical evidence invoked in these policy debates? Second, exactly what does the term "security" mean when it is used in relation to HIV/AIDS? Can this securitization be best understood with reference to national security, or to human security—or does it require an altogether different conceptualization of security that incorporates elements from both of these paradigms but also goes beyond them? Third, what are the political consequences of discussing HIV/AIDS in the language of security? Amid the pressing efforts to assess the complex impact of HIV/AIDS on security, few have reflected on the prior question of whether there are also political dangers associated with construing HIV/AIDS as a security threat. Answers to these questions in the chapters that follow will show that the securitization of HIV/AIDS does not simply mark a significant change in the way that HIV/AIDS is framed in international policy debates; it is also an important attempt to transform the very nature and function of security within contemporary world politics—giving it a much wider significance for our understanding of international relations.

Taking this broader approach to the securitization of HIV/AIDS also benefits those whose primary interest lies in the policy dimensions of responding to the international spread of HIV/AIDS. It provides for a more comprehensive and thorough assessment of the nature of the empirical evidence frequently mobilized in policy debates on HIV/AIDS and security. It also enables those without a background in security to become more familiar with the important analytical and political differences between the various security frameworks used to discuss HIV/AIDS, such as those between the human security and the national security frameworks. Furthermore, it familiarizes policymakers working on HIV/AIDS with the broader insights that security scholars have so far gained about the political benefits and dangers of securitization processes in general. HIV/AIDS, after all, is only the latest in a much longer line of non-military issues, such as migration, drugs, and the environment, to be discussed as security issues in national and international policy forums. Over the past decade we have seen ample precedents of securitization processes occurring outside the field of HIV/AIDS from which scholars have been able to draw important lessons—lessons that may also apply to the question of whether policymakers responding to the AIDS pandemic ought to be doing so in the language of security. Finally, the broader approach also shows how the implicit attempt to transform the function of security, evident in the securitization of HIV/AIDS, brings new political dangers into play that policymakers will need to reflect upon as they seek to respond to the AIDS pandemic. Strategies for responding to such dangers are explored in the conclusion of this book.

THE ARGUMENT

This book makes a deliberate and—as yet—rare attempt to probe the deeper significance that the securitization of HIV/AIDS has for our understanding of contemporary security and world politics. Strictly speaking, therefore, this is not principally a book about the AIDS pandemic, although it has much to say about the international politics of HIV/AIDS. It is primarily a book about security and more specifically still, about what the recent securitization of HIV/AIDS tells us about the nature of contemporary security practices and their wider role within international relations. The main argument of the book is that the securitization of HIV/AIDS is a contemporary manifestation of the *governmentalization of security*. Put differently, recent efforts to frame HIV/AIDS as a security threat mark the integration of security practices with a particular rationalization of political rule that has been gradually emerging in the West since the eighteenth century, and that Michel Foucault described as the "era of governmentality." In order to substantiate this thesis, the book delineates a conceptual framework for understanding the "governmentalization" of security, analyzes how it is unfolding through the securitization of HIV/AIDS, and evaluates its political implications for the international politics of HIV/AIDS.

Chapter 2 begins to develop the overall argument by turning first to the empirical question of whether the inclusion of HIV/AIDS on the security agenda is justified by the evidence. It critically examines arguments considering HIV/AIDS a security threat in the context of three competing frameworks: human security, national security, and international security. It shows that although the empirical case in favor of considering HIV/AIDS to be a human security issue is robust, the evidence for arguments portraying HIV/AIDS as a national and international security threat is considerably weaker. Despite the pressing claims frequently made about the national and international security implications of HIV/AIDS, many of these arguments remain speculative in relation to the social scientific evidence presently available. It would thus be tempting to simply conclude that HIV/AIDS should be viewed only as a human security issue and to end the discussion of HIV/AIDS and security there. Yet the weak nature of the empirical evidence gives rise to the further and much more intriguing question of why this securitization of HIV/AIDS occurred in the first place. If the underlying empirical evidence is presently *not* very strong, and never has been, how is it possible that so many policymakers and researchers are continuing to assert this link? Why, moreover, has the debate about HIV/AIDS and security not simply been abandoned for lack of further evidence? The disjuncture between the nature of the evidence and the fervor with which policymakers are seeking to reposition HIV/AIDS as a security issue reveals that there is much more at stake in this debate than just an empirical question about whether HIV/AIDS is or is not a security issue.

In fact, efforts to frame HIV/AIDS as a security issue are mostly attempts to use the rhetorical power of security in order to mobilize greater political support and financial resources for international initiatives seeking to expand the number of people who have access to life-prolonging medicines, especially in the developing world. The debate about the security implications of HIV/AIDS is primarily driven not by conventional security actors and concerns but by the aspirations of medical, public health, and other progressive political actors who are trying to scale up international responses to the AIDS pandemic. Here the perception that HIV/AIDS is not just a medical and development issue but also a serious international security threat is deemed to be politically advantageous. Labeling HIV/AIDS as a security issue ought to give greater political momentum to international efforts to curb the spread of the virus and generate increased resources for these initiatives. Those perceived benefits also explain why the securitization of HIV/AIDS has been able to unfold even in the absence of firmer empirical evidence. Simply put, many policymakers are going along with arguments about the security implications of HIV/AIDS, or are accepting them uncritically, as a way of scaling up national and international programs addressing the AIDS pandemic.

If this analysis is correct, it also has important implications for our wider understanding of contemporary security practices. The securitization of HIV/AIDS does not merely signal a significant change in how HIV/AIDS is being framed in national and international policy circles; more than that, it also marks an attempt to implicitly transform the very nature and function of security itself. Conventionally seen—especially by political realists—as the primary political objective trumping all other considerations, security is now being asked to perform an almost secondary and subservient role in the quest to improve the health of populations seriously affected by HIV/AIDS. The securitization of HIV/AIDS, in other words, is not just another instance of medicine being deployed in the service of national security; it is conversely also a political process in which the language and imagery of security are being mobilized in the service of public health. In this respect the securitization of HIV/AIDS does not merely perpetuate the—by now very familiar—story whereby the medical professions have been repeatedly enlisted in the service of the state and empire throughout modern history; it is also an instance in which the medical professions are now beginning to assert the political primacy of *their* own public health ambitions and are seeking to marshal the institutions and discourses of security in the service of this endeavor. Mangling Clausewitz, one could even say that security here is effectively becoming the *continuation of medicine by other means*, because the language of security is being deliberately mobilized in order to serve a wider public health and humanitarian purpose. This instrumental use of security language as a quasi-medical and public health tool raises further questions still. What kind of transformation in the practice of security is being attempted in these efforts to securitize HIV/AIDS? How can this instrumental use of security be conceptualized? What, moreover, are the political consequences of encouraging such a transformation in the practice of security?

Chapter 3 argues that the appropriation of the language and imagery of security for the purposes of achieving greater international public health is a contemporary manifestation of the *governmentalization of security*; it marks, in other words, an attempt to integrate current security practices within a wider rationalization of political rule described by Foucault as "governmentality." During this era of governmentality political rule is exercised through a complex triangle of "sovereignty, discipline and governmental management, which has [the] population as its main target and apparatuses of security as its essential mechanism" (Foucault 2007:108–109). The distinctive feature of political rule in the era of governmentality is thus that it takes the *population* (rather than the state) as its primary referent object and that it governs the welfare of populations not just through the deployment of one type of power but through the simultaneous exercise of three different economies of power—sovereignty, discipline, and governmental management. Historically, the emergence of this era of governmentality from the eighteenth century onward thus entailed an important double movement in the West. First, new governmental mechanisms of rule were developed for managing the welfare of populations explicitly *at the level of popula-*

tion. Second, older types of power—referred to by Foucault as sovereign and disciplinary power—were also progressively transformed and redirected in such a way that they began to directly contribute to this goal of enhancing the welfare of populations. For example, the much older institution of law (sovereign power) is increasingly used not just to augment the powers of the sovereign or the state but also to improve the welfare of populations by drafting new regulations—such as making it compulsory to wear seat belts, levying taxes on alcohol, banning smoking in public places, or making it mandatory to take out certain types of insurance. The older forms of sovereign and disciplinary power thus do not cease to operate during the era of governmentality, but they begin to play a much more subservient and "supporting" role for the wider purposes of managing the welfare of populations—giving rise to a complex "triangle" of sovereignty, discipline, and governmental management.

How is the securitization of HIV/AIDS connected to the rise of this era of governmentality? In outlining the broad contours of the latter, Foucault was not principally interested in analyzing the kinds of security practices conventionally studied in international relations. Had he devoted greater attention to those security practices, however, he may well have found that they too are shaped by the rise of the era of governmentality. As the latter unfolds, chapter 3 argues, security practices similarly become governmentalized and integrated within the wider governmental economy of power. The securitization of HIV/AIDS, with its instrumental appropriation of the language of security in order to improve the health of populations, is a tangible manifestation of this very process. Chapter 3 corroborates that core argument by developing a much more detailed conceptual framework for analyzing the governmentalization of security. Drawing in particular upon the recently translated governmentality lectures that Foucault delivered at the Collège de France in 1978, the chapter develops a four-dimensional heuristic of the governmentalization of security. The latter is thus shown to consist, first, of a shift in the orientation of security practices toward a more explicit concern with improving the wider welfare of populations rather than just with the narrower concerns revolving around the deployment of armed force. Second, it transforms security into a practice that simultaneously exercises three different types of power over populations. In the era of governmentality security practices similarly begin to deploy strategies of governmental management that operate at the level of population, as well as continuing to draw upon the older forms of sovereign and disciplinary power. Security too therefore becomes—metaphorically speaking—a complex triangle of sovereignty, discipline, and governmental management. Third, international security agendas become increasingly concerned with a particular category of new threats posed by the unfettered international circulation of a variety of phenomena that could spiral "out of control" in such a way that the welfare of populations would be seriously undermined. Finally, in the era of governmentality the range of security actors begins to broaden significantly beyond the formal military and intelligence institutions to include much wider assemblages of state and non-state actors in the provision of security.

All four of these transformations, chapter 3 concludes, can be traced in the securitization of HIV/AIDS. That process not only constitutes a security practice that mobilizes the language of security in order to protect the welfare of populations against a lethal virus that is circulating internationally; it is also being animated by a wider assemblage of state and non-state actors who concurrently exercise sovereign, disciplinary, and governmental forms of power in this quest. In all four respects, the securitization of HIV/AIDS thus emerges as a crucial site in contemporary world politics where the principles of governmentality are being applied to practices of security, and where these principles are also being disseminated internationally beyond the borders of the West through international institutions such as the UN Security Council, which for the first time in its history has placed a public health issue on its agenda. As a concrete manifestation of this wider governmentalization of security, the securitization of HIV/AIDS also acquires its deeper significance for our understanding of contemporary world politics.

What are the political consequences of encouraging the governmentalization of security? Should this gesture be endorsed and supported by security scholars and policymakers? Or are there also dangers involved in trying to turn security into a "tool" for improving the broader welfare of populations? Foucault once argued: "My point is not that everything is bad, but that everything is dangerous, which is not exactly the same as bad. If everything is dangerous, then we always have something to do. So my position leads not to apathy but to hyper—and pessimistic—activism" (1997c:256). From this perspective it is important not just to trace the governmentalization of security analytically but also to evaluate its political and social consequences. Doing the latter is no small endeavor and in fact requires that a great amount of work be undertaken; if it is true that the securitization of HIV/AIDS is a manifestation of the governmentalization of security, then one would also expect it to simultaneously mobilize three different types of power—sovereign power, disciplinary power, and governmental management. Each of these modalities of power in turn has its own respective dynamics, effects, and associated dangers. Exposing the securitization of HIV/AIDS as a manifestation of governmentalization thus significantly complicates its political evaluation, since it requires one to work simultaneously along three different axes or trajectories of power. Analyzing the dangers accompanying the governmentalization of security necessitates ascertaining whether evidence of these three types of power can indeed be found in the securitization of HIV/AIDS, as well as conducting a more detailed analysis of the dangers to which they give rise. It requires, in short, three separate analyses—one of the dangers associated with sovereign power (chapter 4), one of the dangers associated with disciplinary power (chapter 5), and one of the dangers associated with governmental management (chapter 6).

Chapter 4 undertakes the first of these analyses by examining in greater detail the exercise of *sovereign* power in the securitization of HIV/AIDS. That the securitization of HIV/AIDS does indeed mobilize a sovereign economy of power can be seen in arguments that HIV/AIDS is a threat to *national* security. This national security framework, chapter 4 argues, is itself a contemporary expression of the much older form of sovereign power, since it is a security framework principally concerned with the survival and power of the sovereign and, by way of extension, of the modern state. When political actors claim that HIV/AIDS is a national security threat, they are thus implicitly marshaling a sovereign economy of power in response to the AIDS pandemic. This is a potentially dangerous move—as securitization theorists have long pointed out. Well before the securitization of HIV/AIDS began to unfold, securitization theorists working in the field of security studies had already begun to identify serious dangers associated with such mobilizations of sovereign power—warning that there are "political dangers in simply tacking the word *security* onto an ever wider range of issues" (Buzan, Wæver, and de Wilde 1998:1). On the basis of their analysis of a wide range of securitization processes preceding HIV/AIDS, securitization theorists have found that framing an issue as a national security threat tends to elevate the power of the state that is charged with providing security and can thus lead to the greater domination of society by the state. Specifically, mobilizing sovereign power to address wider social issues risks removing them from routine democratic deliberation procedures by pushing them into the higher echelons of the state's inner circles of power where there is less political transparency and accountability; it also creates the potential for state institutions to invoke the imperatives of "security" to justify the use of heavy-handed or draconian measures in order to confront the threatening condition or to silence opposition to the state (Buzan, Wæver, and de Wilde 1998:21). These risks are present in the securitization of HIV/AIDS, where mobilizing sovereign power through appeals to the national security concerns of states could similarly make it much easier for state institutions to respond to the pandemic by imposing harsh measures overriding the human rights of people living with HIV/AIDS—all in the name of "security." Moreover, it risks pushing the debate on HIV/AIDS in the direction of a knee-jerk, "panic politics" response to the pandemic that may ultimately fail to come to terms with its underlying causes and may therefore not deliver a sustainable response to the disease.

The dangers associated with the mobilization of sovereign power in the securitization of HIV/AIDS are undoubtedly very real. Paradoxically, however, there is only limited evidence to suggest that they have materialized in recent years. With the benefit of hindsight comes the realization that one of the most notable and surprising aspects of the securitization of HIV/AIDS is actually that it does *not* appear to have culminated in such a draconian response to the AIDS pandemic along the lines of responses that states have historically implemented to other infectious diseases (such as leprosy, cholera, or even SARS more recently). The much more interesting question that emerges, then, is why—several years into the securitization of HIV/AIDS—this mobilization of national security language has not exacerbated the kinds of abuses of human rights and civil liberties that securitization theory would lead us to fear. One reason is undoubtedly the strong importance that those involved in the international politics of HIV/AIDS have continuously assigned to human rights considerations in their responses to the AIDS pandemic. Attempts to impose draconian measures on people living with HIV/AIDS have thus been routinely met by counterdiscourses on human rights. But that is not the only reason.

Chapter 4 suggests that there is also another, more subtle, reason for this counterintuitive course of events, a reason that derives from the particular (and modified) way in which sovereign power is actually being deployed in the securitization of HIV/AIDS. Most of the national security arguments about HIV/AIDS are not really trying to enhance the power of the sovereign (and the state) at the expense of people living with HIV/AIDS, but are seeking instead to encourage governments around the world to improve the health and welfare of populations in a way that could benefit those living with HIV/AIDS. A closer examination of the politics of framing HIV/AIDS as a national security threat shows how these national security arguments are being used to highlight the ways in which HIV/AIDS affects the core institutions of the state—such as armed and police forces—so as to demonstrate to political leaders in a very tangible way that it is in their own self-interest to improve the health of their populations. It is a strategy for breaking what former United Nations secretary general Kofi Annan once famously referred to as the "wall of silence" surrounding HIV/AIDS. In addition, the language of national security is being used here to shift responsibility for responding to the pandemic in developing countries away from politically marginalized and underfunded health ministries and toward the center of governments, as well as to make more resources and medicines available in the fight against HIV/AIDS—thus rendering treatment economically more viable for many poorer countries. The language of national security is not being invoked by states in order to maintain their power at the expense of the civil liberties of those who are living with HIV/AIDS; rather it is being invoked by public health and AIDS activists, as well as by well-meaning government officials in the West, in order to pressure states outside of the West into improving the health of their populations.

The mobilization of sovereign power as a way of inciting states to improve (rather than curtail) the welfare of their populations is also exemplary of exactly that crucial shift that sovereign power undergoes in the era of governmentality. Sovereign power ceases to constitute one of the principal devices used by the sovereign in order to augment his power; it becomes progressively redirected toward the goal of managing and improving the welfare of populations. Just as, in the domestic sphere, the sovereign institution of law is increasingly used to protect the welfare of the population (as in making it compulsory to wear seat belts, for example), so too in the international politics of HIV/AIDS, the sovereign language of national security is now being mobilized in order to compel states outside the West to do more to protect the health of their populations. This means that national security arguments about HIV/AIDS are ultimately not so much a manifestation of the attempt to further extend the state's domination of society (*étatisation*) in the manner feared by many securitization theorists, as they are indicative of the attempt to encourage what Foucault in one of his lectures called the *governmentalization* of the state—that is, to transform the state in the developing world from a political entity that governs for its own sake into one that essentially views itself as a manager of the welfare of its population. This, to be sure, does not mean that the concerns of securitization theorists are without foundation; nor does it mean that the governmentalization of security is entirely free of dangers. It does, however, help to explain why the extensive recourse to national security language has not generated a more draconian response to the AIDS pandemic in recent years. Moreover, it implies that the most pressing dangers accompanying this governmentalization of security may not be the obvious ones associated with the language of national security and sovereign power, which are routinely emphasized by securitization theorists; the more serious dangers may reside instead in the concurrent and much more subtle exercise of disciplinary and governmental forms of power.

Chapter 5 thus goes on to show how the securitization of HIV/AIDS simultaneously mobilizes a *disciplinary* economy of power in its quest to internationally extend the availability of treatment and care for people living with HIV/AIDS. Evidence of this mobilization of disciplinary power can in turn be found most readily (although not exclusively) in those arguments positioning HIV/AIDS as a threat to *human* security. Over the past decade many of those who remain concerned about using the language of national security in relation to HIV/AIDS have none-theless been quite willing to openly discuss HIV/AIDS as a threat to hu-man security—viewing that as a safer or "softer" option for discussing the AIDS-security nexus. Yet what does this human security framework represent at its core if not the marrying of the practice of security with a disciplinary economy of power? The human security framework is a contemporary expression of disciplinary power par excellence. Like dis-ciplinary power more generally, the human security framework breaks the provision and analysis of security down to the individual level (in-dividuation), analyzes the existence of human beings with respect to several threats to their physical, corporal survival (also rendering it a technology of the body), and operates according to a "positive" lan-guage of saving lives and empowering individuals. When political ac-tors assert that HIV/AIDS is a threat to human security, they are thus also implicitly mobilizing a disciplinary economy of power in relation to the AIDS pandemic.

Imbuing the practice of security with such a disciplinary logic, and bringing it to bear on the AIDS pandemic, produces additional dangers. What could possibly be harmful about trying to ameliorate the great mortality and human suffering the AIDS pandemic causes by singing the siren song of human security? Chapter 5 argues that the human se-curitization of HIV/AIDS is accompanied by "dangers" that are substan-tially different from those already implicitly identified by securitization theory in discussing the exercise of sovereign power. They reside not in the prospect of excessive state mobilization but rather in the inter-national expansion and intensification of a set of practices that seek to structure the bodies and behaviors of individuals in conformity with a wide range of norms—including biomedical norms about the "healthy" body. Irrespective of whether they are practiced in schools, hospitals, military camps, or factories, such processes of disciplinary "normation" tend to operate by first positing an optimal model (or norm) to which a group of individuals should conform. They then instantiate various forms of surveillance within the social body in order to ascertain which individuals conform to this norm (the normal) and which deviate from it (the abnormal). Finally, they deploy a variety of mechanisms for en-couraging and "disciplining" individuals to conform to the norm. The "danger" with such disciplinary practices is not that they wrest political power away from individuals in such a way that the state might override certain civil liberties but, more subtly, that people's identities and behaviors become implicitly structured in accordance with the norms—often without their full knowledge or awareness. Those who fail to conform to the norm, moreover, can be construed as being lesser or otherwise "dysfunctional," "diseased," or "unhealthy" individuals and can be socially stigmatized as a result. The danger with bringing such a disciplinary economy of power to bear on the AIDS pandemic in the name of greater human security therefore is not so much that this constitutes a new means of direct oppression but rather that it implicitly subjects people to a range of homogenizing, conformist, and "othering" strategies of normation.

Indeed, the human securitization of HIV/AIDS constitutes such a practice of disciplinary normation in that it dramatically instantiates and internationally disseminates a new biomedical norm about what constitutes a "healthy" body—in this case the norm of a body that is HIV-negative. In the urgent quest to ensure that more people conform to this norm, the securitization of HIV/AIDS then also creates greater political pressure to see that the bodies of more and more individuals around the world are subjected to detailed medical surveillance in order to ascertain whether or not they comply with this desired norm of being HIV-negative. As international AIDS initiatives have come under scrutiny to meet their ambitious treatment targets to save lives, they in turn have run into considerable difficulties in having to first "locate" those who need treatment. One of the effects of the securitization of HIV/AIDS has been to generate growing pressure for developing countries in particular to improve (i.e., intensify) their population surveillance by implementing more thorough forms of testing, abandoning voluntary counseling and testing for HIV in favor of much more routine forms of HIV testing so that they can find those who need to be saved by treatment. More and more people will thus need to become aware of how they relate to this biomedical norm and come to terms with being either "HIV-positive" or "HIV-negative." This mobilization of disciplinary power, moreover, creates a political environment in which it is much more permissible for a variety of state and non-state actors to shape people's sexual behavior in a way that is conducive to meeting this norm. Indirectly, the securitization of HIV/AIDS has also bolstered the efforts of an army of faith-based groups, peer educators, and other nongovernmental organizations who have fanned out across many developing countries, spreading a barrage of messages about "good" behaviors that ought to ensure that more people conform to the desired norm of being HIV-negative while at the same time denouncing a variety of other practices as "bad" or "unhealthy." Ultimately, this is just as true of the "condomization" of societies advocated by liberal groups as it is of the monogamy and abstinence-before-marriage messages advocated by more conservative groups in many developing countries. It can also be seen—as has happened more recently—in the recommendation of the more widespread use of male circumcision as a tool for managing the pandemic. Through the rolling out of more routine forms of HIV testing, in conjunction with the abundance of AIDS-awareness posters displayed across the African continent, the securitization of HIV/AIDS has intensified the incitement of individuals to actively seek knowledge about their HIV status and to modify their behaviors in accordance with maintaining the norm. The spread and intensification of such disciplinary practices of normation through the vast international "curing machine" now spurned by the securitization of HIV/AIDS must be added to the list of dangers to which the governmentalization of security can give rise. Realizing the dream of human security for people living with HIV/AIDS around the world will ultimately require a lot of discipline—literally.

Exposing this human security framework as a contemporary manifestation of disciplinary power also implies that the framework is not nearly as novel as many of its proponents frequently claim. Many aspects of the human security agenda remain continuous with the much older practices of *police* that several European states implemented from the seventeenth century onward. These historical practices did not consist of the institutionalized and uniformed police forces that the contemporary usage of the term conjures up; rather they were a host of detailed measures aimed at regulating a wide swath of social life in order to optimize and strengthen the forces of the state from "within." Long before the codification of the human security agenda in the mid-1990s, earlier practices of police were already concerned with optimizing and improving the "vital" capabilities of subjects, and they took a very comprehensive approach to regulating such capabilities—including an emphasis on health. The one crucial respect in which the contemporary human security framework deviates from these older practices of police, however, is that the latter were more explicitly tied to various practices of statecraft, whereas the human security framework again mobilizes disciplinary power as a general tactic for managing the welfare of populations (although within a governmentalized state these two objectives need not be mutually exclusive). Whereas disciplinary power was once engaged primarily with enhancing the military and economic power of the state internally (through training men in barracks to become fitter and better soldiers, by increasing the productivity of the labor force in factories, and so on), in the context of human security it now is incorporated into a wider project concerned with improving and managing the welfare of populations.

It is possible to see very clearly in the securitization of HIV/AIDS how disciplinary power (in the form of the human security framework) can still serve the wider process of managing the welfare of populations in the era of governmentality. First, the disciplining gesture of human security to focus on the individual gives a security presence not just to the state but to each and every member of the population; it is thus a useful device for shifting the practice of security away from a concern with the sovereign and the defense of his territory and toward the population. By moving the referent object of security from the state to the individual, human security also enables a parallel shift from the state to the population, which after all is made up of all these individuals collectively. Second, the human security framework considerably expands the boundaries of the security agenda to deliberately include a broader array of non-military issues directly relevant to the welfare of populations (including health issues). This too allows security not just to be directed at the survival of the state but also to be transformed into a practice that seeks to address the wider welfare of populations much more comprehensively. Finally, because of its humanitarian and progressive language of empowerment, the human security framework facilitates the formation of much wider alliances between states, international organizations, and a range of nongovernmental organizations. Human security can reach actors and elements in the population that the national security framework fails to mobilize. In terms of a governmental project aimed at managing the welfare of populations, the disciplinary framework of human security thus remains a very useful device. Indeed, just as arguments about the national security implications of HIV/AIDS are exemplary of the transformation of *sovereign* power into a tool for managing the welfare of populations by discursively tying the fate of populations to the survival of governments, so do arguments about the human security implications of HIV/AIDS mark the transformation of *disciplinary* power into a tool for managing the welfare of populations. In the securitization of HIV/AIDS both sovereign *and* disciplinary forms of power are being redirected toward the goal of improving the welfare of populations.

Chapter 6 goes on to show how the securitization of HIV/AIDS goes beyond transforming these older forms of sovereign and disciplinary power to also mobilize newer, *governmental* forms of managing the welfare of populations that operate explicitly *at the level of popula-tion*. Evidence of the latter can be found in arguments that portray the armed forces and United Nations peacekeepers as "risk groups" with respect to HIV/AIDS. In terms of the wider history of the international politics of HIV/AIDS, this decision by organizations such as UNAIDS to focus on the uniformed services as a high-risk group is very unusual. Traditionally, most international agencies have tended to avoid re-course to the language of "risk groups" for fear of further stigmatizing groups that often already occupy a marginalized and vulnerable social position—such as injecting drug users, men who have sex with men, and so on. This trend has recently caused some epidemiologists to speak out against the strategy. Although they concede that the option of fo-cusing on populations as a whole ("AIDS is a danger to everybody") is clearly much more palatable to many politicians since it ensures that politically sensitive issues surrounding drug use, gender, and sexuality do not have to be openly discussed with electorates, some epidemiolo-gists argue that such an approach leads to a very wasteful allocation of resources. Because of this strategy, money is now mostly directed at the population as a whole (which is deemed to be at low risk epidemio-logically, except for several states in sub-Saharan Africa), rather than toward those specific groups who are at high risk around the world.

In light of this long-standing determination to avoid using the lan-guage of risk groups, it is all the more surprising that international orga-nizations such as UNAIDS should have played such a key role in the debate about the armed forces constituting a high-risk group in relation to HIV/AIDS. Not wishing to stigmatize other known "risk groups," these organizations have had remarkably little hesitation or compunction about mobilizing the language of risk groups to full effect with respect to the armed forces. In deploying such terminology, moreover, organizations have implicitly introduced a governmental economy of power into the securitization of HIV/AIDS. Contrary to the older forms of sovereign and disciplinary power, this governmental economy of power operates at the level of population in that it begins by assessing statistically the "normal" or "natural" prevalence of HIV *within the population* as a whole. It then uses this "normal" distribution figure to identify those subpopulations whose prevalence levels of HIV are higher than the norm. It is at this point that a governmental economy of power gives rise to the notion of a "risk group" as a marker for precisely those subpopulations that statistically have a higher prevalence of HIV/AIDS compared to the population as a whole. Finally, the governmental form of management operates by designing targeted interventions that focus specifically on the risk groups in order to bring them into line with the population as a whole.

In principle, such direct targeting of risk groups enables various population phenomena (including HIV/AIDS) to be managed more economically, since resources can thus be directed more efficiently to where they can have the biggest impact. Moreover, it allows for a more indirect form of governing the population in that once the relevant risk groups have been statistically identified, one no longer needs to work on each and every member of the population—only on the identified subpopulations. In these respects, the language of risk groups is in and of itself already a revealing sign that a governmental economy of power is at work in the securitization of HIV/AIDS. Indeed, much as the human security framework marks the outcome of applying a disciplinary economy of power to the practice of security, so is the copious language of risk groups deployed for the armed forces and uniformed services in the securitization of HIV/AIDS indicative of the application of a governmental economy of power to the practice of security. Showing that such a governmental economy of power is operating in the securitization of HIV/AIDS also reveals that the latter genuinely represents that complex triangle of sovereignty, discipline, and government management that Foucault

thought to be so characteristic of the era of governmentality; it constitutes a security practice in which all three forms of power—sovereign,
disciplinary, *and* governmental management—are concurrently mobilized with the aim of improving the welfare of populations.

Yet infusing the practice of security with such a governmental rationality and bringing it to bear on the AIDS pandemic gives rise to further dangers. These dangers revolve not so much around the prospect
of excessive state mobilization, nor around the intensification of a set
of disciplinary practices of normation; they derive from the particular
ways in which populations are "normalized" through the identification
and modification of "risk groups" in the population. Unlike disciplinary power, governmental power is not a technology of *normation* but of
normalization (Foucault 2007:63). Foucault's terminology here may seem
somewhat confusing and esoteric (and indeed, it changed over time),
but underlying this differentiation is a crucial divergence in the way in
which disciplinary and governmental economies of power derive the
norms with which they work. In processes of disciplinary normation,
an ideal norm is imposed from the outside, and the distinction between
the normal and the abnormal is undertaken in relation to this "artificial" norm. Put schematically, disciplinary power ideally functions not
unlike a cookie cutter, or an industrial machine that produces identical
goods one after another in the way it is engineered or programmed to
do. In a governmental economy of power, by contrast, this norm is
not so much imposed from above as initially derived by determining
the actual and already existing distribution of a phenomenon—such
as the level of a disease—within the population. The "abnormals" are
consequently not those who deviate from a more abstract norm but
those who deviate from the "natural" and "internal" distribution of a
phenomenon *within* a population. Children under the age of three, for
example, may be a risk group in relation to smallpox, and they are thus
singled out for special interventions in order to better align them with
the more general, and lower, norm in the population.

The danger produced by such risk-based political technologies deployed when implementing processes of population normalization is
threefold. First, as we have already seen, identifying risk groups in such
a manner can lead to the social stigmatization of members of these
groups—irrespective of whether or not they are HIV-positive. Not sur-

prisingly, this has happened with respect to United Nations peacekeepers over the past years, who are now widely associated with the spread of HIV/AIDS—thus corroborating the stigmatizing effects of using a governmental logic of risk. Along with the armed forces in general, the significance of these groups has discursively shifted in the securitization of HIV/AIDS from representing the core institutions of sovereign power to being potentially dangerous "vectors" for the spread of a lethal disease within and between populations. Second, and by way of extension, there is a danger that these groups will be subjected to more intrusive forms of compulsory testing and various other behavioral interventions, with the result that people living with HIV/AIDS may be excluded from these occupations. This has already begun to happen through the introduction of mandatory testing in many armed forces throughout the world.

Finally, there is a danger that the identification of the uniformed services as a "risk group" will have undesirable material effects. Given that governmental management is concerned with governing populations efficiently and economically, the notion of risk groups has an important signaling function in terms of directing the allocation and flow of resources. Rather than spending resources on costly interventions aimed at the population as a whole, they should be "targeted" more efficiently toward the risk groups. The danger that emerges in the securitization of HIV/AIDS, therefore, is that once the armed forces are identified as such a risk group, they move to the front of the line in terms of resource allocation—again at the expense of those who are already struggling to obtain access to resources (such as sex workers, injecting drug users, men having sex with men, and so on). This tendency can also be seen in designated funds being used for programs that specifically address the spread of HIV/AIDS in the armed forces; yet such decisions are being made on the basis of epidemiological information that is often much less reliable than that which exists for the other risk groups. When these additional dangers are taken into account, the securitization of HIV/AIDS emerges as a political practice that gives rise to a complex cocktail of "dangers" associated with its concurrent mobilization of sovereign, disciplinary, and governmental forms of power. Despite ostensibly aiming to reorient security practices toward a more explicit concern with improving the welfare of populations, the attempt to governmentalize security is accompanied by a wide range of more subtle dangers. Everything, as Foucault warned, is indeed dangerous.

Given this, how should scholars and practitioners respond to the securitization of HIV/AIDS? Are the dangers not of such significance that the most prudent and responsible thing to do would be to resist the securitization of HIV/AIDS? Is there, moreover, any way in which Foucault's own cursory reflections on the wider rise of the era of governmentality can help us make this decision with respect to the securitization of HIV/AIDS today? Probably the easiest response would be to simply resist and reject the securitization of HIV/AIDS. That response would echo securitization theory's general preference for "de-securitizing" issues—that is, for shifting them out of "emergency" mode and toward more routine forms of political deliberation and decision making. It would also appear to be consistent with Foucault's reputation for being an iconoclast and a formidable critic of modern power relations. Chapter 7, however, draws upon some of Foucault's late writings and interviews on governmentality to develop a different response to the securitization of HIV/AIDS. Taking into account the distinction that Foucault developed between "power relations" and "states of domination," in conjunction with his views on resistance as well as his own political engagements, the conclusion suggests a response to the securitization of HIV/AIDS that is very similar to the way in which Foucault thought about the medicalization of homosexuality—which he found to be both a means of oppression and something that opened up certain possibilities for resistance. The securitization of HIV/AIDS, chapter 7 concludes, is a similar case in point: it is partially dangerous and therefore should not be endorsed uncritically, yet it simultaneously provides possibilities of resistance to some of the vicissitudes of contemporary world politics. Rather than rejecting the securitization of HIV/AIDS out of hand, therefore, the chapter delineates some of the ways in which this securitization of HIV/AIDS could in the future be conducted in a manner that would at least minimize many of the dangers. Whether this, in the end, is also the best strategy for responding to the wider governmentalization of security that is currently unfolding across a range of other contemporary security practices is a question that will need to be examined more closely in the years ahead.

2 / A NOBLE LIE?

Examining the Evidence on AIDS and Security

Is the designation of HIV/AIDS as a security threat justified by the empirical evidence? The answer to this question depends largely upon which security framework is used as a reference point. The international debate on HIV/AIDS and security has been marked not just by recourse to one overarching security framework but by the intense contestation between at least three different security frameworks: human security, national security, and international security. Each of these competing frameworks posits distinct empirical relationships between HIV/AIDS and security and gives rise to quite different political priorities in relation to the AIDS pandemic. This chapter undertakes a detailed comparative examination of the empirical evidence that has been advanced about HIV/AIDS with respect to all three of these security frameworks. Analysis reveals that even though the empirical case in favor of considering HIV/AIDS as a human security issue is robust, arguments portraying HIV/AIDS as a national and international security threat are considerably weaker. Despite the pressing claims frequently made about the national and international security implications of HIV/AIDS, many of these arguments remain overstated in light of the social scientific evidence presently available. Efforts to frame HIV/AIDS as a national and international security threat are better understood as attempts to use the rhetorical power of security in order to mobilize greater political support and financial resources for international initiatives that seek to expand the number of people receiving access to life-prolonging medicines, especially in the developing world.

HUMAN SECURITY AND HIV/AIDS

One of the most persuasive ways in which many policymakers, non-governmental organizations, and scholars have been able to portray HIV/AIDS as a security issue is by positioning it as a threat to "human security." This has also been the preferred strategy of the Joint United Nations Programme on HIV/AIDS (UNAIDS). UNAIDS is the specialized United Nations agency tasked with addressing the international spread of HIV/AIDS. Established in 1995, UNAIDS is located at the center of a complex network of United Nations programs and affiliated organizations, including the World Health Organization and the World Bank. Its political objectives are to mobilize leadership for effective action against the spread of HIV/AIDS, to monitor and evaluate its spread, and to support an effective response (UNAIDS 2007b:7). "As a global issue," Peter Piot (2001) argued in his capacity as director of UNAIDS, "we must pay attention to AIDS as a threat to human security, and redouble our efforts against the epidemic and its impact."

This human security framework was pioneered by the United Nations Development Programme in its 1994 *Human Development Report* and seeks to redress the perceived imbalance in security thinking that predominated during past decades. By developing a "people-centric" account of security revolving around the needs and welfare of ordinary individuals, rather than around the protection of sovereign states, human security activists wish to challenge the narrow twentieth-century equation of security with the absence of armed conflict between states. Perhaps the most important ramification of this crucial shift in the referent object of security is the resulting breadth of the human security agenda. Not only do individuals arguably confront many more insecurities on a daily basis than states do, but, obviously, there are many more individuals inhabiting the planet than there are states. The sphere of legitimate human security concerns thus includes a variety of non-military threats to the welfare of individuals and societies, including disease, hunger, unemployment, crime, social conflict, political repression, and environmental hazards (UNDP 1994:22).

Specifically the *Human Development Report* initially outlined seven areas or components of human security to which policymakers should henceforth devote greater political attention: economic security (poverty, homelessness), food security (famine and hunger), health security (disease, inadequate health care), environmental security (ecological degradation, pollution, natural disasters), personal security (physical violence, crime, traffic accidents), community security (oppression, discrimination), and political security (repression, torture, disappearance, human rights violations) (UNDP 1994:24–25). Predictably, the breadth of the human security framework has led to charges of analytical confusion, with some analysts now believing the concept to be synonymous with development more generally. For advocates of human security, by contrast, the breadth has proved quite useful politically in that it has enabled the emergence of a wide-ranging coalition of governmental actors, international organizations, and nongovernmental organizations working on a range of issues—all under the umbrella of human security. Moreover, because the human security framework places such great emphasis on health issues, it has also been viewed by many policymakers as a useful vehicle for drawing links between HIV/AIDS and security.

Personal Security

Within the wider framework of human security, HIV/AIDS represents first and foremost a direct threat to the human security of individuals in that the premature loss of life is perhaps one of the greatest human insecurities of all (Chen and Narasimhan 2003:5). It is impossible to determine exactly how many people are living with HIV/AIDS in the world and how many are dying from AIDS-related illnesses. Generating such data would be impossible in light of immense financial and logistical constraints, and would also necessitate testing virtually every member of the human population for HIV—raising difficult ethical questions around compulsory testing. Nevertheless, UNAIDS estimates that around 2 million people die annually of AIDS-related illnesses, while 2.5 million more people become newly infected with the virus every year (table 2.1).

Even these figures are best seen as broad indicators, however. UNAIDS also has a very strong advocacy mission, and some epidemiologists have openly questioned how accurate the UNAIDS figures are (Chin 2007:170). Others have drawn attention to the complex political

Table 2.1 People Living with, Newly Infected, or Dead from HIV/AIDS, 2007

Region	Adults and Children Living with HIV/AIDS	Adults and Children Newly Infected with HIV	Adults and Children Dead from AIDS
Sub-Saharan Africa	22.5 million	1.7 million	1.6 million
Middle East and North Africa	380,000	35,000	25,000
South and Southeast Asia	4 million	340,000	270,000
East Asia	800,000	92,000	32,000
Oceania	75,000	14,000	1,200
Latin America	1.6 million	100,000	58,000
Caribbean	230,000	17,000	11,000
Eastern Europe and Central Asia	1.6 million	150,000	55,000
Western and Central Europe	760,000	31,000	12,000
North America	1.3 million	46,000	21,000
Total	33.2 million [30.6 million– 36.1 million]	2.5 million [1.8 million– 4.1 million]	2.1 million [1.9 million– 2.4 million]

SOURCE: UNAIDS 2007a.

and bureaucratic difficulties associated with generating such figures (Pisani 2008:14–42). Indeed, it is worth noting that recently UNAIDS has itself substantially revised its estimates downward for many countries in light of new studies that have been conducted and new data that have been emerging.

Nevertheless, in sub-Saharan Africa AIDS seems to have already established itself as the leading cause of adult deaths. According to the World Health Organization's *World Health Report 2004*, AIDS-related illnesses have become the world's leading cause of death and loss of life years in the 15–59 age group (WHO 2004:155). In terms of mortality, in 2002 HIV/AIDS was already estimated to be the fourth-largest cause of death in the world (after ischemic heart disease, cerebrovascular disease, and lower-respiratory infections), and it is projected to become the third-largest cause by 2030. In terms of disability-adjusted life years—a measure that takes into account not only direct mortality but also when this mortality occurs in the life span of an individual—HIV/AIDS was estimated to be the third-largest cause in 2002 (after perinatal conditions and lower-respiratory infections) and is expected to be the leading cause by 2030 (Mathers and Loncar 2006). Given that there is no cure for AIDS, and that as of December 2005 roughly 80 percent of the people in clinical need did not have access to anti-retroviral (ARV) treatment, HIV/AIDS constitutes a serious human security threat to the personal security of those living with HIV/AIDS (UNAIDS 2006b:155).

Even when people live for several years with HIV before succumbing to AIDS-related illnesses, moreover, they may not survive the stigma and violence inflicted upon them by fellow human beings, which generate further threats to their personal security. One particularly tragic episode that caught the world's media attention occurred in December 1998, when Gugu Dlamini died at the age of 36 as the result of a beating inflicted by her neighbors in the outskirts of Durban, South Africa, after she revealed her HIV-positive status—on World AIDS Day. Violent attacks continue to occur in many countries, especially where there is still a strong stigma attached to the illness. In 2007 a Tanzanian woman, Tumaini Mbogela, was similarly beaten by her husband after returning home from a voluntary counseling center in Makete, where she had taken the HIV test advocated by the Tanzanian government in a nationwide drive to increase testing (BBC 2007). In the worst-case scenario, such stigma can even lead to the killing of people who are infected or who are erroneously thought to be HIV-positive. Human Rights Watch (2003), for example, has documented how domestic violence frequently erupts in families following confirmation of an HIV infection; in some cases, wives are simply strangled to death after revealing their status. Personal security is therefore one of the components of human security that is affected particularly seriously by HIV/AIDS.

Health Security

HIV/AIDS also has a wide range of social, political, and economic ramifications that generate additional human insecurities beyond the medical condition itself. In countries where prevalence rates are high, HIV/AIDS affects health security more generally by placing additional stresses on health care facilities that are frequently already stretched in the first place. A 2003 study of the impact of HIV/AIDS on the health sector in South Africa found that the AIDS epidemic is having several negative impacts. It is causing the loss of health care workers and generating increased levels of absenteeism, with just under 16 percent of the health care workforce in the Free State, Mpumalanga, KwaZulu-Natal, and North West provinces being HIV-positive. It also found that the rise in the number of HIV/AIDS patients seeking clinical care has led to an increased workload for health care staff, as well as lowering staff morale. With some 46.2 percent of patients in public hospitals being HIV-positive, the study concluded, non-AIDS patients have at times been "crowded out" of the system in order to accommodate patients living with HIV/AIDS (Shisana et al. 2003). A study from Kenya based on a sample of hospitals detected similar trends, with an increase in AIDS-related admissions and 50 percent of the patients on medical wards living with HIV/AIDS. Focus group discussions conducted in the context of the study also revealed that one of the reasons that the Kenyan health care systems had such high levels of attrition, with scores of personnel leaving the sector, was a fear of becoming infected with HIV (in addition to heavy workloads, poor remuneration, and poor working conditions) (Cheluget et al. 2003). A study of the impact of AIDS in Swaziland estimates that up to 80 percent of bed occupancy in medical and pediatric wards is related to HIV/AIDS (Kober and van Damme 2006). The human security ramifications of HIV/AIDS are therefore not confined to the direct mortality caused by the illness, but also reflect the much wider ripple effect of the disease through many social structures—including health care systems.

Economic Security

Defined as "an assured basic income—usually from productive and remunerative work, or in the last resort from some publicly financed safety net" (UNDP 1994:25), economic security is another important component of human security that is affected by HIV/AIDS. Although few household studies have been conducted, those completed suggest that the impact is twofold. Households affected by HIV/AIDS are likely to experience a reduced earning capacity, as people who are ill are unable to work and others in the family are tied down to caring for the affected person. A 2002 comparative study of rural and urban households in South Africa conducted by Frederick Booysen and Max Bachmann (2002) showed that households affected by HIV/AIDS have on average only 50 to 60 percent of the per capita income of non-affected households. Moreover, HIV/AIDS generates new costs for treatment and, in the case of death, for funeral expenditures, legal costs, medical bills, and so forth (Drimrie 2003). Other studies carried out by the World Bank similarly suggest increased expenditure by these households on medical care and funerals, as well as a reduction in spending on non-food items (Barnett and Whiteside 2006:203–205). HIV/AIDS can thus have an additional impact on human security in that it can undermine the ability of individuals and households to ensure their economic security.

Food Security

HIV/AIDS can also affect food security, defined as requiring "that all people at all times have both physical and economic access to basic food. This requires not just enough food to go round. It requires that people have ready access to food" (UNDP 1994:27). The crucial point here is that the physical availability of food is only part of the equation. Even when food is physically available, people may still be hungry and starve if they do not have access or entitlement to the food. During many famines the problem is the lack of purchasing power and the poor distribution of food, rather than the absence of food itself. This distinction is crucial because HIV/AIDS can generate food insecurities by skewing the access of certain individuals and groups to food. The negative impact of HIV/AIDS on food security has prompted the famine researcher Alex de Waal (2002) to advance a "new-variant famine" thesis, arguing that "AIDS attacks exactly those capacities that enable people to resist famine. AIDS kills young adults, especially women—the people whose labor is most needed. When the rains come, people must work 16 hours a day planting and weeding the crop. If that critical period is missed, the family will go hungry." A study carried out by the Food and Agriculture Organization of 1,889 rural households in northern Namibia, southern Zambia, and around Lake Victoria in Uganda found that households affected by HIV/AIDS, particularly if they are headed by women, are finding it increasingly difficult to ensure their food security (FAO 2003). A study of fifteen villages in three districts of Malawi carried out by Shah and colleagues (2002) found that many households affected by HIV/AIDS experienced loss of labor (70 percent), reported delays of agricultural work (45 percent), left fields unattended (23 percent), and changed crop composition (26 percent), but much of the impact depended on when the disease arrived (i.e., before or after the harvest), the existence of other stress factors, and the relative economic status of households. Although HIV/AIDS is therefore unlikely to create a supply shock in terms of food production in and of itself, it can nevertheless have negative implications for households by interacting in complex ways with their ability to secure access to food (de Waal 2006:89–92; Gillespie 2006).

There is reasonably robust empirical evidence, then, to support the view that HIV/AIDS is a human security threat in that it affects several components of human security—personal security, health security, economic security, and food security. Those effects, viewed in conjunction with the large number of lives the disease claims annually, lead many now to consider HIV/AIDS one of the world's most pressing contemporary human security threats. That this should be so, however, is not really that surprising in the end. The human security framework was specifically developed with an eye to highlighting pervasive nonmilitary threats, including those posed by disease. As Lincoln Chen argues, "Health and human security are tightly linked. Good health is 'intrinsic' to human security, since human survival and good health are at the core of 'security.' Health is also 'instrumental' to human security because good health enables the full range of human functioning. Health permits human choice, freedom, and development" (2004:2). Therefore the articulation of HIV/AIDS as a security threat through reference to the framework of human security is really much more a case of definitional fiat, and one of redefining security, than one of making substantially novel empirical claims about the social impact of HIV/ AIDS. What is much more contentious politically, and indeed much more difficult to establish empirically, is whether HIV/AIDS can also be persuasively linked with the older framework of national security. This question is all the more pertinent given that the human security framework has so far made only modest inroads among many countries' more traditional security communities and establishments.

NATIONAL SECURITY AND HIV/AIDS

Do credible empirical links also exist between HIV/AIDS and national security—defined by one analyst as "the protection of [the state's] people and the preservation of territorial integrity, national sovereignty, political, social, economic, and defense institutions against direct or indirect threats" (Garrett 2005:15; see also Buzan 1991:19–20). Security analysts have posited at least two important relationships between HIV/AIDS and national security. First, HIV/AIDS is argued to have a disproportionately high and detrimental impact on the armed forces, thus potentially undermining what for political realists is one of the core national security institutions of the state. Second, HIV/AIDS has also been linked with national security through its perceived potential to generate wider processes of state "failure." For countries with very high civilian prevalence rates, security analysts have thus begun to raise serious questions about the longer-term impact of HIV/AIDS on the institutions on which political stability depends, and on the ability of governments to maintain order and to exert control of their territory in a context of high levels of AIDS-induced mortality.

HIV/AIDS and the Military

International organizations such as UNAIDS have long stated that they expect HIV prevalence rates in the armed forces to substantially exceed those in the civilian population—giving the disease an important national security dimension as well. UNAIDS itself acknowledges in its annual epidemiological reports how difficult it is to obtain precise epidemiological data regarding HIV prevalence rates among the civilian population of many countries where proper surveillance mechanisms are lacking. Yet it is even harder to obtain such data about the armed forces. Particularly in countries where prevalence rates in the military are thought to be high, the armed forces are usually very hesitant to make such information public since it could point to potential security vulnerabilities; very few figures have in fact been made publicly available to date. This lack of data has not, however, prevented the publication of several estimates of HIV prevalence rates, especially in African armed forces,

Table 2.2 Estimated HIV Prevalence in Selected Militaries in Sub-Saharan Africa, 1999

Country	Percentage
Angola	40–60
Congo (Brazzaville)	10–25
Côte d'Ivoire	10–20
Democratic Republic of Congo	40–60
Eritrea	10
Nigeria	10–20
Tanzania	15–30

SOURCE: NIC 2000a.

as well as considerable speculation in the media about the possibility of high rates in many countries (Elbe 2003). Among the most influential of these estimates are those published in a declassified national intelligence estimate (NIC 2000a), which drew upon figures supplied by the Armed Forces Medical Intelligence Center (AFMIC), which is part of the Defense Intelligence Agency of the United States. The estimates pointed to staggering levels of HIV infection in some African armed forces (table 2.2).

These figures, widely cited, constitute the main basis for many arguments about the national security implications of HIV/AIDS. Yet few have questioned exactly how the figures were obtained. In light of their considerable margins, and the classified nature of their source, it is not clear whether they are based on actual testing or on anecdotal evidence. Some of these countries, such as Congo, Eritrea, and Nigeria, reported that at the time they had not yet carried out force-wide surveillance on HIV/AIDS, raising questions about the reliability of the available figures. Some countries—Angola, for example—have also actively disputed the veracity of the figures.

Even though these figures have been widely used in discussions of HIV/AIDS as a national security threat, they cannot be evaluated according to scientific or epidemiological standards. This is part of a larger problem: discussions about the impact of HIV/AIDS on the military are frequently plagued by "factoids." According to Tony Barnett and Gwyn Prins, factoids are

> intellectual viruses of quick and dirty synthetic studies. They are the soft opinions that have hardened into fact. The term describes pieces of data

that look credible at first glance, but which are insecurely grounded in the evidence. They achieve this status as a result of a form of pyramid selling by recycling through publications, grey literature and reports of meetings. (2005:18)

Barnett and Prins single out two such factoids in the debate on HIV/ AIDS and the armed forces in particular. First they examine the frequently made claim that rates of sexually transmitted infections are two to five times higher among the military than among the general population. This is indeed a factoid, although there is a study of the Fort Bragg U.S. Army installation that found that the 1996 adjusted rates for chlamydia "among both male and female active-duty soldiers remained 3- to 6-fold higher than respective rates for the state [North Carolina] and country as a whole" (Seña et al. 2000:746). So there is evidence that in *some* military units, *some* sexually transmitted diseases are indeed significantly higher than in the comparable civilian population. But these studies do not focus directly on HIV, and it still is a far stretch from such narrow studies to much broader geographical claims about the levels of other sexually transmitted infections (with other transmission characteristics) in the many other armed forces that exist around the world. A second controversial claim highlighted by Barnett and Prins is that 45 percent of Dutch peacekeepers deployed in Cambodia in the early 1990s had sexual relations with the local population. Although Barnett and Prins (2005:18) identify that claim as a factoid, it is actually based on a survey carried out by the medical services of the Netherlands navy (Buma et al. 1995). Ironically, in identifying the claim as a factoid, Barnett and Prins may have themselves inadvertently created a new factoid about factoids in the debate on HIV/AIDS and security.

In either case, the NIC figures widely cited about military HIV prevalence rates in sub-Saharan Africa are also at odds with other data that have been subsequently generated in other parts of the U.S. government. Richard Shaffer (2005), executive director of the U.S. Department of Defense HIV/AIDS Prevention Program based in San Diego, who works on a military-to-military basis with many African countries, has presented quite different figures about the prevalence of HIV/AIDS in some of these same countries (table 2.3).

Table 2.3 Prevalence of HIV/AIDS in Some Sub-Saharan Countries, 2005

Country	Military Prevalence (%)	Civilian Prevalence (%)	Ratio
Côte d'Ivoire	9	10	0.9
Togo	14	6	2.3
Nigeria	8	6	1.3
Gabon	4	9	0.4
Congo-Brazzaville	4	7	0.6
Angola	7	6	1.2
Chad	4	4	1.0
Eriterea	5	5	1.0
Ethiopia	7	6	1.2
Uganda	8	5	1.6
Kenya	7	15	0.5
Tanzania	23	8	2.9
Zambia	35	21	1.7
Namibia	33	22	1.5
Botswana	40	39	1.0
South Africa	21	20	1.1
Mozambique	39	13	3.0

SOURCE: Shaffer 2005.

With the exception of the Democratic Republic of Congo (for which there are no figures available) and Tanzania (which falls within the range estimated by the Armed Forces Medical Intelligence Council), the other figures are either substantially lower or at the very low end of the estimates initially provided by the AFMIC. Moreover, even these figures are unverifiable estimates in the sense that they remain beyond public scrutiny because the country reports generated by this Department of Defense program often do not cite the sources for the estimates or indicate that they were generated from limited samples conducted predominantly in one city. Although there is some evidence of elevated levels of HIV in African armed forces as indicated by publicly cited figures (Ba et al. 2008), the fact that such divergent figures are circulating within various U.S. government agencies means that much uncertainty remains about the actual HIV prevalence in many of the armed forces.

There are also grounds to suspect that, on the contrary, HIV prevalence rates in some armed forces may increasingly become lower than in comparative civilian cohorts because studies show that the male age cohorts from which militaries predominantly recruit (males aged 17–22) generally have lower HIV prevalence rates than female cohorts of the same age, and because many militaries have introduced mandatory testing at the recruitment stage and no longer recruit those who are HIV-positive (Whiteside, de Waal, and Gebre-Tensae 2006). Arguments about the impact of HIV/AIDS on the armed forces, though intuitively plausible, remain shrouded in a high degree of uncertainty, and there is very little publicly available and verifiable evidence to corroborate them at present. The same is true about the impact of HIV/AIDS on state capacity.

HIV/AIDS and State Capacity

Analysts have also presented HIV/AIDS as a national security threat by speculating about its potential longer-term ramifications for social and political stability in the worst-affected countries. "Declining health, particularly in the form of the spread of infectious diseases," one report concluded, "will work in combination with other factors to promote instability" (CBACI 2000:13). As early as 1990 the CIA had already added AIDS incidence to the list of variables that should be considered when analyzing which states were likely to become unstable or collapse in the future (Gellman 2000). UNAIDS, too, has warned with reference to sub-Saharan Africa that "the risks of social unrest and even socio-political instability should not be under-estimated" (2001a:18). How could HIV/AIDS weaken a state to the point of instability or failure? Discounting some of the more outlandish speculation, there are four separate arguments advancing such a link by claiming that HIV/AIDS might: (1) undermine the economy, (2) weaken state institutions, (3) produce new tensions over access to life-prolonging medicines, and (4) generate a socially unsustainably high number of orphans. Each of these arguments is considered in greater detail below.

Macroeconomic Impact

AIDS is widely predicted to have a negative long-term macroeconomic impact in states that are severely affected by the disease. According to the National Intelligence Council (NIC 2000b) report, the worst-affected countries will suffer from a reduction in economic growth of up to 1 percent of gross domestic product (GDP) per year as a result of AIDS, and the disease will consume more than half of the health budgets of those countries. This assessment was shared at the time by the secretary-general of the United Nations, Kofi Annan (2001:5), whose report found that in the next twenty years the worst-affected countries could well lose up to a quarter of their projected economic growth. A World Health Organization (2001:31) report in turn "conservatively" estimated that the economic value of life years lost because of AIDS in sub-Saharan Africa amounted to 11.7 percent of the region's gross national product in 1999.

Reasons frequently invoked for this expected macroeconomic impact are that HIV/AIDS affects the demographic groups that are most productive economically—including the economic elites that provide capital and strategic input for developing the economy—that it increases levels of morbidity, mortality, and absenteeism in local economies; that it introduces new costs for medical care; that it results in higher indirect costs with respect to contributions to pension plans and training new personnel; and that, in seriously affected countries, it may undermine the belief in the long-term sustainability of the economy. Yet here too it is important to bear in mind that these figures are only estimates derived from economic models, many of which display an alarming sense of uniformity in their assumptions—despite the varied nature of the economies of the worst-affected states. All other things being equal, one might reasonably expect economies that are primarily reliant on manufacturing and small-scale agriculture, for example, to be more seriously affected by HIV/AIDS than those that are structurally dependent on foreign aid, minerals, and oil (de Waal 2006:88–89). Whereas the former economies depend on a large and healthy workforce to generate their economic revenue, the latter predominantly rely on outside sources of funding or on key industries that do not require a large and healthy population of workers.

The analytical complexity involved in assessing the macroeconomic impact of HIV/AIDS emerges particularly clearly when considering the diverging results that have been generated through the use of different economic models applied to a single African country—South Africa. In 2000, ING Baring commissioned research papers that concluded that

GDP growth for the period 2002–2010 would be only about 0.3 percent lower in the "AIDS-scenario" than in the "no-AIDS scenario" and that per capita GDP might actually *rise* (Quatteck 2000). This result would not appear to be sufficiently severe to undermine the stability of the state. A different study carried out in the same year, however, projected an impact closer to 2 percent over the same period, with a *decline* in per capita GDP (Arndt and Lewis 2000). In 2001 yet another study, conducted by the Bureau for Economic Research (Laubscher et al. 2001), used a forecasting model to simulate the impact of HIV/AIDS and found that GDP growth would be 0.47 percent lower between 2002 and 2015 compared to a "no-AIDS" scenario, but also found an expectation that the demographic impact on the population would outweigh the economic effects, resulting in a positive per capita GDP effect. A more recent study—sponsored by the same institutions and incorporating updated demographic data—then projected an average decline of GDP growth from 4.4 to 4 percent for the period 2000–2020—a growth reduction of 0.4 percent, which would be ameliorated by 17 percent if anti-retroviral therapies were provided and there was at least a 50 percent uptake (Smit and Ellis 2006). Although all four studies point to a negative macroeconomic impact, there is considerable disagreement about the extent of the impact and about whether per capita GDP—a potentially more crucial indicator in terms of any source of potential instability—will be affected negatively or positively. Moreover, it is worth bearing in mind that none of these studies actually point to a reduction in the overall size of the economy; they point "merely" to reduction in the rate of growth in the "AIDS" scenario compared to the "no-AIDS" scenario. This casts further doubt upon whether the impact is sufficient to cause failure of the state, however that is defined.

The picture is complicated further still by the fact that economists presently do not even agree as to whether the macroeconomic implications of such a long-wave event can be properly modeled within the context of neoclassical economics, especially given the epidemic's long cycle and its anticipated wider impact on non-standard economic indicators. Tony Barnett and Colette Clement (2005:239) have rightly argued that formal economic modeling runs into serious difficulties when trying to grapple with a long-term demographic event such as the AIDS epidemic. If one diversifies the economic models away from such formal modeling, then the variation in the predictions of the economic impact of HIV/AIDS becomes even larger. A more unconventional study by Clive Bell, Shantayanan Devarajan, and Hans Gersbach (2003:76–77), based on an overlapping-generations model (albeit assuming full employment and no measures to reduce the spread of HIV/AIDS), predicts that the average South Africa income would fall from R26,266 in 1990 to R12,901 in 2080. The point here is not to deny the validity of either of these economic models—many of which come to terms with the issue innovatively under conditions marked by a paucity of data—but to show that the foundations on which such estimates rest are at present still shaky and that the economics in this area is still very much in its infancy. While this is understandable given the novelty of this area of research and the complexity of the phenomenon to be analyzed, it must at this stage also caution against positing any simple relationships between HIV/AIDS and national security on the basis of the disease's macroeconomic effects.

State Institutions

It is also frequently argued that HIV/AIDS weakens the national security of states by having negative personnel implications that undermine the functioning of core institutions. In terms of the personnel numbers, a representative of the development assistance organization Crown Agents testified before the UK Select Committee on International Development that, in the government departments of several sub-Saharan African countries, the organization had witnessed a reduction in "staff resources" of between 25 and 50 percent (Select Committee 2001:Section 2 §116). In addition to this loss of personnel, other analysts have also argued that the culture of state institutions can change as a result of HIV/AIDS. George Fidas (2001), one of the authors of the National Intelligence Estimate (NIC2000a), states: "Once you know you have HIV, and we know these militaries have huge rates including the officer corps, you develop a short-term life span mentality, and you want to provide for your family, provide for your status and glory, whatever, in a shorter period of time, so that accentuates the process. It accentuates corruption." The reduction of life expectancy is thus expected to have a variety of more subtle, but important, institutional effects—including outside the armed forces as well. As de Waal argues more generally:

> The creation and functioning of complex institutions depends upon long career trajectories. Institutions such as government ministries, large corporations, armies, and universities all depend upon the skills, experience, and networks built up by their senior staff over many years. . . . As working lives shorten, it follows that levels of institutional complexity will shrink as well. (2003a:132)

He became concerned therefore that HIV/AIDS could initiate a process of running—metaphorically speaking—a "Max Weber in reverse" (2003a:133).

Yet these arguments too need to be scrutinized. One problem with them is that they often do not pay sufficient attention to the crucial difference between prevalence rates and mortality rates. The country data on HIV/AIDS presented by international organizations usually focus on the prevalence rate of HIV/AIDS is the *adult* population—that is, those between 15 and 49 years of age. This is certainly justified in that the primary route of transmission in many countries is through sexual intercourse. Yet it also means that these figures can give a slightly exaggerated impression of the extent of the epidemic if audiences unfamiliar with such epidemiological categories do not discriminate sufficiently between prevalence in the *adult* population and prevalence in the *total* population. The latter will invariably be lower by definition because it also contains members of the population who are younger than 15 years of age, as well as those who are older than 49 years of age. In the case of HIV/AIDS, "shocking" prevalence rates of close to 30 percent or more in the *adult* population thus translate into a smaller prevalence rate when calculated for the population as a whole. In Botswana, for example, a national HIV estimate in 2003 illustrated this difference very clearly. It estimated that HIV prevalence among the *adult* population was 25.3 percent (UNAIDS estimated 37.3 percent among the adult population) and 17.1 among the entire *national* population (Chin 2007:97).

What is more, prevalence rates are different from mortality rates, especially given the long cycle of the progression from initial HIV infection to developing AIDS. Mortality rates in any given year will not amount to 30 percent or more; rather the figure will be substantially lower, because the mortality from AIDS is spread over many years. In South Africa, for example, the annual number of AIDS deaths in 2010 is estimated to be (depending on which data sources are used) between 1 and 3 percent of the population (Rehle 2003). This comment is not at all intended to minimize or downplay the extent of the pandemic, nor to deny that for many countries these figures are clearly very serious and represent an immense humanitarian tragedy, especially because they will occur year after year (Whiteside and Whalley 2007). But the data do raise difficult questions as to whether the gradual onset of this mortality will produce state and social instability, even if it is sustained over many years. There is some historical evidence that in the past, epidemics like the plague did indeed culminate in the breakup of social cohesion, albeit when *mortality* rates reached around 40 percent. Yet, in the case of cholera, even where localized mortality rates reached 25 to 30 percent, such widespread breakdown of social cohesion did not occur (Evans 1988:143–144). Although the loss of human capital can indeed be crucial, especially with respect to highly skilled or specialized workers, HIV/AIDS is unlikely to reach such mortality levels. More important still, many of these arguments make a variety of very strong assumptions about the nature of the African state. De Waal himself realized as much when he recently amended his "Max Weber in reverse" thesis, acknowledging that there is considerable literature on the state in Africa that shows how many state institutions in Africa do not function according to the "Weberian" model (2006:76). Although the loss of large numbers of personnel in government departments, especially those with substantial experience, will undoubtedly cause protracted governance problems, it is far from established at this stage that the impact will be severe enough to lead to state collapse. At present, these arguments too remain premature.

Conflicts over Medicines

Some analysts have argued that HIV/AIDS could also destabilize states by provoking new intrastate political conflicts over access to expensive life-prolonging medicines. Infectious diseases, of course, have ravaged

many countries for decades without necessarily leading to political instability. Unlike diseases that are strongly linked with poverty, however,
HIV/AIDS afflicts the educated and moderately wealthy middle classes
as well. Given the current availability of anti-retroviral treatments,
many elites with access to resources will be able to extend their life
expectancy substantially by purchasing medicines. The plight of the
middle classes, however, is less certain. If the elites are not seen to be
working in the interests of the middle classes and securing the availability of medications for them as well or if the elites cannot afford the
medications at current prices, this could contribute to further polariza-
tion between the classes. Randy Cheek has argued that the "uneven
distribution of essential HIV treatment based on social, ethnic, or political criteria could well put unmanageable pressures on social and political structures, threatening the stability of regimes throughout Southern
Africa" (2001:20).

One of the main problems with this argument is that even though it
was already advanced in 2001, there is no sound evidence available to
show that HIV/AIDS produces new conflicts over access to medicines.
In fact, there is actually evidence against that idea. The ability of South
Africa's government to be reelected in 2004 with an overwhelming majority despite its controversial stance and slowly evolving response to
HIV/AIDS surely has to act as a caution in this regard. The explanation lies partly in the fact that although many countries are being seriously affected by HIV/AIDS, their people are not making the issue a
political priority. Available data for these countries indicate that public
opinion has not yet reached levels at which it might provoke political unrest. Afrobarometer (2004:4) data show that among fifteen African countries, many of which have high HIV prevalence rates, only
11 percent of respondents mentioned AIDS as one of the three most
important issues facing their country. Moreover, contrary to what one
would expect according to this argument, in some of the most heavily
affected countries the percentage of respondents mentioning AIDS as
an issue is substantially lower still, such as in Lesotho (5 percent), Malawi (3 percent), and Zambia (3 percent) (Afrobarometer 2004:5). More
recent data from the beginning of 2006 for South Africa—the African
country worst affected in terms of the absolute number of people living with HIV/AIDS—shows that 25 percent of respondents there men-

tioned AIDS, but this still places the issue in only the fourth position, after unemployment (63 percent), housing (28 percent), and crime (27 percent) (Afrobarometer 2006). The data reveal no evidence as yet that HIV/AIDS is generating sufficient political saliency and friction to provoke such conflicts over the disease and access to medicines.

Orphans and Crime

A final argument linking infectious diseases to state instability, and thus to national security, was advanced by Richard Holbrooke when he argued that the disease will "create a unique, new untouchable caste" that could provoke violence and civil strife (quoted in Schoofs 2000). According to such arguments, the AIDS pandemic could lead to a growing number of people who will become increasingly disengaged from their respective societies and might seek alternative and potentially violent ways of securing their existence. AIDS orphans are frequently singled out in this respect, as it is argued that they are vulnerable to exploitation and radicalization and might turn toward crime and militias in order to maintain their existence in the face of inadequate support from their families and communities (Kasselow 2001). Martin Schönteich (1999), of the Institute for Security Studies in South Africa, has linked this rise of HIV/AIDS with an exponentially increasing crime rate for the next five to twenty years. Given the large number of orphans that HIV/AIDS is likely to generate, such a development would be of considerable concern.

Yet this argument too is not, as of yet, backed by evidence. In her detailed review of the evidence for South Africa, Rachel Bray (2003:43) finds very little reliable data to support such an association. The evidence that does exist shows instead that orphanhood increases poverty levels primarily in households that are already poor, and it mostly means that many orphaned children will henceforth have to play a greater role in maintaining the livelihood of the household (Bray 2003:19). Although the numbers of orphans are rising, it is not clear at present how many will become street children, as this in turn will depend on the abilities of the society to absorb the orphans. What is more, some scholars anticipate that the growing size of populations, coupled with the decline in the number of orphans resulting from other causes, could actually mean that the proportion of orphans within society as a whole may not increase substantially (de Waal 2006:84). Nor, for that matter, is there strong evidence that an increase in the number of street children will necessarily destabilize societies. Many countries and cities in the world have a high number of street children and do not destabilize as a result. As with the impact of infectious diseases on the armed forces, the processes through which HIV/AIDS might lead to political instability and state collapse are actually far more complex than is usually acknowledged by these advocates. Many such scenarios are based on logical deduction, extrapolation, and speculation, rather than on empirically observed developments, and there is, as yet, no evidence that a single country has become unstable because of HIV/AIDS. In the case of all four arguments, the evidence base for claiming that HIV/AIDS is a national security threat remains limited at present. At most, it is possible to establish HIV/AIDS as an indirect stressor on various other factors that shape national security, or as something that may further exacerbate other already existing sources of insecurity.

INTERNATIONAL SECURITY AND HIV/AIDS

International security is yet a third framework that has been invoked to discuss HIV/AIDS as a security issue. A report by the Center for Strategic and International Studies argues that HIV/AIDS also affects the institutions that "safeguard the international system as a whole" (CSIS 2002:5). Although the notion of international security shares many affinities with the national security framework, in this case the referent object is not the stability of an individual state but the wider stability of the international order—that is, what some scholars refer to as "international society." Analysts have argued that there are at least three ways in which this international order could be weakened by HIV/AIDS. First, if great powers such as Russia, China, and India, which occupy positions of strategic significance and play important roles within the international order, were to experience wider epidemics in the "next wave" of HIV/AIDS, the international order could potentially be destabilized. Second, HIV/AIDS could create pervasive zones of instability in the worst-affected regions of Africa, possibly requiring difficult outside intervention. Finally, United Nations peacekeeping operations that play an important role in policing the international order are also being adversely affected by HIV/AIDS. As in the case of national security, however, all three of these arguments require further critical examination.

HIV/AIDS and the "Great Powers"

From the perspective of international security, the potential destabilization of great powers by a rampant AIDS epidemic would be a matter of grave concern, and this is precisely what a growing number of scholars and security think tanks have been predicting might happen in the future. In an influential *Foreign Affairs* article, Nicholas Eberstadt warned that the coming "Eurasian" pandemic in China, India, and Russia will "derail the economic prospects of billions and alter the global military balance" (2002:22). In a similar vein, others have predicted a "second wave" of HIV/AIDS undermining these "big" states:

> The first wave of the AIDS pandemic has hit east and southern Africa hardest—with dire results. The second wave now threatens countries both in and outside of Africa, including a number of big states—most notably India, China, Russia, Nigeria, and Ethiopia—with a combined population of 2.8 billion people, where instability will have enormous regional and global ramifications. (CSIS 2002:2)

Russia, India, and China are frequently singled out in the debate on HIV/AIDS and security because of the greater role they play in the maintenance of international security.

In 2005, Russia's deputy prime minister, Alexander Zhukov, argued that AIDS was no longer just a medical problem but also a national security threat (Garrett 2005:25). The potentially threefold impact of HIV/AIDS on Russian national security was further analyzed by Vladimir Frolov, who at the time was deputy staff director of the Committee on Foreign Affairs of the Russian State Duma. First, a declining population will mean that Russia has a smaller male population cohort available for military service (Frolov 2004; Feshbach 2005; Holacheck 2006). Second, HIV/AIDS will accelerate the depopulation of Russia's most-affected regions, many of which are along the borders, thus creating, in Frolov's view, an important international security dimension, since several of these regions border China, which in contrast has considerable surplus population in its corresponding border areas. "Although the threat of Chinese aggression seems remote at the moment," Frolov warns, "uncontrolled Chinese migration into the bordering Russian territories is becoming a serious socio-political issue for the local and regional governments. . . . Thus their stalled development and a shrinking population (due in part to HIV/AIDS), could become a factor in Russia-Chinese relations" (2004:92). Finally, Frolov draws a link between the estimated negative macroeconomic impact of HIV/AIDS and Russian national security. Citing figures from the World Bank stating that Russia's GDP will be 4.15 percent lower by 2010 than it would be without the epidemic, and adding to that the costs of anti-retroviral programs, Frolov finds that these projects will reduce Russia's available resources for national security needs. Specifically, it will be difficult under such circumstances to maintain the goal of dedicating 3 percent of Russia's GDP to defense spending. Even though further study is clearly required, Frolov concludes that "the epidemic needs to be thought of as a major national security issue affecting every aspect of Russia's security for the next 50 years" (2004:96). This makes HIV/AIDS not only an "African" problem but a wider international security concern as well (Ambrosio 2005:2; Grisin and Wallander 2002).

Similar arguments have been advanced with respect to China. Andrew Thompson (2004) identified five threats to Chinese security that could result from HIV/AIDS: (1) areas with a high number of former plasma donors might experience security breakdowns; (2) HIV/AIDS could affect military and police forces; (3) HIV/AIDS could undermine the abilities of states bordering China to control illicit activities and population flow into China; (4) HIV/AIDS could weaken the armed forces of neighboring countries; and (5) HIV/AIDS could generate risks to the army from deployments abroad and to high-prevalence areas. Although Thompson finds it premature to speculate about the impact of HIV/AIDS on the Chinese army, there is already a wider regional or Asian dynamic at play; with militaries in Cambodia, Vietnam, and

Thailand being affected, HIV/AIDS could shape "the military balance in the region in the medium term" and could undermine the delicate balance of power that prevents "regional militaries from initiating hostilities" (2004:302). Like the investigators in many of the other studies, Thompson is keen to emphasize that these are concerns not only for China's national security but also for international security in general, given the important status of China in the region and in contemporary world politics (see also Huang 2003).

Analysts have speculated in the same vein about the security implications of HIV/AIDS for India. There is no need to repeat the arguments in great detail, as they usually follow a very similar course to the ones already explored in discussing Russia and China; India, like Russia and China, is singled out precisely because it is deemed to occupy a crucial position on key strategic issues. To cite one illustrative example, a report by the Center for Strategic and International Studies argues not only that India has become an important security partner for the United States since 2001, but that as "the largest power in a turbulent neighborhood, a nuclear weapons state with an unresolved dispute with a less-stable and less-prosperous nuclear neighbor, India can tilt the region toward greater peace or greater turmoil. The success of its efforts against HIV/AIDS will in part determine in which direction it goes" (CSIS 2004:3; see also CSIS 2006 and Happymon 2005). Again HIV/AIDS is portrayed not only as an African issue, nor even just an Indian one, but as a wider threat to international security and the international order, for if a generalized epidemic breaks out in India, it "will have grave consequences for its national interests, ours, and the region as a whole" (CSIS 2004:2).

Despite their prominence, these international security arguments remain highly speculative—often by the admission of their own authors. As yet there is very little empirical evidence to corroborate the security ramifications of HIV/AIDS for these states. The arguments are mostly exercises in considering "worst-case scenarios" of what might happen *if* these states follow the trajectory of some of the African states that have experienced very large epidemics. As epidemiologist James Chin notes wryly on the basis of his own insider experience with the international politics of HIV/AIDS,

[a] pandemic of AIDS "experts," most without any epidemiological training, have used a variety of epidemic models to project large heterosexual
epidemics in countries where HIV prevalence rates in the general population are still very low. These "experts" sound alarms that the "next
waves" of HIV epidemics are imminent, or HIV is "on the brink" of
jumping into the general population from existing foci in MSM [men
having sex with men] and IDU [injecting drug user] populations. The
"next waves" of HIV epidemics predicted for the general heterosexual
populations in developed countries during the 1980s have never materialized. Most of these AIDS "experts" have given up sounding alarms
about heterosexual HIV epidemics in developed countries and have
turned their attention to large populous countries in Asia. For countries
such as India and China they project severe heterosexual HIV epidemics,
if any sex outside of marital sex is permitted to occur, and education of
the general public, especially youth, on how HIV is transmitted, [is] not
aggressively implemented. (2007:166)

Many studies of the international security ramifications of HIV/AIDS
focusing on the great powers are thus insufficiently sensitive to the underlying drivers of the epidemic in different countries.

Even according to the annual reports compiled by UNAIDS
(2006a:39), the main risk factor in Russia's epidemic, for example, remains the use of non-sterile drug-injecting equipment, and the number
of new HIV infections overall has fallen substantially in this group compared to the levels in 2001. Of course, concern remains that the proportion of heterosexual transmissions among those registering new infections is increasing as a result, and rates may again rise in the future, but
this is still a very different picture from the "runaway" epidemic crip-
pling Russia presented by advocates of the "second wave" thesis. With
respect to both India and China, moreover, UNAIDS (2006a:24–31)
similarly argues that it is actually more accurate to think about these
countries in terms of a series of different epidemics, with some provinces
being largely spared while others experience higher concentrations of
HIV/AIDS, primarily among risk groups. The point here is not for the
governments of these countries to become complacent; the point is to
show that many of the arguments about the impact of HIV/AIDS on the

"great powers" are more keen to make the case that HIV/AIDS is indeed such a potential international security threat than they are to carefully weigh the possibilities that such scenarios might actually emerge.

HIV/AIDS and Regional Instability

Within the framework of international security, HIV/AIDS is often also presented as potentially fueling wider regional instability, especially in parts of Africa. Here it is argued that HIV/AIDS will shift the balance of power between rival states and could provoke new conflicts, thus destabilizing the international order and possibly requiring outside intervention. This concern has even been expressed by some senior military officials in sub-Saharan Africa. Major General Bakwena Oitsile of the Botswana army has argued that the high prevalence rates in the region "could be a source for intra- and inter-state conflict. . . . If the security forces become weaker due to ill health, the countries' constitutions could easily be challenged" (AFP 2003). A report from the Center for Strategic and International Studies similarly warns that "weakened militaries leave a vacuum, at home and abroad, which gangs, terrorist organizations, and guerrilla groups will be only too tempted to fill" (CSIS 2002:6; Singer 2002:149). The International Crisis Group broadened this argument even further by pointing out that the mere *perception* that a neighboring country is experiencing a severe pandemic could be taken as a tactical advantage and could thus lead to hostilities on the basis of misinformation or miscalculation (ICG 2001:21).

Again, however, the empirical basis for such claims is at present quite limited, if not nonexistent. There is no evidence to date that HIV/AIDS is already having international security implications in the sense of either inspiring or preventing the outbreak of armed conflicts. There are no current or recent armed conflicts that were initiated primarily because of HIV/AIDS. Moreover, several important factors raise considerable doubt about whether HIV/AIDS would on its own ever contribute to the outbreak of conflict in this manner. First, there is the regional nature of the spread of HIV/AIDS. In light of the important role of proximity in armed conflicts, it is likely that if one country were affected by prevalence rates high enough to have an impact on military capabilities, the neighboring state would also have similar problems. In sub-Saharan Africa, in particular, many countries are facing such high prevalence rates. In this case the difference between parties would not be expected to be that great, or asymmetrical, unless it became significant through accumulation over time or because one party to a potential dispute had been able to reduce prevalence significantly. Second, the majority of conflicts over the past decade on the continent have been internal ones, further dampening the prospect of such a scenario.

Furthermore, even if a considerable discrepancy in the balance of power were to emerge over time, this scenario still loses some of its probability in light of the fact that it is difficult to identify any historical precedents in which the prevalence of disease alone caused the outbreak of conflict. Induction is not foolproof, of course, but it does raise questions about whether the prevalence of HIV/AIDS alone is sufficient for the outbreak of armed conflict, and it does cast doubt on the scenario that any state would initiate armed conflict on these grounds and no others. All in all, HIV/AIDS seems a rather negligible factor compared to other variables in determining and constraining any confrontation that might take place between two countries. The deployment of armed force always occurs in a larger political context, and discrepancies in force strength are rarely the only reason for the outbreak of conflict or the sole determinant of battle outcomes. Not only does it therefore remain unclear whether the combat capabilities of armed forces would actually be significantly diminished by HIV/AIDS, but other political and strategic factors would be much more important and decisive than the HIV prevalence among the respective armed forces. HIV/AIDS is unlikely to generate new wars along these lines, and arguments to the contrary remain highly speculative.

HIV/AIDS and United Nations Peacekeeping Operations

Finally, HIV/AIDS has become a concern for international security also because it is feared that United Nations peacekeepers could be serving as a vector of the disease. "Here," Richard Holbrooke (2000b) argued, "we get into one of the ugliest secret truths . . . about AIDS: it is spread by UN peacekeepers." The composition of peacekeeping forces has gradually changed over the past decade from a majority contribution by European and North American armed forces to a majority contribution by armed forces from Asia, Africa, and the Middle East. According to Christian Halle, of the United Nations Department of Peacekeeping Operations (DPKO), HIV/AIDS was at the same time also spreading rapidly through several of these newer contributing countries. In recent years the largest contributors to peacekeeping operations have thus included what Halle refers to as "endemic countries" such as Kenya, Nigeria, and Ghana, as well as "high risk" countries such as Ukraine, Pakistan, Bangladesh, and India (2002:17–18). Of course peacekeepers are rarely the only source for spreading the infection, and it is in fact very difficult to quantify this problem because many of the epidemiological preconditions cannot be properly met in areas experiencing complex emergencies where peacekeepers are deployed. There have been six confirmed HIV-positive peacekeepers deployed in East Timor and six in Kosovo, although it remains unclear whether they were already HIV-positive prior to deployment (GAO 2001:24). According to the U.S. General Accounting Office, roughly 14 percent of peacekeepers in 2001 were drawn from countries where prevalence in the general population was estimated to be over 5 percent (GAO 2001).

Roxanne Bazergan (2003:30), working at the time for the UN Department of Peacekeeping Operations, countered that such calculations are not really very informative, since some of the militaries with high HIV prevalence rates do follow UN recommendations of deploying only soldiers who are HIV-negative. Her case study conducted in Sierra Leone found that the Nigerian armed forces, which contributed more than 3,000 troops to UNAMSIL in 2001 and had an adult prevalence rate of 5.8 percent, implemented a predeployment screening policy that should have prevented most HIV-positive soldiers from being deployed in the first place (Bazergan 2003:30). Even Bazergan (2002:5) had to concede, however, that there are serious weaknesses in existing national testing procedures, given that between November 1999 and March 2002 four peacekeepers died from AIDS-related illnesses and ten others were repatriated with AIDS symptoms. This concern is exacerbated when viewed in conjunction with a behavioral study carried out among Nigerian forces in 2001, which found that almost half (48 percent) of the respondents who had participated in peacekeeping operations had sexual partners while deployed, that the probability of their doing so increased the longer they were posted on such operations, and that of those with sexual partners only half used a condom (Adebajo 2002:1–2, 26). The risk that peacekeepers could spread, or indeed acquire, HIV while on deployment thus remains.

The UN Security Council has since begun to take this issue seriously enough to address it formally by passing Resolution 1308, with the result that UNAIDS now encourages member states to provide predeployment voluntary counseling and testing and has developed training modules to communicate key information about HIV/AIDS to countries that contribute troops. UNAIDS also provides financial and technical support to various AIDS programs in the uniformed services, allocates AIDS advisers to peacekeeping operations, and distributes AIDS awareness cards that contain the basic information about HIV/AIDS. Nevertheless, even today the United Nations is still not in a position to discern exactly how many of the peacekeepers deployed in its name are HIV-positive. Because the UN has a policy of voluntary testing, and makes this testing the responsibility of individual troop-contributing countries, it is simply impossible to establish the extent to which the impact of HIV/AIDS on peacekeeping operations does in fact pose a threat to international security. There is no official record publicly available (UNAIDS 2003c:6).

Scrutiny of the empirical evidence about HIV/AIDS and security shows, then, that although the case in favor of considering HIV/AIDS a human security issue is robust, arguments additionally claiming that HIV/AIDS is a national and international security threat traverse quite complex analytical terrain and are much more difficult to corroborate empirically than is usually assumed in the literature. Here, it is at best possible to suggest so far that HIV/AIDS is a factor that contributes indirectly to these types of insecurity or that must be taken into account alongside a wide range of other factors. Of course it is possible that stronger evidence for the latter two claims may emerge in the future, especially as the new AIDS, Security, and Conflict Initiative (ASCI) was launched in September 2006 precisely in order to strengthen the evidence base on the links between HIV/AIDS and security. Moreover, some analysts advancing these connections in the absence of firmer evidence make the precautionary point that waiting for such evidence to emerge may well mean it will be too late to take meaningful action (Garrett 2005:13). Nevertheless, at present there is clearly a considerable disjuncture between the weak nature of the empirical evidence base and the fervor with which policymakers are seeking to reposition HIV/AIDS as a security issue. This disjuncture is significant in and of itself, as it gives rise to the further—and more intriguing—question of why the debate on HIV/AIDS and security has not simply been abandoned, or at least restricted to considering HIV/AIDS solely as a human security issue. The disparity between the nature of the evidence and the strength with which claims about the security implications of HIV/AIDS are asserted suggests that there is much more at stake in the debate about HIV/AIDS and security than simply an empirical question about whether HIV/AIDS is, or is not, a security issue.

The most plausible explanation is that those advancing the securitization of HIV/AIDS are deliberately attempting to use the rhetorical power and connotations of security in order to increase political support and resources for international initiatives seeking to reduce the spread of HIV/AIDS among populations. Despite their weak empirical foundation, arguments about the national and international security implications of HIV/AIDS are deemed advantageous in terms of bolstering international efforts to combat the spread of the disease and increasing the number of people in the world who have access to life-prolonging medicines. Peter Singer concedes as much when he points out that presenting HIV/AIDS as a security threat "strengthens the call for serious action against the menace of AIDS. It is not just a matter of altruism, but simple cold self-interest" (2002:158). Many policymakers concur, among them the director of UNAIDS, who has similarly argued that framing HIV/AIDS as a security issue is not merely an academic exercise but in fact "defines how we respond to the epidemic, how much is allocated to combating it, and what sectors of government are involved in the response" (Piot 2000). In the debate on HIV/AIDS and security, interest in analyzing and understanding the wider social dynamics of the AIDS pandemic therefore frequently goes hand in hand with an underlying commitment to bolster, enhance, and promote international efforts to respond to the disease, and many AIDS activists are concerned that without such frightening scenarios, governments will simply become complacent once again. In order to prevent this, the use of even patchy data seems justified in many quarters. Chin (2007:1) has called this wider strategy of peddling "doom and gloom" scenarios a *splendide mendax*—that is, a noble lie, or a lie told for a good cause. In no small measure, the securitization of HIV/AIDS is an important extension of this process—perhaps even its logical endpoint.

It is not actually that difficult to establish the deliberate and instrumental nature of this framing of HIV/AIDS as a security threat. In the United States, Richard Holbrooke played a leading role in the securitization of HIV/AIDS when he was U.S. ambassador to the United Nations. On the flight home from a trip to Africa with Senator Russ Feingold (D-Wis.) in December 1999, Holbrooke reportedly picked up the telephone and, according to Feingold, "just started doing what Dick Holbrooke does. I watched him call up the Secretary-General (Kofi Annan) and tell him we have to have a Security Council meeting on AIDS. The Secretary-General said, 'We can't do that. AIDS isn't a security issue'" (quoted in Sternberg 2002). Despite serious reservations from China and Russia, the UN Security Council held its historic meeting on HIV/AIDS only one month later, in January 2000. In this sense Holbrooke played a crucial role in framing AIDS as a security issue; he deliberately helped to transform HIV/AIDS—an issue previously thought of primarily in terms of health and development—into a security threat by placing it on the agenda of the UN Security Council. He was joined in this endeavor by the director of UNAIDS, Peter Piot (2005a), who admits that from the very beginning one of his goals as director was to make sure that "we redefined AIDS from a medical curiosity into an issue for economic and social development, an obstacle for that, and as a security issue." Arguments positioning HIV/AIDS as a national and international security issue are thus best understood as deliberate attempts to instrumentally use the language of security in order to increase political support and resources for international programs seeking to reduce the spread of HIV/AIDS among populations.

If that is true, then the securitization of HIV/AIDS marks much more than just a significant change in how HIV/AIDS is being framed in national and international policy circles. It reflects an implicit attempt to encourage an important transformation in the nature and function of security itself. Conventionally seen as the primary political objective trumping all other considerations, security is now being asked to perform an almost secondary and subservient role to the more pressing aim of improving the health of populations seriously affected by HIV/AIDS. Mangling Clausewitz, one could even say that security here is effectively becoming the continuation of medicine by other means, because the language of security is now being deliberately mobilized in this debate to serve a wider public health and humanitarian purpose. The much more challenging questions that the politics of securitizing HIV/AIDS gives rise to, therefore, are exactly what kind of transformation in the nature and function of security is being implicitly attempted in these efforts to securitize HIV/AIDS, how can this transformation be conceptualized, and what are the political consequences of encouraging such a "medical" transformation of security?

3 / SECURITY IN THE ERA OF GOVERNMENTALITY

AIDS and the Rise of Health Security

What kind of transformation in the function of security is the securitization of HIV/AIDS implicitly encouraging? This chapter argues that the instrumental use of security arguments as a strategy for scaling up international AIDS initiatives is a contemporary manifestation of the *governmentalization of security*. Put differently, the securitization of HIV/AIDS is a site in contemporary world politics where practices of security are being absorbed within a broader rationalization of political rule that has been unfolding in the West since the eighteenth century and that was described by Michel Foucault as the era of "governmentality." During this era of governmentality political rule is practiced through a complex triangle of "sovereignty, discipline and governmental management, which has [the] population as its main target and [uses] apparatuses of security as its essential mechanism" (Foucault 2007:108–109). The distinctive features of the era of governmentality are that it takes the population (rather than the sovereign or the state) as its primary referent object and that it simultaneously governs the welfare of populations through three different economies of power. The gradual emergence of this era of governmentality from the eighteenth century on involved an important historical double movement in the West: (1) older forms of sovereign and disciplinary power were increasingly redirected toward the goal of enhancing the welfare of populations, and (2) new mechanisms of rule were developed for managing the welfare of populations directly *at the level of population*. Although Foucault's primary interest in analyzing the era of governmentality was to capture an important change in the nature of political rule more generally, the security practices conventionally studied in international relations are shaped by the rise of the era of governmentality as well. As the latter unfolds, security too eventually becomes absorbed within the governmental economy of power and is gradually, if unevenly, transformed into a practice that is more explicitly concerned with managing the wider welfare of populations and that concurrently deploys sovereign, disciplinary, and governmental forms of power toward that end. The securitization of HIV/AIDS has a greater significance for our understanding of world politics because it is a contemporary manifestation of this very process. This core argument is further corroborated below by the delineation of a more detailed framework for analyzing the governmentalization of security, derived from Foucault's recently translated lecture series *Security, Territory, Population*, which he delivered at the Collège de France in 1978.

SECURING THE WELFARE OF POPULATIONS: SECURITY IN THE ERA OF GOVERNMENTALITY

It is increasingly recognized that Foucault's concept of governmentality is also useful for studying contemporary world politics (Cerny 2003; Dean 1999; Merlingen 2006). The notion has already informed a range of studies on globalization (Larner and Walters 2004; Lipschutz and Rowe 2005), European integration (Barry 1993; Huysmans 2004; Walters and Haahr 2005), refugees (Lippert 1999), and civil society (Lipschutz 2005). Less frequently, the notion of governmentality has been directly utilized by security scholars (Dillon 1995, 2004), who have adopted it to analyze the securitization of migration (Bigo 1998, 2002; Huysmans 2006), the trafficking of women (Aradau 2008), the privatization of security (Leander and van Munster 2006), and terrorism (Aradau and van Munster 2005, 2007). Mirroring the evolution of Foucault's own thinking about governmentality, these studies show that the notion can be interpreted in a variety of ways. At the broadest level, governmentality can refer to the "conduct of conduct" (Gordon 1991). It can also be used more narrowly to designate different mentalities of rule that emerged throughout various periods of human history—as in the case of authoritarian, liberal, or neoliberal governmentality (Dean 1999).

For the purposes of this book, however, the notion of governmentality is deployed more narrowly still, as designating a historically specific transformation in the rationalization of political rule that has been unfolding in the West since the eighteenth century and that Foucault referred to in his lectures as the "era" of governmentality (Walters and Haahr 2005; see also Dean 1999; Merlingen 2006). "We live," Foucault proclaimed in one of these lectures, "in the era of governmentality discovered in the eighteenth century" (2007:109). The distinctive feature of this governmental epoch is that it takes the population as its primary referent object. The "population will appear above all else as the final end of government," and it now "appears as the end and instrument of government rather than as the sovereign's strength" (Foucault 2007:105). The principal aim of political rule in this era of governmentality is to "improve the condition of the population, to increase its wealth, its longevity, and its health" (Foucault 2007:105).

The historical rise of the era of governmentality in the eighteenth century thus presupposes the emergence of the "population" as a meaningful social, economic, and political category, superseding older social categories and units such as the family. This crucial shift resulted in part from the application of statistical methods to the study of the social body, which showed that there were also dynamics at play within society that could not be reduced to the family alone:

Statistics, which had hitherto functioned within administrative frameworks, and so in terms of the functioning of sovereignty, now discovers and gradually reveals that the population possesses its own regularities: its death rate, its incidence of disease, its regularity of accidents. Statistics also shows that the population also involves specific, aggregate effects and that these phenomena are irreducible to those of the family: major epidemics, endemic expansions, the spiral of labor and wealth. Statistics [further] shows that, through its movements, its customs, and its activity, population has specific economic effects. Statistics enables the specific phenomena of population to be quantified and thereby reveals that this specificity is irreducible [to the] small framework of the family. Apart from some residual themes, such as moral or religious themes, the family disappears as the model of government. (Foucault 2007:104)

From the eighteenth century onward, the population increasingly became understood in the West as something that, beyond all the individual occurrences of a particular phenomenon, also has collective or aggregate properties. Illness, for example, is not only manifested individually—that is, as occurring in this family or in that family—but occurs at a regular rate within the entire population as a whole. By gathering detailed statistical knowledge about such phenomena it becomes possible to discover that on average and in any given year, a certain number of people will be born, will become ill, will have an accident, will die, and so on, and these aggregate constants can in turn inform the ways in which populations are governed. For this reason Foucault also spoke of the emergence of a whole series of new knowledges (*savoirs*) within the era of governmentality, the function of which was precisely to detect such constants and to understand how they affect and shape the various elements of the population. This task effectively becomes the primary preoccupation of the human and social sciences more generally, and the knowledge they yield shows very clearly that despite the apparent randomness of these events at the individual level of analysis, there are deeper regularities traversing the population as a whole.

The central category of "population" should not, therefore, be understood as simply referring to a numerical sum of individuals inhabiting a particular territory, nor even as just an aggregate body of legal subjects. Rather—and this will also constitute its historical specificity for Foucault—the category of population refers to a totality of elements, in the midst of which one can find certain constants and regularities and in relation to which one can detect a certain number of variables that influence and mold the population and that are amenable to productive modification (Foucault 2007:74–75). At the one end of the spectrum this "population" denotes a biological mass consisting of "living beings, traversed, commanded, ruled by processes and biological laws. A population has a birth rate, a rate of mortality, a population has an age curve, a generation pyramid, a life-expectancy, a state of health, a population can perish or, on the contrary, grow" (Foucault 1981:161). At the other end of the spectrum this notion of population also entails what one might call its "public" attributes—that is, the behavioral patterns of a population, the opinions of its members, its habits and customs, its religious beliefs, its prejudices and fears, its aspirations, and so on (Foucault 2007:75). Armed with knowledge about these various population dynamics, the wise art of governing in the era of governmentality consists of working with, and through, these multiple variables in order to improve the welfare of the population; it entails the knowledgeable modulation of a complex set of biological and social processes that make the population develop and unfold in a way that increases its overall welfare. Once this way of governing becomes the dominant mode of politics, one has crossed the threshold of the "era of governmentality," which gives birth not just to this new art of government but also to a whole new range of political tactics and techniques (Foucault 2007:106).

In historical terms the emergence of this specific understanding of "population" as the central referent object of politics is a fairly recent development. It was really only in the eighteenth century that the population emerged as an "absolutely new political figure" in a way that it had not been conceptualized before (Foucault 2007:67). Foucault acknowledged that there were of course much older, even ancient, references to "population," but they were mostly confined to questions of repopulating territories following epidemics, crises, wars, famines, and other unexpected shocks to the size of populations. Foucault also had no qualms about conceding that prior to the eighteenth century, populations were frequently seen by mercantilists as an important resource to be exploited by rulers—having a large population was necessary to ensure a large supply of troops, well-populated cities, abundantly attended markets, and so on. What changed from the eighteenth century onward was that the population was no longer viewed merely as a resource to be exploited by the sovereign in terms of his economic and military power; it became something autonomous, something that had its own internal dynamics and distributions that needed to be understood and properly governed. The population was seen less as the legal or juridical subject of the sovereign ruler that could be shaped simply according to his will and more as something "natural" that could not simply be altered by decree of the sovereign (Foucault 2007:70–71).

What happens to the practice of security when the social body begins to be conceptualized and governed in this particular manner? To the extent that security practices too eventually become absorbed and integrated within this governmental economy of power, one would initially expect them to move away from their more traditional goal of ensuring the survival of the sovereign and to become increasingly redirected toward the goal of managing the overall welfare of populations. Security practices too would increasingly have to contribute to improving the welfare of populations rather than just revolving around the preservation of the state, maintaining the stability of the international order, and controlling the deployment of armed force in international politics. These more narrow goals would gradually have to be complemented by a range of concerns crucial to the welfare of populations that would increasingly find their way onto the security agenda. In the first instance, the governmentalization of security would thus signify a transformative process whereby the traditional division of labor between security and politics becomes progressively blurred and where institutions of security are increasingly called upon to contribute to the goals of improving the welfare of populations. The most tangible expression of this transformation would be an expansion of the formal security agenda beyond military force to include a growing range of social issues crucial to the welfare of populations.

HOW ARE POPULATIONS SECURED? THE TRIANGLE OF SOVEREIGNTY, DISCIPLINE, AND GOVERNMENTAL MANAGEMENT

Foucault also argued in his lectures that the rise of the era of governmentality is further characterized by a quantitative and qualitative diversification in the different types of power that are used for managing the welfare of populations. Increasingly, the latter goal is achieved not just through the exercise of one type of power but by the concurrent deployment of at least three different modalities of power. Political rule in the era of governmentality essentially consists of a complex triangle of "sovereignty, discipline and governmental management" (Foucault 2007:107). One of the valuable contributions of Foucault's lecture series is that it schematically illustrates the differences among these three different types of power in greater detail, and that it does so specifically in relation to how issues such as crime and disease can be governed.

Crime can be governed firstly through the use of a simple penal code, according to which "you are not allowed to murder, you are not allowed to steal," which is associated with particular penalties for breaking these laws, such as hanging, a ban, or a fine (Foucault 2007:4). This system is an example of a straightforward binary type of *sovereign* power; it differentiates between what is permitted and what is forbidden, and the sovereign punishes those who deviate from the law—often through spectacular and public displays.

A second way of dealing with crime employs this same prohibition but is accompanied, on the one hand, by a variety of surveillance mechanisms and controls that seek to ascertain whether the thief will or will not steal and, on the other hand, by a set of much less "spectacular" exercises and penal practices, such as confinement, aimed at transforming and improving the behavior of the thief through, for instance, forced labor, rehabilitation programs, and so on. This is an example of *disciplinary* power in that it gives rise to the idea of a "criminal" subject or individual, and rather than simply expelling such individuals from the society by hanging or expulsion, it subjects criminals to a whole set of police, medical, and psychological policies aimed at surveying, diagnosing, and potentially transforming them so that they become peaceful, law-abiding, and productive citizens (Foucault 2007:4).

A third type of power includes the first two dimensions but additionally seeks to govern the population in relation to crime by conducting a variety of complex statistical inquiries into the phenomenon. It seeks to ascertain the average level of this type of criminal offense in the population as a whole, and it further breaks down the phenomenon according to its occurrence in particular regions, among different social classes, in urban versus rural areas, and so on (Foucault 2007:5). It also tries to determine what other factors drive the aggregate level of crime—that is, whether economic crises, famines, and wars increase or decrease the average level of crime. The third type of power then also analyzes these phenomena from the perspective of cost, making an effort to ascertain what the social and economic costs of the crimes are, as well as analyzing how crime can be managed in the most cost-effective manner. Once one has caught a thief, for example, is it more economical to penalize and try to transform the criminal or just to let him go unpunished? Through such a series of extensive and extended questioning, a governmental economy of power tries to discover how criminality (such as theft) can be efficiently and economically contained within boundaries that are socially and economically tolerable (Foucault 2007:5). This mode of governing crime is indicative of a third modality of power, which Foucault referred to as *governmental management.*

In a way that is even more directly relevant to the securitization of HIV/AIDS, Foucault went on in his lectures to illustrate the crucial differences among the three types of power in relation to the governing of disease, where they can be identified by considering the divergent public responses to leprosy, the plague, and smallpox, respectively. The societal exclusion of lepers until the end of the Middle Ages can be understood according to the first, *sovereign* model of power. A host of laws, regulations, and religious rituals provoked a simple binary division between those who were suffering from leprosy and those who were not, enabling the exclusion of those with leprosy (Foucault 2007:9). The responses to plague that emerged toward the end of the Middle Ages, by contrast, worked according to a different logic and deployed other methods. Here, the mechanism was not primarily one of exclusion—of banning those who were infected—but one of subjecting the towns and regions where plague was prevalent to a whole host of detailed regulations stipulating when and how people were permitted to leave their houses, what they needed to do at home, including what kinds of food to consume, and forbidding certain forms of human contact. All of these detailed regulations, moreover, were in turn supported by a host of inspectors who would regularly visit the homes to ensure that the regulations were observed. Here, then, there is no longer merely a sovereign model of power at play; there is also a *disciplinary* one, concerned with regulation and surveillance of individuals and space in order to achieve forms of behavior conducive to containing plague, albeit without the need to physically remove sick individuals from society (Foucault 2007:10).

By the time of the eighteenth century, yet a third mode for managing disease was being pioneered with respect to smallpox—one that again worked at the level of population. Although this form of disease management also relied in part on disciplinary mechanisms, its key objective was (as with the earlier example of crime) to obtain detailed statistical knowledge about how many people suffered from smallpox, at what age, with what social consequences, and with what mortality rate. The discovery of a vaccine, moreover, meant that one could raise additional statistical questions about what chances an individual had to succumb to smallpox, or to acquire smallpox when vaccinated, and indeed how the vaccine would affect the distribution of the disease in the population. Here the logic was not one of exclusion, as in the case of leprosy; nor was it the logic of quarantine, as in the case of plague; rather, it was the question of efficiently managing diseases within the population and keeping them within socially and economically acceptable limits. This last way of dealing with disease is again indicative of the governmental modality of power that operates at the level of population (Foucault 2007:10).

Taken together, these two examples of crime and disease also highlight the four central principles that collectively constitute a governmental economy of power and set it apart from older forms of sovereign and disciplinary rule. First, phenomena such as theft or disease need to be considered at the level of population (rather than at the individual or family level) and within the context of a whole series of complex probability calculations. Authorities, "experts," and scholars thus try to statistically anticipate the rate of incidence and prevalence of a phenomenon within a population, to understand how it relates to other variables shaping the population, and to isolate the key drivers of it (Foucault 2007:6). Second, such population phenomena are to be governed economically in the sense that they are subjected to cost-benefit analysis. They are thus no longer seen primarily in religious, moral, or legal terms; nor are they grounded in a defective concept of mankind or human nature (Foucault 2007:49). Rather, they are considered as natural phenomena in relation to which one needs to calculate the costs, the required level of expenditure to manage these costs, and the likelihood that the expenditure will achieve the desired ends (Foucault 2007:6). For example, even if it has been determined in the courts that an individual has behaved reprehensibly and has violated the law, governments may nevertheless decide on cost grounds that it is inefficient to incarcerate criminals who have committed only a "lower" category of offense. Third, and contrary to the binary divisions between things that are lawful and those that are prohibited according to sovereign power, governmental management works by trying to determine the optimal mean of the population phenomena, as well as setting the outer boundaries of the acceptable deviation from this mean. It will thus be necessary to ask, for example, what level of disease or crime is acceptable and what is a worthwhile expenditure in order to address it. Governing the population thus does not consist of completely eradicating a phenomenon like disease or crime; instead it involves planning for the regular rate at which it occurs and putting in place policies and institutions (such as health insurance and public health measures) that ensure that the levels and consequences of the phenomenon remain within a socially acceptable and tolerable range (Foucault 2007:6).

Finally, a governmental economy of power operates according to the principle of *laissez-faire* or *laissez-passer*. Unlike a disciplinary economy of power, which tries to regulate phenomena in every detail, a governmental economy of power ideally allows things to take their own course, permitting a certain "freedom of movement" (Foucault 2007:41). Insofar as possible, members of the population ought to be left to pursue their desires in a largely uninhibited way, and social life should be permitted to unfold in a fairly unconstrained manner (Foucault 2007:48). In part, this approach stems from the understanding of the population as an organic entity marked by the amalgamated interplay of different variables that shape its inner contours and dynamics—such as climate, levels of commerce, laws (including those relating to marriage and taxes), customs, religious beliefs, and so forth (Foucault 2007:70). The continuous interaction between the population and these multiple variables is extremely complex and escapes the possibility of complete comprehension by any sovereign or government. The proper way of governing them economically, therefore, is not at the level of minute detail, through direct and general decree, but by allowing as much as possible the free play of things and carefully modulating these complex factors. If, for example, one wants to ensure that the population benefits and stands in a productive relationship to the resources of a state, one needs to influence wider financial flows—assessing whether all elements of the population are benefiting from them and whether certain regions are being ignored or circumvented by them. It may subsequently become necessary to influence imports or exports in ways that will stimulate additional employment in certain regions (Foucault 2007:72). The population's economic behavior can then be regulated not by forcing people to behave in a particular way but by, for instance, modulating interest rates or by creating new tax incentives. A governmental economy of power does not try to force people or businesses to move into particular regions but shapes economic processes and incentives in a manner that encourages people and businesses to do so of their own accord.

It is in this context that Foucault understood the rise of modern liberalism not so much as a political ideology but as essentially a technology of governmental management:

> The game of liberalism—not interfering, allowing free movement, letting things follow their course; *laisser faire, passer et aller*—basically and fundamentally means acting so that reality develops, goes its way, and follows its own course according to the laws, principles, and mechanisms of reality itself. . . . Freedom is nothing else but the correlative of this development of apparatuses of security. . . . I think it is this freedom of circulation, in the broad sense of the term, it is in terms of this option of circulation, that we should understand the word freedom, and understand it as one of the facets, aspects or dimensions of the deployment of apparatuses of security. (2007:48–49)

In this respect a governmental economy also departs from the historical relationship between the sovereign and the subject. Governmental management does not primarily "make use of a relationship of obedience between a higher will, of the sovereign, and the wills of those subjected to his will" (Foucault 2007:65). Instead of principally working through such a logic of vertically imposed prohibition, and coercively "nullifying" various phenomena, proper government of the population now consists of exercising a more horizontal form of power that seeks to modulate these various "natural" processes of population, and indeed to play them off against one another, in such a manner that they remain within acceptable limits and do not threaten the overall welfare of the population (Foucault 2007:66). This represents the proper art of government in the era of governmentality.

What ultimately distinguishes the era of governmentality from earlier epochs, however, is not just the recourse to this third form of governmental management but that it simultaneously draws upon *all three* economies of power in order to improve the welfare of populations. Foucault was unambiguous in his view that the era of governmentality should not be thought of as "the replacement of a society of sovereignty by a society of discipline, and then of a society of discipline by a society, say, of government"; rather the era of governmentality should be thought of as a triangle of sovereignty, discipline, and governmental management (2007:107).

The mutual interplay of these three types of power has been widely emphasized by other scholars drawing upon Foucault's work on governmentality (Brown 2006; Butler 2004:52–53, 95)—including those who have used the notion to critically interrogate a range of contemporary security practices. In his groundbreaking analysis, Michael Dillon rightly argued that governmentality refers to a "manifold power that traverses in its compass, and so reproblematizes the juridical and territorial practices of statecraft . . . as well as introducing to us the notions of biopower and population management" (1995:334–335). Similarly, Jef Huysmans observes that a governmentality perspective "moves attention away from the state as an apparatus of unity to a multitude of situated practices that form and apply a variety of governmental techniques that modulate the conduct of freedom in situations of insecurity" (2006:43). While these characterizations are undoubtedly accurate, it possible on the basis of Foucault's lectures to delineate an even more radical reading of the precise arrangement of these three forms of power during the era of governmentality.

In *Security, Territory, Population*, Foucault repeatedly indicated that although all three modalities of power continue to operate in the era of governmentality, they do not stand on an equal footing. Schematically, it is the newer, governmental economy of power that dominates and resides—metaphorically speaking—at the top of the triangle, whereas the older forms of sovereign and disciplinary power play a much more subsidiary, supporting, and subaltern role. Such an arrangement was already implicit in Foucault's lecture from February 1, 1978 (translated into English in 1991), in which he defined "governmentality" as the tendency that "has constantly led towards the *pre-eminence* [emphasis added] over all types of power—sovereignty, discipline, and so on—of the type of power we can call 'government'" (2007:108). Here Foucault already referred explicitly to the "pre-eminence" of government over older forms of sovereign and disciplinary power. This reading is further corroborated when considering the first lecture of Foucault's series from 1978. Again he argued: "What above all changes is the dominant characteristic, or more exactly, the system of correlation between juridico-legal mechanisms, disciplinary mechanisms and mechanisms of security [operating at the level of population]" (2007:8). The era of governmentality thus "consist[s] to a great extent in the *reactivation* and *transformation* [emphasis added] of the juridico-legal techniques and the disciplinary techniques I have talked about in previous years" (Foucault 2007:9). This is an important qualification because it points not just toward the mutual coexistence of these three types of power during the era of governmentality, but also toward a particular arrangement between them. In the era of governmentality, sovereign and disciplinary forms of power become progressively transformed so that they too begin to serve this governmental purpose of enhancing the welfare of the population. It is a way of "making the old armatures of law and discipline function in addition to the specific mechanisms of security [based on the population]" (Foucault 2007:10). The historical emergence of the era of governmentality thus entailed what was effectively an important double movement. On the one hand, it saw the development of new forms of governmental mechanisms of political rule that managed the welfare of populations explicitly *at the level of population*. On the other hand, it also involved increasingly redirecting older forms of sovereign and disciplinary power in such a way that they now explicitly contributed to this governmental goal of enhancing the welfare of populations.

This reading of Foucault's governmentality lectures also has important ramifications for how we further understand the more specific governmentalization of security. To the extent that practices of security become governmentalized as well, one would expect that they too would gradually become sites in which three different types of power— sovereignty, discipline, and governmental management—are concurrently exercised. In this sense the "governmentalization of security" does not just demarcate a transformative process whereby the security agenda broadens to include a number of other issues bearing directly upon the welfare of populations. It also refers, in the second instance, to a process by which security practices themselves become infused with new tactics of governmental management operating at the level of population, which in turn are flanked by the concurrent recourse to sovereign and disciplinary forms of power that now are enlisted in this same effort to manage the welfare of populations.

PROTECTING POPULATIONS FROM NEW SECURITY THREATS:
THE FUTURE CRISES OF CIRCULATION

The particular rationalization of political rule that is characteristic of the era of governmentality also leads to the identification of a new category of threats to the welfare of populations—which Foucault referred to in his lectures as "crises of circulation" (2007:64). At a level of considerable abstraction, one could say that the older form of sovereign power was primarily concerned with pinning things down and with making sure things do *not* circulate. The central political question was usually cast in terms of how territory could be "demarcated, fixed, protected, or enlarged" (Foucault 2007:65). This was essentially the problem that still preoccupied Machiavelli, who was concerned with the question of how to secure the power of the prince over a fixed territory. For this very reason, Foucault also thought that Machiavelli represented not the first modern political thinker but in fact the last great thinker of sovereignty. By contrast, a governmental economy of power seeks to achieve pretty much the opposite; it tries to incite and preserve circulation understood "in the very broad sense of movement, exchange, and contact, as form of dispersion and also as form of distribution, the problem being: How should things circulate or not circulate?" (Foucault 2007:64). Proper governmental management therefore consists of managing circulation and ensuring that everything remains in motion in order to maximize the prosperity and welfare of the population (Foucault 2007:65). Here, too, Foucault's lecture series is valuable in that it provides concrete illustrations of how this concern with fostering circulation emerged historically in the eighteenth century, within the larger context of the rise of the era of governmentality.

In the French city of Nantes, for example, several important changes were made to the spatial layout and organization of the town during this time in order to better facilitate various processes of circulation. The town was effectively to become "a perfect agent of circulation" (Foucault 2007:17) through, for instance, the development of wider roads that traversed the city and that would have to fulfill four important functions (Foucault 2007:18). First, the streets would have to perform a hygienic and public health function—that is, be wide enough to allow the circulation of air through the city in order to purge it of miasmas and thus help keep inhabitants healthy. Second, the major traffic arteries would have to be able to process the volume of traffic needed to conduct all the trade in the city. Third, these roads would have to be integrated into a wider network of surrounding country roads to allow goods to easily enter and exit the city, albeit without relinquishing too much control over customs. Finally, the roads would also have to allow for the policing of the town. In this way the city of Nantes was being positioned within a much broader set of important processes of circulation—the circulation of wealth, of people, of diseases, of climate, and so on. This process of spatial transformation is also indicative of the quintessential political challenge in the era of governmentality, namely how to shape complex and interdependent processes of circulation within and between populations.

Yet precisely because a governmental rationality works according to the principle of laissez-faire and seeks to effectively incite the circulation of goods, people, capital, food, and so on, various circulatory phenomena will emerge that, left to their own devices, will threaten to spiral "out of control" in a way that could undermine the welfare of the population. Again consider the historical example of Nantes: its integration into wider systems of circulation also generated some novel problems. The new roads and the growth in travel made it impossible for Nantes to close the city at night, which in turn made the town more vulnerable to beggars, vagabonds, delinquents, criminals, thieves, and murderers who could come into the city from the countryside. It was thus necessary to better organize these processes of circulation, to distinguish between good and bad circulation, to maximize the good circulation, and to minimize or even eliminate the bad circulation. In this case the proper art of government consisted of making sure that all remained in motion—but in a way that minimized the dangers inherent in processes of circulation (Foucault 2007:65). One of the greatest challenges that a governmental economy of power thus confronts in its efforts to incite the circulation of various goods and people is how to cope with the emergence of "bad" circulatory processes that, left uncontrolled, could undermine the population as a whole. The latter would constitute a new type of *crisis*, which Foucault broadly defined as essentially that "phenomenon of sudden, circular bolting that can only be checked either by a higher, natural mechanism, or by an artificial intervention" (2007:64). These crises of circulation are the result of concrete new praxiological challenges that emerge, but they are also the correlative of a particular way of rationalizing political rule. In many ways, these problematizations surrounding a range of circulatory crises effectively constitute the "dark side" of a rationalization of political rule that is bent on maintaining efficiency while simultaneously allowing the free play of phenomena and stimulating circulation.

During the era of governmentality, the art of governing well also consists of undertaking considerable forward planning in order to anticipate the potential emergence of such crises of circulation in relation to what is a contingent and open "future that is not exactly controllable, not precisely measured or measurable and that . . . takes into account precisely what might happen" (Foucault 2007:24). Foucault argued in this respect that "security will try to plan a milieu in terms of events or series of events or possible elements, of series that will have to be regulated within a multivalent and transformable framework. The specific space of security refers then to a series of possible events; it refers to the temporal and the uncertain, which have to be inserted within a given space" (2007:20). Herein also lies the third element of the governmentalization of security. To the extent that security practices too become integrated within this governmental rationalization of rule, one would further expect them to become sites in contemporary world politics where political actors increasingly seek to problematize and avert the emergence of such future "crises of circulation." The most tangible expression of this third dimension to the governmentalization of security would be an expansion of the formal security agenda to include not just a range of wider social issues, as we have already seen; more specifically still, it would also entail the inclusion of a particular type, or category, of threat that essentially derives from a circulatory phenomenon that, left to unfold freely, could at some future point become unmanageable and directly undermine the welfare of populations; therefore it also requires some more direct form of intervention upon the population. In the era of governmentality, the task of security now effectively becomes to manage such "bad" circulation and to prevent it from getting to the point that it could culminate in a "crisis" of circulation.

WHO SECURES POPULATIONS?
ASSEMBLAGES OF STATE AND NON-STATE ACTORS

Finally, the rise of the era of governmentality entails important changes in terms of *who* governs the welfare of populations and the constellation of political actors involved in the process. First, although the state continues to be a significant political actor (perhaps even the most important one), it too undergoes an important transformation during the era of governmentality. Foucault disagreed with his contemporaries who clung to what he called the "cold monster" view of the state, whereby the state is deemed to be dominating an ever-growing proportion of social life. He also parted company with those who sought to reduce it to a certain number of functions, such as the development of labor or the reification of the modes of production (2007:109). What was important about the state for Foucault was not that it was trying to encroach upon a growing proportion of society but rather the rearticulation and insertion of the state in this new governmental economy power—that is, precisely its "governmentalization," whereby the state becomes increasingly repositioned as a multifaceted manager of the welfare of populations. "What is important for our modernity, that is to say for our present," he chided in his lectures, "is not then the state's takeover [*étatisation*] of society, so much as what I would call the governmentalization of the state" (2007:109). Schematically, he referred to this governmental transformation of the state as its third "incarnation":

> First, the state of justice, born in a feudal type of territoriality and broadly corresponding to a society of customary and written law, with a whole interplay of commitments and litigations; second, the administrative state that corresponds to a society of regulations and disciplines; and finally, a state of government that is no longer essentially defined by its territoriality, by the surface occupied, but by a mass: the mass of the population, with its volume, its density, and for sure, the territory it covers, but which is, in a way, only one of its components. The state of government, which essentially bears on the population and calls upon and employs economic knowledge as an instrument, would correspond to a society controlled by apparatuses of security. (2007:110)

Continuing to subscribe to the "cold monster" theory of the state would be to overlook three crucial characteristics of the state that impose inherent limits on the extent to which it can dominate society in the era of governmentality. First, as we have just seen, governmental management is premised on a certain concept of freedom in which one should allow, insofar as is possible, for the free movement and circulation of goods and people, as well as allowing individuals to pursue their desires in as unconstrained a manner as possible. This is one important limit that restrains governmental power from seeking to interfere too much with the daily workings of society. Second, because the population is understood in "natural" terms, and as being penetrated by complex internal dynamics, great care is taken within a governmental rationality not to govern too much—that is, to respect these natural processes and allow them to unfold as much as possible. A governmental economy of power will only set the outer limits, which these processes should not be allowed to transgress—lest they have negative implications for the welfare of the population as a whole. This too restrains the extent to which the state will try to intervene in the unfolding of these population dynamics. Third, the interventions that the state will undertake within this governmental economy of power often do not bear directly upon individual members of the population by trying to restrict their actions; instead they tend to operate more indirectly. As Foucault put it, the state "will be acting directly on the population itself through campaigns, or, indirectly, by, for example, techniques that, without people being aware of it, stimulate the birth rate, or direct the flows of population to this or that region or activity" (2007:105). These kinds of interventions are not social or political interventions in the strict sense of the word; rather, they mark attempts at the aggregate population level to influence, stimulate, or relieve certain population dynamics "behind the scenes." They will not necessarily be perceived by individual members of the population as direct state interventions. Although the state gradually begins to act in a wider range of issues relating to the welfare of the population, therefore, that is not the same thing as the state encroaching upon a growing proportion of social life in the way envisioned in the "cold monster" view of the state.

This transformation of the state into more of a manager of the welfare of populations is accompanied, secondly, by the growing involvement of a much wider range of social and political actors in the governing of populations. In part this expansion is necessary because governmentality demands a "scientific" and "economic" approach to government; population dynamics need to be empirically observed and statistically evaluated in much the same way that the natural sciences observe physical, biological, and chemical processes (Foucault 2007:350–351). This way of governing necessitates continuous study and observation of the population, the creation of social scientific models, and their evaluations against empirical data. Effectively, anyone engaged in the "analyses," "reflections," "calculations," and "*savoirs*"—that is, social scientific knowledge that has to be generated in relation to the population— is also participating in this form of governmental management. This group includes not only formal state institutions but also experts, scholars, universities, "think tanks," analysts, charitable organizations, and so on. The same is true of those experts generating the knowledge required for understanding the intricate workings and interactions of these multiple population dynamics and how the various population variables relate to and affect one another. This larger assemblage also includes all those involved, in one capacity or another, in managing various population dynamics—such as actuaries who maintain insurance schemes and the doctors and managers who run hospitals ensuring public health, for example. In a sense, governmental power is even exercised implicitly by individual members of the population, who through their desire for security, health, and wealth actively demand the maintenance of such governmental apparatuses and thus seek out and participate in such schemes—like taking out insurance or seeking vaccinations.

To the extent, then, that practices of security become increasingly governmentalized, one would expect these transformations to be mirrored by the political actors involved in the provision and discourses of security. These practices would become sites where states were urged to conduct their political activities in such a manner that they become better and more efficient managers of the welfare of their populations, rather than seeking primarily to ensure their own power and wealth. Moreover, the governmentalization of security would also entail a considerable expansion in the number of actors involved in security practices to progressively incorporate a range of non-state entities such as nongovernmental organizations, scholars, medical workers, and charities. There would, in short, be a sizable expansion of "security" assemblages and networks.

Viewed in conjunction with the previously discussed dimensions to the governmentalization of security, the four principal ways in which one would expect the governmentalization of security to manifest itself are these: (1) security practices become more explicitly concerned with improving the wider welfare of populations; (2) security practices concurrently exercise a combination of sovereign, disciplinary, and governmental forms of power toward this end; (3) international security agendas become increasingly populated with a new category of threat posed by phenomena that are essentially circulatory in nature and that threaten to spiral out of control; and (4) the range of security actors begins to broaden significantly beyond the formal military and intelligence institutions to include much larger assemblages of state and nonstate actors in the provision of security.

HIV/AIDS, HEALTH, AND THE GOVERNMENTALIZATION OF SECURITY

The securitization of HIV/AIDS is one important site in contemporary world politics where this governmentalization of security can be seen to be unfolding in all four respects. First, the emergence of HIV/AIDS on the agenda of the UN Security Council is indicative of precisely that widening of the formal security agenda so as to include broader issues that are crucial to the welfare of populations. In more than four thousand meetings, the Security Council had never before considered a health issue to constitute such a threat to international peace and security. In the historic meetings of the Security Council on HIV/AIDS, international political actors securitizing AIDS are effectively calling upon governments around the world to make the health and longevity of their populations a matter of highest governmental priority— echoing Foucault's (2007:105) earlier observation that in an age of governmentality the population rather than the power of the sovereign is the end of government. This concern with the welfare of populations is evident in the specific ways in which HIV/AIDS has been discussed by international institutions. Although it was politically a very controversial move, Western leaders were able to place HIV/AIDS on the agenda of the Security Council by drawing attention to the potential role of peacekeepers in spreading the virus. The concern expressed was not just that HIV/AIDS would undermine the functioning of international peacekeeping operations in a way that would inhibit the effective policing of the international order but also that this important instrument of maintaining international security (peacekeeping) was potentially spreading a lethal virus to various populations around the world. As Richard Holbrooke put it at the time, that possibility gave rise to "almost the greatest irony of all: in the cause of peacekeeping to spread a disease which is killing 10 times as many people as war" (quoted in Schoofs 2000). In this case, the referent object of the security arguments about HIV/AIDS made at the Security Council was not just the stability of the international order per se but also the welfare of populations adversely affected by the international circulation of peacekeepers who might be carrying HIV across borders.

This expansion of the security agenda at the Security Council to include the health of populations mirrors a deeper transformation in the nature of political rule that also accompanied the rise of the era of governmentality in eighteenth-century Europe, during which the biological life of populations became a matter of more explicit political concern:

> For the first time in history, no doubt, biological existence was reflected in political existence; the fact of living was no longer an inaccessible substrate that only emerged from time to time, amid the randomness of death and its fatality; part of it passed into knowledge's field of control and power's sphere of intervention. Power would no longer be dealing simply with legal subjects over whom the ultimate dominion was death, but with living beings, and the mastery it would be able to exercise over them would have to be applied at the level of life itself; it was the taking charge of life, more than the threat of death, that gave power its access even to the body. (Foucault 1976:142–143)

The debate on HIV/AIDS and security is a site where such biological aspects of existence are now passing into the field of knowledge not just of politicians but of security practitioners as well and where the practices and institutions of security are being explicitly invited to contribute to the wider goal of enhancing the welfare of populations—including their overall levels of health. To be sure, this art of government does not yet prevail in the Security Council; it has clearly not risen to preeminence and still remains heavily contested—especially by countries with veto power, such as Russia and China. Nevertheless, the securitization of HIV/AIDS may turn out to be indicative of the beginning of an important transformation that may unfold rapidly or, as in the case of European societies, only gradually and unevenly over a much longer period of time. Indeed, it is worth noting that even Russia and China have already overcome some of their initial skepticism and have subsequently come to the table to join in the debate on HIV/AIDS and security.

Beyond providing evidence of how the security agenda is expanding to include issues relevant to the welfare of populations; the securitization of HIV/AIDS also offers a pertinent example of precisely the kind of future *crisis of circulation* that poses particularly grave challenges to a governmental economy of power. The way in which HIV/AIDS is problematized in various national and international security forums is precisely as a *circulatory* threat—that is, as a phenomenon that, according to the frequently invoked cliché, does not stop at national borders. HIV, it is argued, is something that in the absence of more direct intervention upon the population threatens to escalate dangerously and reach unmanageable dimensions. In this respect the securitization of HIV/AIDS also marks the identification of a more specific type of circulatory threat, what is effectively an international crisis of (viral) circulation. This understanding of HIV/AIDS as essentially constituting a "crisis of circulation" is implicit in the way the pandemic has been characterized by the director of UNAIDS:

> I see it as an extremely smart creature. It's diabolic certainly, but in a way that it makes use of all the opportunities—I mean globalization. People travel, and there's the networks. When you think of it that in, let's say, 25 years roughly that about 70 million people have become infected with this virus, probably coming from one at some point, it's mind-blowing. It tells you also about the networks that exist, tells you another story about globalization. All these people are connected with each other by definition, because they had sex with each other; they shared needles; they got a blood transfusion from someone who got it, or their mother had it. That's it. There are no other ways of transmission. That virus has made

optimal use of let's say communication networks and contact among people. . . . So the potential for the epidemic and the spread of the virus is—we haven't reached the end yet. We are only at the beginning from a historic perspective, and we are now entering into the true globalization phase of this epidemic. We're spreading it all over the world. It's not only the West and Africa alone. It's the whole world now. (Piot 2006)

In a way that is all too representative of many daily characterizations of, and pronouncements on, the AIDS pandemic, Piot considers HIV/AIDS to be located at the nexus of various international processes of circulation that continually amplify its global spread, with potentially devastating consequences. Just as the fostering of processes of circulation through the spatial reorganization of the town historically created novel problems in Nantes, so too states that are today trying to position themselves optimally with respect to various processes of international circulation (be it labor, capital, or tourism) are thereby also potentially exposing themselves to seeing "dangerous" increases in the levels of HIV/AIDS among their populations—the AIDS pandemic as the "dark side of globalization" if you wish.

Travel is one such system of circulation that undoubtedly inter-acts synergistically with HIV/AIDS. Beyond the obvious points about the growth in air travel, a key component of trying to position states well in relation to various processes of international circulation is the development of a good and reliable transport infrastructure. Unfortu-nately, such improvements in the developing world also facilitate the circulation of HIV across territories and populations. Truckers traveling long distances often sleep in their trucks and use part of their wages, or the promise of a meal, to entice women to sleep with them when they are away from home. This pattern is confounded when local men sub-sequently have sex with the same women who also had sex with the truck drivers, thus driving the virus further into the local populations living along the truck routes (Clarke 2004; Lurie et al. 2004:209). In Af-rica, high HIV prevalence rates have been detected among truck drivers in Kenya, Tanzania, Sudan, Côte d'Ivoire, and Nigeria, and the spread of the pandemic across Africa shadowed the building of the Kinshasa Highway, which traverses the African continent from east to west, from Congo to Kenya. Keith Suter notes: "If the virus had been noticed earlier, it might have been named the 'Kinshasa Disease' to note the fact that it passed along the Kinshasa Highway during its emergence from the African forest" (2003:120). In this respect the circulation of goods and people goes hand in hand with the circulation of the virus.

The international market in blood transfusions and blood products is another important system of circulation that has helped to spread the virus around the globe, particularly in the early stages of the pandemic. Although screening procedures for blood transfusions have greatly improved since then, this problem reemerged in China during the 1990s, when several Chinese companies trading in the international market for blood and blood products began to collect blood plasma from poor farmers in Henan province. The problem was not only that these companies used collection methods that were not sterile and safe; it was also that the collection of the blood plasma entailed separating the red blood cells from the plasma and then returning the former to the donors after it had circulated in contaminated machines, thus greatly increasing the chances of infection. The farmers, ignorant of the dangers of the disease, viewed selling their blood plasma as a very lucrative proposition. The average farmer in Henan lives on around seventy-eight U.S. cents a day, whereas villagers were paid six dollars for a donation, so they were able to achieve a week's worth of pay with one donation—and at a fraction of the usual physical exertion. Not surprisingly, Henan province quickly became a "blood farm," and hundreds of farmers lined up, often giving multiple donations. Many of these villagers from the countryside have since been heading to the major cities of China in search of employment (Grasso, Corrin, and Kort 2004:315–316). Similar practices have also been reported in Hebei, Anhui, Shaanxi, and Guizhou provinces (Akella, Singhal, and Rogers 2003:76). In this way the global circulation of blood and blood products has generated new risks that are fueling the AIDS pandemic.

HIV/AIDS does not simply act synergistically with wider processes of circulation; it is also driven specifically by those international processes of circulation fostered by security institutions, such as the armed forces. As we have already seen, HIV/AIDS is probably also being spread around the globe by the international circulation of peacekeepers. Here the problem confronting the Security Council is precisely that it needs to modulate two different systems of circulation—the circulation of peacekeepers and the circulation of HIV. The cognitive and policy challenge of studying such processes of circulation is not only to understand these flows in their singularity but also to grasp the complex interdependencies that exist between various systems of circulation (such as the microbial, economic, and military). Policymakers at the Security Council must now confront the difficult task of modulating different, interdependent, and highly complex systems of international circulation in order to prevent the future emergence of a viral crisis of circulation.

Even the governmental concern with taking precautionary measures in order to prevent such crises of circulation from emerging in the future is evident in the securitization of HIV/AIDS. In the era of governmentality, Foucault argued, governing focuses on "a possible event, an event that could take place, and which one tries to prevent before it becomes reality" (2007:33). In the securitization of HIV/AIDS, the pandemic is usually presented not so much as an immediate and present existential security threat but more as an underlying and longer-term security "risk." If insufficient action is taken now, it is argued, the pandemic could potentially develop serious national and international security implications in the future. Many of the security arguments about the impact of HIV/AIDS on the armed forces, on the stability of states, and on peacekeepers function by identifying various risk factors and then speculatively linking them in such a way that HIV/AIDS can be seen to potentially produce a security crisis *in the future*. For example, one of the preambulatory clauses of Security Council Resolution 1308—the first resolution ever to be passed on HIV/AIDS by the council—warns that HIV/AIDS, "if unchecked, *may* pose a *risk* to stability and security [emphasis added]" (UNSC 2000a). Frustrated with the speculative nature of many such arguments, some social scientists working on HIV/AIDS have recently insisted that "those who write on AIDS and security are advised to avoid, if at all possible, using the word 'may' or at least to note that while the epidemic may do x, it may also not do x" (Whiteside, de Waal, and Gebre-Tensae 2006:215). If this advice were followed, the securitization of HIV/AIDS would probably have to stop dead in its tracks; for it works mostly on the basis of a precautionary risk logic in which the future is permitted to determine the actions taken in the present. These speculative statements made in the context of the securitization of HIV/AIDS are significant precisely because they illustrate the governmental postulation of a possible series of events that could, if the free circulation of HIV is left unchecked, threaten to escalate into a crisis. In this respect, the securitization of HIV/AIDS is not merely an example of a wider social issue relevant to the welfare of populations that has now been explicitly placed on the international security agenda; it is also indicative of the new category of threat resulting from circulatory overloading, the kind of future "crisis of circulation" that a governmental economy of power essentially seeks to plan for and avert.

Finally, the securitization of HIV/AIDS reflects the widening assemblage of actors that are becoming involved in the practice and provision of security. Those involved in attempts to present HIV/AIDS as a security threat certainly include state institutions, such as national governments, heads of state, and government institutions. Yet they also include a much broader range of actors—international institutions such as the Security Council, the World Bank, UNAIDS—all of which have contributed to the debate on HIV/AIDS and security. They include a range of public health institutions, such as various national health ministries, the World Health Organization, and members of the medical profession, who have participated in these debates. They further include think tanks such as the Center for Strategic and International Studies, the Chemical and Biological Arms Control Institute, the International Crisis Group, the International Institute for Strategic Studies, and others, all of which have contributed to the process of generating knowledge about the ways in which the international circulation of HIV/AIDS has implications for security. They even include scholars, social scientists, epidemiologists, and demographers working at universities who are engaged in generating the necessary empirical knowledge about how the welfare of populations is affected by the circulation of the lethal virus within and between populations. The securitization of HIV/AIDS has thus been facilitated by a wide network and assemblage extending far beyond the traditional military and intelligence institutions that have historically tended to be the primary actors in the field of security. In all of these ways, the debate on HIV/AIDS and security becomes a crucial site in contemporary world politics where the principles of governmentality are being applied to practices of security and are also being disseminated internationally beyond the borders of the

West through international institutions such as the Security Council, which for the first time in its history has placed a public health issue on its agenda. The securitization of AIDS emerges, in short, as a concrete contemporary manifestation of the governmentalization of security.

What are the political ramifications of encouraging the governmentalization of security? Does the immense scale of the humanitarian tragedy of HIV/AIDS justify the appropriation of security as a tool for improving the health and welfare of populations? Or does the attempt to respond to HIV/AIDS in the language of security produce more dangerous political effects that, irrespective of the well-meaning intentions that animate such securitization, ought to be avoided? Foucault once famously argued: "My point is not that everything is bad, but that everything is dangerous, which is not exactly the same as bad. If everything is dangerous, then we always have something to do. So my position leads not to apathy but to hyper—and pessimistic—activism" (1997c:256). From this perspective it is important not just to trace the governmentalization of security analytically but also to evaluate its political and social consequences. Doing so is no small endeavor and in fact requires a great amount of work. If it is indeed true that the securitization of HIV/AIDS is a manifestation of the governmentalization of security, then one would also expect this practice to be simultaneously infused with at least three different economies of power—sovereign power, disciplinary power, and governmental management. Each of these modalities of power in turn has its own dynamics, effects, and associated dangers. Exposing the securitization of HIV/AIDS as a manifestation of governmentalization thus significantly complicates its evaluation, as it now effectively requires one to work simultaneously along three different trajectories of power. Analyzing the dangers accompanying the governmentalization of security requires ascertaining whether signs of these three types of power can indeed be found in the securitization of HIV/AIDS, as well as conducting a more detailed analysis of the dangers to which these modalities of power give rise. It requires not just one but three separate analyses. Each of the next three chapters therefore focuses on the operation of one of the economies of power in the securitization of HIV/AIDS and analyzes its potential dangers.

4 / NATIONAL SECURITY
Sovereignty, Medicine, and the Securitization of AIDS

That the securitization of HIV/AIDS draws upon a *sovereign* economy of power can be seen in those arguments claiming that the AIDS pandemic is a threat to *national* security. This is because the national security framework invoked in such arguments is itself a legacy of the much older form of sovereign power; it is a security framework principally concerned with the survival and power of the sovereign and, by modern extension, of the state. When political actors claim that HIV/AIDS is a threat to national security, they are thus implicitly marshaling a sovereign economy of power in response to the AIDS pandemic. This is potentially a very dangerous move. Within security studies the political dangers associated with such mobilizations of sovereign power have already been highlighted by securitization theorists, who have long warned that securitization processes can strengthen the power of the state over its society and its citizens. National security justifications, for example, may be invoked by the state in order to override the individual rights of citizens. This chapter draws upon securitization theory in order to analyze the extent to which such dangers are present in the securitization of HIV/AIDS. Paradoxically, the analysis finds that although the securitization of HIV/AIDS is indeed accompanied by such potential dangers, they have for the most part failed to materialize to date—despite the fact that the AIDS pandemic has been publicly framed and discussed as a national security threat for several years now. That observation gives rise to the much more intriguing question of exactly why the mobilization of national security language has *not* exacerbated the kinds of abuses of human rights or civil liberties that securitization theory would lead us to fear.

A more detailed analysis of the politics of framing HIV/AIDS as a national security threat provides an explanation. The national security arguments are not actually calling for states to preserve their power by curtailing the civil liberties of people living with HIV/AIDS. Rather, they are trying to convince governments—especially those in the developing world—that they need to ensure their survival by improving the overall health of their populations. Public health advocates are thus deliberately deploying the language of national security in order to both compel and materially enable states in the developing world to move away from being neo-patrimonial entities largely serving their own narrow interests and toward becoming political entities that are much better at managing the health of their populations. This mobilization of national security arguments as a strategy for persuading states to improve—rather than restrict—the welfare of their populations is exemplary of precisely the crucial shift that sovereign power begins to undergo in the era of governmentality, when sovereign power comes to serve less and less the power of the sovereign and is increasingly redirected toward the task of managing the welfare of populations.

That development can be seen in the domestic sphere, where the institution of law, which historically has been used to serve the power of the sovereign, is increasingly deployed to manage the welfare of the population (for example, in making it compulsory to wear seat belts). It can also be seen today in the international politics of HIV/AIDS, where the sovereign language of national security is being mobilized to compel states to do more to improve the health of their populations. This mobilization of sovereign power through the language of national security is not so much a manifestation of the *étatisation* of society in the manner that securitization theory would lead us to fear as it is an indication of the attempt to encourage the *governmentalization of the state* in the developing world. At a deeper level, this explains why the extensive use of national security language has not animated a more draconian international response toward people living with HIV/AIDS. It also means, however, that the most pressing political dangers associated with the securitization of HIV/AIDS may not be the obvious ones that securitization theory routinely warns about; the much more important dangers may reside instead in the concurrent and subtle mobilizations of disciplinary and governmental forms of power in the broader international quest to scale up international AIDS programs.

NATIONAL SECURITY AS SOVEREIGN POWER

The notion of national security that is frequently invoked in the debate on HIV/AIDS and security is significant not only because of the kinds of empirical relationships it posits between HIV/AIDS and security. In many ways this framework is, in and of itself, a contemporary legacy of the much older form of sovereign power, which historically had the sovereign or king at its center and was concerned with securing, defending, and at times expanding the sovereign's control over his territory and subjects. These subjects stand in either submission to or transgression of the sovereign's authority. This notion of sovereign power originated in the Middle Ages, when it initially served to justify the rule of the feudal monarchies and, later, the great monarchical administrations. It is a theory of power that was quintessentially expressed by Machiavelli, who was concerned precisely with the question of how in a given territory (be it conquered or inherited, and irrespective of whether rule was legitimate or not) one could ensure that the power of the sovereign is not threatened, or at least that the sovereign would be in a position to protect himself from danger. This, in effect, was the problem of *The Prince* (Foucault 2007:65).

As a modality of power, sovereign power has several important characteristics. First, it is a form of power exercised by individuals, be it the sovereign himself (a king, a prince, a head of state) or agents acting on behalf of the sovereign in an official capacity. Second, sovereign power is exercised in a highly visible manner. Those exercising it—if not the sovereign himself—will be identifiable as such (through uniforms or other means of identification); they are agents of the sovereign and they are aware of this. Third, sovereign power is exercised intermittently; it is enacted at certain crucial points in time, when it is displayed in a spectacular and elaborate fashion, especially when enforcing law, punishing crimes, raising armies, or going to war. Michel Foucault (1975:48) referred, for example, to the spectacular rituals of torture and execution that sovereigns used to display publicly, but the display of sovereign power also includes other public ceremonies such as a coronation or the entry of a king into a conquered city. Finally, sovereign power is fundamentally a "negative" power of subtraction or deduction; it is a power that essentially functions by taking things away from its subjects—be it goods, labor, money in the form of levies and taxes, or in the most extreme case, life itself (Foucault 2003:240–241).

Although this notion of sovereign power may seem quite antiquated today, it survived well into the era of parliamentary democracies (Foucault 2003:35). It is true that from this time ever onward, the actual sovereign (king, queen, prince) played a less important role, but this form of power nevertheless continued to operate in the form of the state, public law, prohibitions, and compulsion. It also continues to reside in the theory of the social contract where, even after the democratic revolutions, individuals relinquish part of their personal sovereignty to a common sovereign (in Hobbes's case, a Leviathan) or to the state in return for their collective protection (Constantinou 2004; Odysseos 2002, 2007). Even in liberal democracies the state continues to exercise a significant degree of sovereign power—this power has "merely" become democratized. Nor does sovereign power disappear in the era of governmentality. Although the era of governmentality entails the rise to preeminence of governmental economies of power concerned with (and operating at the level of) population, that does not imply that sovereign power ceases to play a role. Rather sovereign power is increasingly transformed and mobilized in a redirected manner so that it no longer principally serves the selfish interests of the sovereign but contributes instead to the greater goal of enhancing the welfare of the population.

Within contemporary international relations, the continuing legacy of sovereign power is evident in the notion of national security. Like sovereign power more generally, the national security framework is principally concerned with the preservation of the power of the state. As we have seen, arguments that HIV/AIDS is a national security threat speak directly to the concerns of the sovereign by positing that HIV/AIDS undermines the ability of the sovereign and/or the state to maintain control over its territory, since it is argued that HIV/AIDS weakens its military institutions. Such arguments also warn sovereigns and heads of state that HIV/AIDS will undermine their ability to visibly exercise power in terms of enforcing laws and punishing crimes by weakening the police force and the judiciary as a result of increased mortality in these sectors. Analysts working with the national security framework argue further that HIV/AIDS will undercut the sovereign's economic power base by causing mortality in the economically most productive age groups, thereby diminishing the ability of the sovereign to extract taxes, revenues, and labor from his population. In all of these ways national security arguments about HIV/AIDS testify to the continuing operation of the older form of sovereign power in the securitization of HIV/AIDS. Indeed, they effectively mark the incitement of a sovereign economy of power in relation to the AIDS pandemic.

HIV/AIDS, SECURITIZATION THEORY, AND THE DANGERS OF SOVEREIGN POWER

What political dangers arise when a sovereign economy of power is marshaled in response to the AIDS pandemic? Within security studies, one school of thought has been concerned for some time (albeit indirectly) with answering precisely this question—although it has not explored it specifically in relation to HIV/AIDS. Long before HIV/AIDS was articulated as a national security threat, securitization theory sought to probe the implications and dangers of expanding the security agenda to include a range of social issues (Buzan, Wæver, and de Wilde 1998; Deudney 1990). Jef Huysmans (2006) has usefully summarized the way in which securitization theory tends to critically approach such securitization processes by illustrating them in relation to the securitization of migration. Here, the development of security knowledge is viewed as

> a political and normative practice of representing policy questions in an existential modality. In this understanding, security knowledge is not simply an analytical lens. It is a political technique of framing policy questions in logics of survival with a capacity to mobilize politics of fear in which social relations are structured on the basis of distrust. In this interpretation, security studies is not primarily about evaluating whether the political identification of threats rests on a true or an imagined danger and about developing instruments for controlling threats or for rec-

tifying a misperception. The key question was not whether immigrants or asylum seekers posed a real or imagined threat to the member states of the European Union or to the proper functioning of the Internal Market. What seemed to matter more was the idea that security knowledge implied a particular way of arranging social and political relations. It has a specific capacity for fabricating and sustaining antagonistic relations between groups of people. Framing refugees as a humanitarian question introduces different relations to refugees than framing it as a security question, for example. While the former allows for compassion or for relating to the refugee as a rights holder, the latter sustains fear of refugees and policies of territorial and administrative exclusion. (xi–xii)

What specific dangers have these securitization scholars identified in relation to other securitization processes? On the basis of their analysis of case studies from the 1990s, securitization theorists warn that the securitization of an issue usually leads to a greater level of state mobilization, enabling the state to encroach to an increasing degree upon social life where it might not be desirable (Buzan, Wæver, and de Wilde 1998:4). First, states can employ the language of security to remove an issue from routine democratic considerations and elevate it to the higher echelons of the state's inner circles of power, where there is less political transparency and hence less democratic scrutiny of issues. Second, state representatives often also invoke the term "security" in order to justify the use of any necessary means to confront the threatening condition or to silence opposition to the state (Buzan, Wæver, and de Wilde 1998:21). Any emergency measures taken by the state can thus potentially be used to override the rule of law and infringe upon valued civil liberties. Hence securitization theorists are generally concerned about how the language of security has historically served to silence opposition to the state, how it has given state representatives special powers that could be exploited for domestic purposes, and how it can lead to the suspension of important democratic control mechanisms (Buzan, Wæver, and de Wilde 1998:29).

Those framing HIV/AIDS as a national security threat will need to devote greater attention to this outcome of past securitization processes. In the case of HIV/AIDS, too, framing the issue as a national security threat could push responses to the disease away from civil society and toward the much less transparent workings of military and intelligence organizations, which also possess the power to override human rights and civil liberties—including those of people living with HIV/AIDS. One analyst has pointed out that the designation of HIV/AIDS as a national security issue is "a bit frightening and a bit scary . . . because that means you're going to begin to call in the FBI, you can call in the CIA. If people are talking about things which are decided to be a national security issue, they in fact can be spied upon and civil rights protections can be suspended" (Chowka 2000). Although many would not want to go quite that far, it is true that in the United States the armed forces and the CIA have become increasingly involved in assessing the security implications of HIV/AIDS. Throughout history, moreover, people suffering from illnesses have endured some fairly draconian measures imposed by the state—be it the quarantining of cholera victims or the forced institutionalization of lepers well into the twentieth century (Baldwin 2005:2).

State responses to people living with HIV/AIDS have also frequently been undemocratic and characterized by periods of great insensitivity. Calls for quarantining such people, subjecting them to various forms of violence, attempting to bar them from serving in state institutions, and refusing to issue visas to HIV-positive foreigners are only a few of the ways in which those living with HIV/AIDS have been ostracized and even persecuted by some states for their illness. In his historical account of state responses to the AIDS pandemic, David Baldwin (2005) chronicles how countries ranging from Iraq and Syria to China have demanded testing of aliens entering the country, as well as of nationals who have spent considerable amounts of time abroad. In China citizens were required to report anyone they suspected of having AIDS for isolation and treatment, and—in confirmed cases—movements and activities were restricted and obligations to carry registration cards imposed. In the Indian state of Goa, people suspected of having AIDS could not refuse testing, while those living with HIV/AIDS were forced to book entire compartments in order to travel on trains. Cuba, too, imposed screening measures on various "at risk" populations and isolated those living with HIV/AIDS in sanatoriums (Baldwin 2005:35–36). Portraying HIV/AIDS as a national security threat risks fueling such exclusionary and dehumanizing responses and could inadvertently serve as an implicit legitimization of any harsh or unjust "emergency" policies that states may adopt in relation to those living with the virus.

Nor are such measures confined to the dustbin of history. In the United States, the Institute of Medicine not long ago proposed a policy of introducing mandatory screening for tuberculosis (TB)—a common condition among people living with HIV—for immigrants from countries with high prevalence rates, and it even made the case in favor of linking the permanent residence card (green card) to taking preventative treatment (Coker 2003:2). As recently as February 2003, the British government similarly considered implementing compulsory HIV screening for prospective immigrants amid alleged worries that HIV-positive foreigners were traveling to the United Kingdom to seek treatment (Hinsliff 2003:2). Such moves undoubtedly justify the political concern of securitization theorists that the involvement of the state in the management of broader social issues can have a detrimental effect by placing the management of such issues behind closed doors and by paving the way for overriding the civil liberties of persons living with HIV/AIDS if it is deemed necessary by the state.

Even where such draconian measures are not imposed, the state-centric nature of the language of national security may have other political drawbacks. Susan Peterson fears that responding to HIV/AIDS as a national security issue transforms the logic of international action on HIV/AIDS into one based on narrow self-interest, which historically has not proved very effective in addressing global health issues. Indeed, it creates the impression that global health issues are worth addressing only to the extent that they touch upon the core security interests of states, which may mean that in the long run states will actually cease to be concerned about global health in areas where health issues do not affect their core national security interests (Peterson 2002/2003:46, 80). These potentially important side effects of using the language of national security need to be kept in mind by those who make a connection between HIV/AIDS and national security. Indeed, Peterson warns that "if well-intentioned people seek to rally support among western governments for anti-AIDS efforts in Africa, portraying disease as a security issue may be exactly the wrong strategy to employ" (2002/2003:81).

Securitization theory also identifies a second political danger associated with the mobilization of sovereign power when it urges securitizing actors to "ask with some force whether it is a good idea to make this issue a security issue—to transfer it to the agenda of panic politics—or whether it is better handled within normal politics" (Buzan, Wæver, and de Wilde 1998:34). The potential problem with the language of security here is that it encourages the adoption of a hasty and urgent response—that is, a "panic politics"—that may preclude an analysis of the deeper factors driving the AIDS epidemic. Framing HIV/AIDS as a national security threat is likely to fuel a vertical, "quick fix" approach to the disease that is insufficiently sensitive to the local experience of HIV/AIDS in the affected communities (Seckinelgin 2008). As the AIDS researcher Tony Barnett argues:

> Suggestions either that AIDS is a threat to "national security" or that it necessarily leads to political and governance problems are facile and may be self-fulfilling. We can speculate but we just do not have the evidence on this, either way, for countries in sub-Saharan Africa or, for that matter, anywhere else. Such simple-minded perspectives may move national security organs. They fail to engage with the key problem of the 21st century: living together on one small, diverse and increasingly crowded planetary homeland. (2006:313)

There is also a deeper problem here. In the case of HIV/AIDS, arguments about the national security implications of the disease focus predominantly on the dire consequences and the long-term effects of the pandemic; they have very little to say about the causes of the pandemic. For efforts to ameliorate the extent of the current pandemic, this emphasis is undoubtedly problematic, since the international community can respond successfully to this pandemic only through an analysis of what is actually driving the pandemic, rather than just an awareness of what its longer-term consequences might be.

Precisely because of such dangers, securitization theorists generally try to avoid the excessive securitization of issues and suggest that "security should be seen as negative, as a failure to deal with issues as normal politics. Ideally, politics should be able to unfold according to routine procedures without this extraordinary elevation of specific 'threats' to prepolitical immediacy" (Buzan, Wæver, and de Wilde 1998:29; Williams 2003:523). It is better to aim for "de-securitization"—that is, for shifting issues out of emergency mode and returning them to routine political processes. In so doing, securitization theory implicitly recognizes that the mobilization of sovereign power—through the language of national security—could also have dangerous and undesirable political consequences for people living with HIV/AIDS, and that those engaged in the securitization of HIV/AIDS need to take care not to replicate these dangers.

TRANSGRESSIVE POLITICS: SOVEREIGN POWER
AND THE GOVERNMENTALIZATION OF THE STATE

The benefit of some hindsight, however, shows that one of the most notable and counterintuitive aspects of the securitization of HIV/AIDS is precisely that it does *not* appear to have fueled the same kind of draconian response to the AIDS pandemic that characterized the response to other infectious diseases (such as leprosy, cholera, or even SARS) in the past. It is certainly true that throughout the history of HIV/AIDS, and especially in the early stages of the pandemic, there were many instances of draconian measures being imposed upon people living with HIV/AIDS, but there is little evidence that the more recent use of national security language at international institutions such as the United Nations Security Council has substantially exacerbated this situation to the extent that securitization theory would initially make us fear. That such dangers have largely failed to materialize gives rise to the much more interesting question of exactly why the invocation of national security language has not generated a harsher response to the pandemic, as securitization theory would lead us to expect.

An important part of the explanation undoubtedly lies in the strong human rights culture that pioneering civil servants such as Jonathan Mann, who founded the World Health Organization's initial Global Program on AIDS in 1986, imprinted on international AIDS initiatives from the outset—insisting on the paramount importance of democratic consent and *voluntary* behavior change (de Waal 2006:48). This approach has meant that attempts to impose more-stringent political measures on people living with HIV/AIDS could be continuously met with counterdiscourses on human rights. Yet there is also another and more subtle reason for this counterintuitive course of events—one that is linked more closely to the particular ways in which sovereign power is being mobilized in the securitization of HIV/AIDS. A closer examination of the national security arguments about HIV/AIDS shows that they are not trying to protect the power of states by calling for the civil liberties of persons living with HIV/AIDS to be curtailed. Rather, they are being mobilized as part of a comprehensive strategy for transforming states into better managers of the welfare of their populations—that is, essentially for governmentalizing the state in the developing world.

Such a national security argument about HIV/AIDS is being used as a political technology for encouraging governmentalization of the state in the developing world in at least two ways. First, these arguments deliberately mobilize the strong rhetorical power of national security language in order to break through the "wall of silence" that historically has surrounded HIV/AIDS in many developing countries, thereby opening the way for these states to become more proactive in managing the health of their populations. Whereas securitization theorists—working largely within the context of Western liberal democracies—are understandably concerned to ensure that the state should not forcibly interfere with democratic deliberation processes, outside of the West the relationship between state, society, and security is often more complex.

In some of the countries most seriously affected by the AIDS pandemic, the main danger is not excessive state mobilization; on the contrary, it is the absence of a more meaningful state response to the disease. In several southern African countries there is a widespread desire among people living with HIV/AIDS for more action to be taken to ensure the provision of medicines—a prominent example of which is the Treatment Action Campaign in South Africa (Sell and Prakash 2004). In many other African countries there are millions of people who do not even have the privilege of being informed about this illness, let alone knowing whether they have contracted the virus or not; yet their governments remain unable or unwilling to take leadership on the issue, to make such medical provisions, or even to prioritize the illness politically. Over the past years, Thabo Mbeki's refusal to instruct the South African government to prioritize efforts to address the AIDS pandemic has been a case in point (Youde 2007). It is, unfortunately, only one example among many. In Cameroon, too, the state has remained fairly isolated from the concerns of its people; and the interruption of its democratization process has enabled it to ignore HIV/AIDS (Eboko 2005).

Because of the stigmatized nature of the illness, and the long illness cycle, the avenue of denial has been a particularly convenient course for many governments to pursue in the past—albeit with fairly catastrophic humanitarian consequences. In an influential speech, former UN secretary-general Kofi Annan referred to this strategy as the "wall of silence" surrounding HIV/AIDS in many countries. Annan (2004) directly challenged heads of state to demonstrate greater leadership on HIV/AIDS by: (1) breaking this deadly wall of silence that engulfs the epidemic, (2) encouraging the cultural shift required for responding to it effectively, and (3) scaling up the response to disease, including providing treatment to all those who need it. Indeed, he insisted:

> We need leaders everywhere to demonstrate that speaking up about AIDS is a point of pride, not a source of shame. There must be no more sticking heads in the sand, no more embarrassment, no more hiding behind a veil of apathy. Your leadership must then translate into adequate resources from national budgets. It must mobilize the entire state apparatus, from Ministries of Finance down to local governments, from Ministries of Education to Ministries of Defence. And it must generate partnerships with every sector of society—business, civil society, and people living with HIV/AIDS. (Anan 2004)

In a context where a widespread and stigmatized disease remains largely ignored by governments in the developing world, the primary concern of many working in the international politics of HIVAIDS understandably is not a fear of excessive state mobilization; on the contrary, the main concern is the striking absence of a more adequate and proportionate state response.

Here, the language of national security—with its connotations of immediacy and urgency—is deemed to perform a useful transgressive function in terms of breaking down the wall of silence. If HIV/AIDS is a threat to national security, governments can no longer afford to ignore it; they must develop commensurate responses. Persuading the UN

Security Council, with its high profile and unique status in international law, that it should designate HIV/AIDS as a threat to international peace and security in Africa was one way in which various political actors have tried to achieve this goal. Speaking at the Security Council in January 2001, Peter Piot (2001) argued as much when, as director of UNAIDS, he pointed out that "the simple fact that the Security Council regards AIDS as a significant problem sends a powerful message: AIDS is a serious matter for the global community." Later that same year, the Abuja Declaration on HIV/AIDS, Tuberculosis, and Other Related Infectious Diseases was adopted by several African heads of state and by the Organization of African Unity. The declaration reasoned that it was now necessary to break the silence around HIV/AIDS precisely because HIV/AIDS is not just a health issue but also a threat to Africa's political stability, and that, consequently, fighting illnesses such as HIV/AIDS must form a part of Africa's strategy for ensuring durable peace and political security on the continent (OAU 2001). Thus, where securitization theorists see dangers to democracy emanating from securitization processes because of the potentially oppressive role they accord to the security institutions of states, for some of those involved in the international politics of HIV/AIDS, using the language of national security to compel states hitherto unresponsive to the needs of their people to take greater action is an equally important political goal. However imperfect, it is deemed to be a way of representing the silent voices of those living with HIV/AIDS at the highest levels of government.

Beyond its connotations of urgency, the language of national security is also deemed useful for breaking through the wall of silence in other ways. It can connect the health needs of populations with their governments' own self-interest in power and survival. Such a discursive alignment can be seen, for example, in comments made by former U.S. secretary of state Colin Powell (2001), who argued that the security implications of HIV/AIDS mean that AIDS is no longer solely a question of altruism; it is a question of national interest as well:

No longer is such devastation simply a cause for our sympathy, our charity, our reaching out to care for fellow humans—although these altruistic motivations are still vital to us as humans. Increasingly meeting such challenges successfully, appeals to even more basic instincts—caring for our own interests, paying attention to our own hope for survival on this earth.

Aligning the health of populations with the self-interest of governments in this manner is also important in the context of many African states where political power remains centralized and where individual leaders often have a heightened importance when it comes to making policy. In terms of extending and scaling up various HIV/AIDS programs it is crucial to demonstrate to these leaders in a very tangible way that their own ability to govern their countries depends to a large extent on the health of their populations (Patterson 2006:22).

Using national security arguments to highlight the impact of HIV/AIDS on the armed forces can thus serve as an important initial trigger for placing HIV/AIDS on the larger political agenda (UNAIDS 1998). There is evidence from countries such as Uganda, Ethiopia, and Malawi that highlighting this military relationship was crucial in securing wider political leadership on the issue of HIV/AIDS. In Uganda, President Museveni began to take the issue seriously when, in 1986, Fidel Castro took him aside at a meeting of the Non-Aligned Movement in Harare and informed him that eighteen of the sixty military staff that Museveni had sent to Cuba for military training had tested HIV-positive. This spurred Museveni (1995) to commence a more extensive social program on HIV/AIDS in Uganda. Commenting on the response to HIV/AIDS by the Ethiopian army in 1996, Alex de Waal similarly observes that "within the military such as the quasi-democratic 'council of commanders,' a legacy of the army's roots as a revolutionary guerrilla army, allowed the institution to develop and implement its own distinctive AIDS program" (2003b:22). There is also some evidence from Malawi indicating that the impact of HIV/AIDS on the army and members of parliament was crucial in prompting political leadership on this issue (Lwanda 2004:40). Here, national security arguments highlighting the impact of HIV/AIDS on the armed forces can present a very tangible way of persuading leaders in developing countries that they need to put HIV/AIDS on the political agenda, as well as marking an entry point for wider HIV/AIDS programs and efforts.

The same is true about the impact of HIV/AIDS on police forces. Among the effects of HIV/AIDS on the police forces that have been highlighted by researchers are increased absenteeism, staff attrition, overwork and understaffing, decrease in operational efficiency, and increased recruitment costs (de Waal 2007:2–3). At the same time, police forces stand in a critical relationship to other high-risk groups such as commercial sex workers, trafficked women, illegal immigrants, street children, and injecting drug users, and thus it is important to educate them about HIV/AIDS. A recent report notes that there are clearly challenges in drawing upon police forces—possibilities of corruption, their active involvement in commercial sex work, criminalization of some of the groups at risk for HIV/AIDS in many countries— but goes on to say:

> Law enforcement practices can [nevertheless] influence the course of the epidemic, either for good or ill, especially with regard to policing practices concerning injecting drug use, commercial sex work, SGBV [sexual and gender-based violence] and migrant populations. Police services can also influence social and health policies that in turn determine national responses to HIV/AIDS. (de Waal 2007:4)

Again, therefore, where those who are skeptical of the securitization of HIV/AIDS have lamented the state-centric and self-interested nature of many national security policies, some of those advocating the links between HIV/AIDS and security view exactly this aspect of national security language as a useful tool for encouraging states in developing countries to take better care of their populations. "It is a simple truth," notes de Waal in reflecting on his experience with many African governments over the past decades, "that governments act when they perceive real threats to their power" (2003b:21).

Finally, the language of national security can also help to break down the aura of complacency surrounding the AIDS pandemic by provoking governments to adopt a more comprehensive response to HIV/AIDS. It can do so by bureaucratically shifting responsibility for addressing HIV/AIDS away from ministries with only very little political clout and toward political bodies that wield greater influence on the political process. Dennis Altman (2000) has observed that in countries such as Nigeria, Côte d'Ivoire, and South Africa, where health ministries enjoy only a modest degree of political influence and are perennially short of financial resources, the securitization of the pandemic has helped to move the issue higher up on the political agenda, and HIV/AIDS has subsequently become the responsibility of ministries or committees with greater political clout and more resources at their disposal. This change is crucial because the African state often centralizes power in the executive, which in turn has strong influence over the party and bureaucratic apparatuses (Patterson 2006:22). Whereas securitization theorists generally see dangers in pushing issues higher up the echelons of state bureaucracies—and thus away from civilian control—many AIDS activists see that as precisely the course that is needed in order to get many African governments to undertake more sustained efforts and to commit more resources to addressing a pandemic within their populations. In none of these instances, moreover, is national security language being invoked in order to persuade states that they now ought to introduce more draconian measures against people living with HIV/AIDS as a way of preserving state power. Rather, it constitutes a vehicle for encouraging a particular kind of statecraft in the developing world whereby devoting greater attention to the health of populations is viewed as a component of proper government. These national security arguments implicitly assert, in short, that a properly secure state is a governmentalized state.

Beyond asserting this ideal of a governmentalized state, national security arguments also seek to bring about the material conditions under which it would be economically feasible for developing states to address the health needs of their populations. National security arguments thus play an important role in freeing up the resources—both financial and medical—for responding to the AIDS pandemic. This too is crucial, for there would be little point in mobilizing greater levels of leadership on HIV/AIDS in developing countries if the provision of treatment remained financially unfeasible. Elizabeth Pisani wryly notes in this regard that "there's no better way to open the purse strings than to have a threat to national security up your sleeve" (2008:33). Indeed, in the United States, arguments about the long-term security implications of AIDS reportedly informed President Bush's decision to launch his five-year $15 billion Emergency Plan for AIDS Relief (Stolberg 2003). Not only is the language of "emergency" reflected in the title of the program, but his announcement in the State of the Union speech of 2003 made similar references to an "urgent *crisis* abroad [emphasis added]." Amy Patterson argues that "PEPFAR's rapid passage reflects the fact that US citizens and policymakers viewed AIDS in Africa to be an emergency, not a long-term development problem" (2006:138).

There has been much controversy about this programs in terms of (1) the strings attached to this money, (2) the emphasis on bilateral rather than multilateral programs, (3) the considerable delay in its appropriation, (4) the stipulation that medicines for treatment had to be purchased from U.S. pharmaceutical companies when cheaper generic drugs were available from Brazil and India, and (5) the fact that these programs were frequently channeled through various "Beltway Bandit" organizations based around Washington, D.C., which invariably take a significant slice of the funds. Nevertheless, such financial resources are crucial for international efforts to respond to the pandemic, and to do so sustainably, given that treatment, once commenced, must be maintained for life (Pisani 2008:290). The securitization of HIV/AIDS has coincided with a substantial increase in global funding for HIV/AIDS, from $300 million in 1995 to $8.3 billion in 2005 (UNAIDS 2006b:224). While this amount still falls short of the sums that are required, it nevertheless indicates that the language of security may have helped leaders to justify the appropriation of considerable sums and the general expansion in AIDS funding that has taken place in recent years. The funding, in turn, has led to an increase in the number of people receiving treatment through life-prolonging anti-retroviral therapies (ARVs), to just under 2 million people in middle- and low-income countries— although this still falls short of the 7.1 million persons estimated to be in urgent need of ARVs in these countries (WHO 2007:5). To the extent that national security arguments help to free up such financial resources and make it economically more viable for developing countries to improve the provision of health care for their populations, they do implicitly encourage the further governmentalization of the state in the developing world.

It is not only financial resources that these national security arguments seek to gain access to, however. National security arguments also play an important role in the controversy over patents that apply to many AIDS-related medicines. One of the well-known problems that emerged in the 1990s was that many of the AIDS medicines are under patents that are now protected internationally through the World Trade Organization's Agreement on Trade-Related Aspects of Intellectual Property Rights (TRIPS). This restriction initially barred many poorer countries from producing generic anti-retroviral therapies and other AIDS medicines at lower prices or even from importing them from other countries that can procure them at lower costs. In the past, countries that tried to circumvent these restrictions were threatened with a variety of political, economic, and legal sanctions. In 1997, for example, some thirty-nine pharmaceutical companies attempted to legally challenge the South African Medicines and Related Substances Control Amendment Act, which would have enabled South Africa to "parallel" import much cheaper generic HIV/AIDS medicines.

Here the language of national security can also assist groups that wish to weaken the grip of patents on life-prolonging medicines, since such patents could potentially be overridden in the light of national security considerations. The TRIPS agreement contains an important set of "security exceptions," including article 73(b), which notes that nothing contained in the agreement should be construed to "prevent a Member from taking any action which it considers necessary for the protection of its essential security interests" (World Trade Organization 1994). Although no formal dispute has yet occurred under article 73 since the establishment of the World Trade Organization, the devastating social and economic impact of HIV/AIDS is raising the possibility of invoking these security provisions. A report by the United Nations notes that it might be possible to do so because "it could be argued that pandemics such as HIV affect a nation far beyond purely economic interests and might therefore justify action otherwise inconsistent with the TRIPS Agreement" (Roffe and Meléndez-Ortiz 2005:10). If states do wish to override these patents on expensive lifesaving medicines in the future, or at least maintain pressure on the pharmaceutical companies when negotiating prices, it will be essential for them to demonstrate that the AIDS pandemic constitutes an emergency affecting the security of states, especially as attempts to protect such access to medicines through widening the public health provisions of TRIPS agreed at Doha in 2001 are proving increasingly ineffective and are being actively sidestepped through bilateral free trade agreements (Medecins Sans Frontiers 2005; Oxfam 2004).

Some participants in the UN Security Council debates on AIDS and international security have already been able to use that forum to make precisely this point. The Indian representative urged the Security Council, in line with its responsibility for maintaining international peace and security, "to rule that Article 73 of the TRIPS Agreement must be invoked to urgently provide affordable medicines that help in the treatment of the epidemic" (Sharma 2001). Thus, where securitization theorists point to the danger of security arguments being used to override the rule of law (e.g., through the restriction of civil liberties), this "transgressive" ability of national security to occasionally override the law is deemed by some working in the international politics of HIV/AIDS to be a potential advantage.

Beyond article 73, moreover, the language of national security is useful for invoking the less radical provisions under TRIPS contained in article 31, which allows states to bypass certain provisions if they declare a national "emergency" in relation to HIV/AIDS—the medical equivalent of "martial law." In South Africa, the leader of the Opposition Democratic Alliance, Tony Leon, asked Thabo Mbeki in 2001 whether he would "consider proclaiming HIV/AIDS a national emergency in terms of Section 1 of the State of Emergency Act, 1997 (Act No. 64 of 1997) so as to allow South Africa to act in terms of article 31 of the World Trade Organization's Agreement on Trade-Related Aspects of Intellectual Property Rights (TRIPS) to gain access to generic drugs used in the treatment of HIV/AIDS; if not, why not; if so, when?" (Lindhal and Sundset 2003:45). In the end Mbeki refused to take this route, but the episode nevertheless shows the political complexity behind the securitization of HIV/AIDS in terms of potentially unlocking the legal constraints to the import or production of cheaper, generic medicines.

The legal dimension to the securitization of HIV/AIDS remains important because of the strong role that Indian pharmaceuticals have recently been playing in providing generic and affordable AIDS medicines to many developing countries. Because India's Patent Act of 1970 did not apply to medicines, Indian pharmaceutical companies have been able to produce generic versions of AIDS drugs for some time. India effectively became the pharmacy of the world's poor, producing generic copies of medicines that were still patented in other countries—and at much lower prices. The pressure of the Indian generic products has meant that prices for ARVs have dropped from more than $10,000 annually to, in some instances, $140 annually; but this has been possible only because some of the provisions of the TRIPS agreement have not applied to India. Indian pharmaceutical companies have also been at the forefront of developing the three-in-one cocktail pill, which means that patients need to take only two pills a day instead of six, making the medication regimen considerably easier. Yet as members of the Affordable Medicines and Treatment Campaign point out, India has been in the process of changing its Patent Act in a way that would comply with TRIPS, which requires all governments to grant developed countries a twenty-year monopoly patent on all essential medicines, including HIV/ AIDS drugs. Several proposed amendments to the act would potentially impede generic competition. Moreover, nine thousand patents are now being examined in India (Cook 2007). If the supply of cheap Indian medicines dries up in the near future, it will make the ability to invoke the security exceptions of TRIPS all the more pressing (Grover 2004).

In this context, anything that helps to maintain pressure in making the case that HIV/AIDS constitutes an emergency could be deemed helpful from the perspective of those who wish to make more comprehensive treatment available to people in poorer countries who are living with HIV/AIDS. Indeed, it is worth noting that in November 2006 Thailand took the bold step of issuing a compulsory license for Efavirenz (produced by Merck), and in February 2007 announced its intent to infringe the patent for Kaletra (produced by Abbott) as well. The response by Western governments and the pharmaceutical companies has been predictable, with Abbott subsequently ceasing to introduce new products in the Thai market—including an improved version of Kaletra that is more heat resistant and needs to be taken only once a day. Thailand was also placed on the Office of the United States Trade Representative's "priority watch list" because of its infringements of intellectual property rights (AVERT 2008b). In May 2007 Brazil nevertheless followed suit by announcing that it too would be issuing a compulsory license to produce a lower-cost version of Efavirenz. Previously, Brazil had repeatedly used the threat of invoking compulsory licenses as a key tool in bringing down the costs of medicines, a strategy that, in conjunction with its ability to produce many medicines domestically, meant that Brazil has a very high level of treatment coverage

(85 percent)—a level much more representative of a developed country than of a middle-income country (AVERT 2008a). Even today, invoking the connotations of "crisis" and "emergency" that are associated with the language of national security continues to play into the hands of countries that wish to invoke the legal provisions necessary for procuring lifesaving medicines at lower costs, thereby also enabling governments in the developing world to take better care of their populations. In all of these instances, the language of national security is being mobilized not just as a way of compelling states in developing countries to take better care of their populations but also as a way of materially enabling them to do so, thereby further encouraging the governmentalization of the state outside of the West.

That the mobilization of sovereign power can also have such beneficial consequences for populations is readily conceded by securitization theorists, who grant that "one has to weigh the always problematic side effects of applying a mind-set of security against the possible advantages of focus, attention, and mobilization" (Buzan, Wæver, and de Wilde 1998:29). Although de-securitization remains the ideal, securitization theorists are nonetheless prepared to concede that occasionally "in specific situations one can choose securitization, only one should not believe this is an innocent reflection of the issue *being* a security threat; it is always a political choice to securitize or to accept a securitization" (Buzan, Wæver, and de Wilde 1998:29). HIV/AIDS may well represent such an exception because the political dangers identified above in the mobilization of a sovereign economy of power apply in only a qualified manner and because they also have to be balanced with a wide range of competing political, economic, and legal advantages that national security arguments about the AIDS pandemic could accrue for persons living with HIV/AIDS. Many of the actors securitizing HIV/AIDS are not merely blindly tacking the word "security" onto yet another issue; they are trying to deliberately provoke very specific political and economic effects that would make the provision of medicines to populations in many developing countries more viable. Unlike, say, the securitization of migration, the securitization of HIV/AIDS is therefore not mobilizing sovereign power in order to protect the state by excluding certain "dangerous" population groups, but is seeking to assist people living with HIV/AIDS who do not presently enjoy access to life-prolonging medicines.

This also means that the mobilization of sovereign power in the securitization of HIV/AIDS is, in the end, really not so much an example of the further *étatisation* (state domination) of society feared by securitization theorists as it is a manifestation of the *governmentalization of the state* sketched by Foucault. National security arguments about HIV/AIDS, in other words, exemplify precisely that crucial transformation that sovereign power undergoes in the era of governmentality, when it becomes increasingly redirected toward managing the welfare of populations. Just as the sovereign institution of law is used a tool to manage the welfare of populations by making it compulsory to take out certain forms of insurance, to prohibit driving under the influence of alcohol, and so on, so too in the domain of security the sovereign language of national security is now being widely mobilized as a way of encouraging states to become better managers of the welfare of their populations, and as a way of creating the political and economic conditions that would make the extension of health care to people living with HIV/AIDS more viable. It is for this reason too that the securitization of HIV/AIDS has not provoked the kind of draconian response that securitization theory would lead us to fear, given the results when other issues were securitized over the past decade.

None of this, to be sure, invalidates the broader concerns that securitization theorists have raised about the mobilization of sovereign power. Bringing the language of national security to bear on HIV/AIDS ultimately remains a very risky gamble that depends on the ability of those presenting HIV/AIDS as a national security issue to maintain control over the uses to which this language will be put. What all of this does imply, however, is that for the time being the much more pressing dangers associated with the governmentalization of security may actually reside in concurrent exercise of disciplinary and governmental modalities of power that is required for internationally extending the provision of AIDS-related health care—economies of power with which securitization theory has traditionally not engaged very deeply.

5 / HUMAN SECURITY

Discipline, Healthy Bodies, and the Global Curing Machine

The securitization of HIV/AIDS not only draws upon sovereign power, but also mobilizes a *disciplinary* economy of power. This can be seen in arguments claiming that the AIDS pandemic is also a threat to *human* security. Over the past decade many of those who remain uneasy about using the language of national security in relation to HIV/AIDS have nevertheless been quite willing to openly discuss HIV/AIDS as a threat to human security—the seemingly "softer" option for analyzing the AIDS-security nexus. Yet what is this human security framework at its core if not the marrying of a disciplinary economy of power to the practice of security? The human security framework is a contemporary expression of disciplinary power par excellence. Like the older form of disciplinary power, the human security framework breaks the provision and analysis of security down to the individual level (individuation). Like disciplinary power more generally, it is a political technology of the body in that it further analyzes the security of individuals in relation to seven threats to their corporal existence, ranging from food to health insecurities. And like disciplinary power, human security practitioners gain access to the body by invoking a "positive" and "progressive" language that promises to "save" lives and "empower" individuals. When political actors involved in the international politics of HIV/AIDS claim that the disease is a threat to human security, they are thus implicitly mobilizing a disciplinary economy of power in response to the AIDS pandemic.

This exercise of disciplinary power in the securitization of HIV/AIDS gives rise to further dangers—albeit different dangers than the ones previously outlined by securitization theory in relation to sovereign power. What could possibly be harmful about singing the siren song of human security in order to ameliorate the mortality and human suffering caused by the AIDS pandemic? Here the danger is not principally one of excessive state mobilization; rather it is that disciplinary power ultimately diminishes the range of human possibilities by characterizing certain activities, actions, and behaviors as normal and others as deviant. The danger with the securitization of HIV/AIDS is therefore that it animates a variety of disciplinary practices that seek to internationally structure the bodies and behaviors of individuals around the biomedical norm of being HIV-negative. The spread and intensification of such homogenizing practices of disciplinary normation through the vast international "curing machine" fueled by the securitization of HIV/AIDS represents a further "danger" inherent in the contemporary governmentalization of security.

DISCIPLINING SECURITY: HUMAN SECURITY AS DISCIPLINARY POWER

Disciplinary power differs from sovereign power in several key respects. First, whereas sovereign power is exercised primarily (although not exclusively) over territory, disciplinary power is mostly exercised over individual bodies. It is more corporal than territorial (Foucault 2003:36). Disciplinary power is aimed not at seizing goods and wealth but at increasing the productivity of individuals through continuous and meticulous modes of surveillance. Second, disciplinary power works through "breaking down" individuals, places, times, gestures, acts, and processes into their constituent elements, which is the precondition for their optimization. Third, once it has broken processes down into their constituent elements, disciplinary power then reorders and reclassifies these elements according to particular goals. It tries to determine which gestures are best adopted in order to achieve particular ends. Which motion, for example, is best for rapidly loading a rifle? What are the most suitable workers for a particular job? Discipline seeks to establish the optimal sequences of these individual gestures for the purpose of achieving the desired goal. Finally, disciplinary power makes use of evaluation and sorting mechanisms in order to distinguish between those who are capable and suitable for a task and those who are not. The former are usually designated as being "normal," whereas the latter are not (Foucault 2007:57–58).

Within contemporary international relations, this older form of disciplinary power finds one of its most prominent expressions in the framework of human security. This claim may initially seem counterintuitive. Those already familiar with the history of disciplinary power will know that it is usually associated with the confined and circumscribed spaces of modern institutions—such as military barracks, schools, universities, hospitals, workshops, factories, and prisons. Michel Foucault (1981) referred, for example, to the historical transformation that militaries underwent between the seventeenth and eighteenth centuries, especially the Prussian army during the reign of Frederick II. From that time on, the military ceased to consist of small collectives, usually under the command of a single leader, in which soldiers were mostly unskilled and little more than "cannon fodder" that could, in principle, be easily replaced by other men. Henceforth, soldiers had to be properly trained, and the military became a much more complex hierarchical and differentiated organization, with a vertical and multilayered chain of command—including lieutenants, corporals, commanders, generals, and so on. It also saw the emergence of specialized units focusing on particular combat skills. A proper soldier now required substantial investment and had to be trained in how to discharge his weapon, how to coordinate his movements with other soldiers, and other such skills. Discipline and training were thus used as a means for making the modern military more efficient and effective. These same techniques were also introduced in a wide range of other social institutions, such as modern schools. Here, too, one began to see the parallel emergence of differentiated education systems catering to different abilities and aptitudes. Here, too, the formless mass of students was grouped into more manageable classes, each allocated a teacher who monitored students' progress and abilities and ranked them through the use of graded examinations (Foucault 1981). In this sense, it is certainly true that the emergence of disciplinary power initially manifested itself in relatively enclosed institutional spaces such as barracks and schools.

Yet Foucault was also quite clear in his analysis of disciplinary power that despite these historical origins, it should not be equated with the workings of such confined institutions alone:

> "Discipline" may be identified neither with an institution nor with an apparatus; it is a type of power, a modality for its exercise, comprising a whole set of instruments, techniques, procedures, levels of application, targets. . . . And it may be taken over either by "specialized" institutions . . . or by institutions that use it as an essential instrument for a particular end . . . or by pre-existing authorities that find in it a means of reinforcing and reorganizing their internal mechanisms of power . . . or by apparatuses that have made discipline their principle of internal functioning . . . or finally by state apparatuses whose major, if not exclusive, function is to assure that discipline reigns over society as a whole (the police). (1975:215–216)

It would be a mistake therefore to view the exercise of disciplinary power as something that is restricted solely to such enclosed or confined spaces; disciplinary power can also be found circulating in other social spheres—including the framework of human security.

Perhaps the most fundamental principle of a disciplinary economy of power is that it operates according to an individuating logic; it works by allocating to each individual his or her own space and by breaking up collectivities into their constituent elements (Foucault 1975:143). What is the human security framework if not the application of this very principle to the practice of security? Like disciplinary power more generally, the human security framework takes the notion of security and breaks it down to the level of the individual. "The concept of security," the 1994 *Human Development Report* lamented in this regard, "has for too long been interpreted narrowly: . . . It has been related more to nation-states than to people. . . . Forgotten were the legitimate concerns of ordinary people who sought security in their daily lives" (UNDP 1994:22). The human security framework thus focuses not on political collectives such as states, or even on the sovereign himself, but breaks security down to its most fundamental level by focusing on the lives of each and every individual human being. Human security advocates argue that the state-centric nature of much realist security think-

ing has failed to capture the extent to which the state, rather than being a universal "Hobbesian" guarantor of security as assumed in much
security literature, can also act as a source of insecurity for many individuals around the world. At the outset of the twenty-first century,

> both the challenges to security and its protectors have become more
> complex. The state remains the fundamental purveyor of security. Yet
> it often fails to fulfill its security obligations—and at times has even be-
> come a source of threat to its own people. That is why attention must
> now shift from the security of the state to the security of the people—to
> human security. (Commission on Human Security 2003:2)

The human security approach allows for a shift in emphasis to the individual in those countries where the state has largely abandoned, or become sufficiently removed from, the greater needs of its population, or
where the crucial security dynamics occur within the borders of a state,
rather than between states. The notion of human security is "based on
the premise that the individual human being is the only irreducible
focus for discourse on security" (MacFarlane and Khong 2006:2). Human security, in short, undertakes what is effectively the *individuation*
of security.

Second, the human security framework tends to conceptualize this
individual largely in a corporal or bodily manner—another important
hallmark of disciplinary power. Although the human security framework is frequently invoked by human rights activists as well, it is not
principally based on a language and philosophy of rights (i.e., democratized, universalized sovereign-juridical power), but on a more material conception of the individual human being as a physical body with
certain vital, biological, and material needs that have to be satisfied in
order to ensure survival. Like disciplinary power, human security is also
a "political technology of the body" (Foucault 1975:24). The human
security framework compartmentalizes the vital corporal presence of
individual human beings into its various components or dimensions.
Much like the process of a soldier loading a rifle can be broken down
into a series of individual bodily gestures, so too the human security
framework takes the security of each individual, divides it into a series

of elements that are vital for achieving security, and tries to regulate this life in all of its detail and minutiae (Foucault 2007:45). When the *Human Development Report* first outlined the idea of human security in 1994, it identified seven components of human security that policy-makers should henceforth focus upon, ranging from food security to health security (UNDP 1994:24–25). Thus the life of each individual human being is further broken down into seven subcomponents that collectively make up his or her "vital" needs and that must be met in order to ensure the survival and flourishing of corporal existence.

Third, the human security agenda shares with disciplinary power its more general tendency to structure bodies according to certain norms in order to decide which bodies are normal and which are "abnormal." The human security framework does this by internationally promoting an idealized and universal conception of what it means to be a human being. This ideal currently resembles most closely the wealthy citizens of the developed world who have access to health care, affordable food in plentiful supply, good wages, and so on (Duffield and Waddell 2004; MacFarlane and Khong 2006). The human security agenda then evaluates, or "judges," states—particularly in the South—against this standard of what it means to be a human being and to live a "proper" life. Implicitly, it even distinguishes between normal and abnormal states—those that meet the minimum requirements of human security and those that do not. An entire network of states and nongovernmental organizations is now devoted to identifying those countries that deviate from this norm, while those that already conform to these human security standards are held up as good examples of governments that are ensuring the security of their citizens. The *Human Security Report 2005*, for instance, drew upon three existing data sets in order to undertake a "Human Security Audit," which concluded by identifying the world's thirty "least-secure" countries (HSR 2005:92). Not surprisingly, the list was mostly (though not exclusively) made up of non-Western countries in Africa, Asia, and the Middle East. Just as the larger disciplinary society has its arbiters of "normality" in the form of doctors, judges, teachers, and others, so too does the human security framework now have officials and activists judging which states are normal, in the sense of complying with human security standards, and which are not.

Finally, the human security agenda is inherently disciplinary in its deployment of a "positive" model of power. Disciplinary power works "to incite, reinforce, control, monitor, optimize and organize the forces under it: [it is] a power bent on generating forces, making them grow, and ordering them, rather than one dedicated to impeding them, making them submit, or destroying them" (Foucault 1976:136). Unlike sovereign power and its associated language of national security, disciplinary power seeks not to detract or seize things from life but to enhance and empower it. According to the *Human Development Report*, human security thus acknowledges "the universality of life claims . . . [and] is embedded in a notion of solidarity among people" (UNDP 1994:24); it is "not a defensive concept—the way territorial or military security is. Instead human security is an integrative concept. . . . It cannot be brought about through force, with armies standing against armies" (UNDP 1994:23). This "positivity" of power also enables the human security agenda to "open up" states and to politicize aspects of their internal politics that would otherwise be deemed, under the provisions of the United Nations charter, to fall under the sovereign jurisdiction of member states. Human security thus obtains access to the human body not by appearing threatening but, on the contrary, by promising to take charge of life, by empowering and improving it, by "saving" it and by increasing its vitality (Foucault 1976:143). As Mark Duffield argues, the human security framework produces "'humans' requiring securing" and empowers "international institutions and actors to individuate, group and act upon Southern populations" (2005:2–3).

In these ways arguments that HIV/AIDS is a threat to human security testify to the continuing operation of a disciplinary economy of power in the securitization of HIV/AIDS. They show that the debate between those who prefer to think of HIV/AIDS as a national security threat and those who are more in favor of a human security framing of the disease is not just a contest about the appropriate referent object of security, or about the proper breadth of the security agenda in the twenty-first century, or even about the kinds of empirical relationships to analyze in relation to HIV/AIDS; more fundamentally, it is a contest about which economy of power to mobilize in the international effort to rein in the AIDS pandemic.

MANUFACTURING SUBJECTS: FROM THE POWER OF THE STATE
TO THE PRODUCTION OF THE SUBJECT

Imbuing the practice of security with a disciplinary logic and marshaling it in response to the AIDS pandemic generate additional dangers. Given the evident humanitarian concern of those who wish to invoke the notion of human security in response to the AIDS pandemic, prima facie it seems difficult to object to them. Yet it would be a mistake to assume that just because advocates of human security employ a progressive and "soft" language of humanitarian empowerment and do not habitually invoke coercive measures to achieve their goals the human security framework does not have important disciplining effects. Disciplinary power, Foucault argued,

> is not a triumphant power, which because of its own excess can pride itself on its omnipotence; it is a modest, suspicious power, which functions as a calculated, but permanent economy. These are humble modalities, minor procedures, as compared with the majestic rituals of sovereign or the great apparatuses of the state. And it is precisely they that were gradually to invade the major forms, altering their mechanisms and imposing their procedures. (1975:170)

Evaluating these more subtle effects of disciplinary mechanisms in the context of the securitization of HIV/AIDS will require conceptual tools that are quite different from those developed by securitization theory.

As we have already seen, securitization theory tends to evaluate securitization processes largely in terms of how they affect the relationship between the individual and the state—effectively juxtaposing the power of the state with the rights and civil liberties of citizens, and expressing concern about how the use of security language can shape the power relations in favor of the state. Yet casting the political question about securitization processes primarily in this manner is already to firmly locate the discussion within an economy of *sovereign* power. The politics of sovereign power, Foucault pointed out, tend to revolve exactly around this relationship between the individual and the state, and around the question of where the proper limits of political authority rest. In liberal democracies the relationship between the state and the individual is usually expressed in the form of a social contract whereby individuals sacrifice a certain amount of their liberty to a sovereign state in return for their security. This social contract, codified in the form of constitutions or laws, also delineates what the legitimate and illegitimate uses of power by the state are. In this model, power is thus almost regarded

> as a right which can be possessed in the way one possesses a commodity, and which can therefore be transferred or alienated, either completely or partly, through a juridical act or an act that founds a right—it does not matter which, for the moment—thanks to the surrender of something or thanks to a contract. Power is the concrete power that any individual can hold, and which he can surrender, either as a whole or in part, so as to constitute a power or a political sovereignty. (Foucault 2003:13)

Historically, this understanding of power is still derived from the political theory of sovereignty, which initially served as the legitimizing basis of the European feudal monarchies. When Enlightenment critics such as Rousseau later took on absolutist despotism, they did not abandon this conception of power in their antimonarchical struggles; they in fact used this same model of power in order to oppose the monarchy. The notion of sovereignty was "merely" shifted to a more popular or democratic conception of the sovereign body, and in this process the juridical conception of power was never questioned or challenged by the opponents of monarchy. At bottom, the sovereign model of power is thus "all about the king: the king, his rights, his power, and the possible limits of his power. . . . No matter whether the jurists were the king's servants or his adversaries, the great edifices of juridical thought and juridical knowledge were always about royal power" (Foucault 2003:25–26). In warning that securitization processes can increase the power of the state over the individual in a dangerous manner, securitization theory is still casting the political question about securitization processes broadly within this economy of sovereign power.

Why is this an insufficient way of analyzing the politics of securitizing HIV/AIDS? Although the focus on sovereign power is not wrong in and of itself, it does not generate a complete account of the multiple power relations at play in the securitization of HIV/AIDS. Specifically, it does not take into account the exercise of disciplinary power and how it in turn plays an important role in the very "production" of the individual subjects that the sovereign model of power takes for granted. As Foucault argued,

> In order to conduct a concrete analysis of power relations, one would have to abandon the juridical notion of sovereignty. That model presupposes the individual as a subject of natural rights or original powers; it aims to account for the ideal genesis of the state; and it makes law the fundamental manifestation of power. . . . [I]nstead of asking ideal subjects what part of themselves or what power of theirs they have surrendered, allowing themselves to be subjectified, one would need to inquire how relations of subjectivation can manufacture subjects. (1997f:59)

In other words, the "free" subject or individual located at the basis of social contract theory (and indeed of securitization theory) cannot simply be assumed. This subject is itself produced through complex and continuously operating power relations. "Discipline," Foucault insisted in this regard, "'makes' individuals: it is the specific technique of a power that regards individuals both as objects and as instruments of its exercise" (1975:170).

If this is true, then it is not sufficient merely to trace the ways in which this securitization of HIV/AIDS may recalibrate the power relationship between the individual and the state in favor of the latter; it becomes just as important to probe how the exercise of disciplinary power in the securitization of HIV/AIDS animates practices that in turn shape the very identities and behaviors of individuals. Power, in this sense, can no longer be conceived as something that is predominantly or essentially negative (i.e., as something that excludes, represses, or conceals); it is something that "produces; it produces reality; it produces domains of objects and rituals of truth. The individual and the knowledge that may be gained of him belong to this production" (Foucault 1975:194).

Paying attention to these subtle processes also demands a very different analytics of power—which Foucault subsequently tried to develop by thinking about power not so much as a commodity, but as a "relationship of force" or a "warlike clash between forces" (2003:16).

Here the analysis of power centers not on "the king in his central position, but [on] subjects in their reciprocal relations; not sovereignty in its one edifice, but the multiple subjugations that take place and function within the social body" (Foucault 2003:27). Power is now conceptualized as an essentially *relational* phenomenon that circulates widely within, and penetrates deeply into, the social fabric:

> Power must be analyzed as something which circulates, or rather as something which only functions in the form of a chain. It is never localized here or there, never in anybody's hands, never appropriated as a commodity or piece of wealth. Power is employed and exercised through a net-like organization. And not only do individuals circulate between its threads; they are always in the position of simultaneously undergoing and exercising this power. (Foucault 1980:98)

Shifting the analysis of the securitization of HIV/AIDS from the operation of sovereign power to that of disciplinary power thus culminates in a greater questioning of how individual subjects are themselves "produced" through a whole range of complex power relations circulating throughout modern societies.

Viewed in this light, contemporary liberal-democratic societies no longer emerge as the zenith of a progressive culture of individual rights and autonomy; it is these same societies that have developed, refined, and perfected the broader disciplinary means of social control. Behind the facade of liberal societies there operates a pervasive network of disciplinary power relations that continuously monitors, shapes, and regulates the behavior of individuals. In no small measure, the "free" individual of liberal societies is itself the product of this "panoptic" network of disciplinary surveillance and training methods that are deployed in a variety of institutions and that virtually every citizen will have passed through from childhood—be it schools, universities, hospitals, the military, or some other institution. Yet these are more subtle power relations that securitization theory does not readily address. It remains anchored largely in the "cold monster" theory of the state and is mostly concerned to prevent the "*étatisation*" of society. Securitization theory has not yet cut off the king's head; it does not analyze how society's control of the individual is achieved not just at the level of consciousness or ideology but also "in the body and with the body" (Foucault 2000a:137). Therefore it cannot capture the ways in which the securitization of HIV/AIDS today similarly forms an integral part of this network of disciplinary power that is circulating in and between contemporary societies.

HUMAN SECURITY, AIDS, AND THE INTERNATIONAL NORMATION OF BIOMEDICAL BODIES

Viewed from the perspective of disciplinary power, the securitization of HIV/AIDS is "dangerous" because it facilitates the geographic expansion and intensification of various disciplinary practices of normation that seek to structure the bodies and behaviors of individuals in developing countries around the biomedical norm of being HIV-negative. Such processes of disciplinary "normation" tend to operate by first positing an optimal model (or norm) to which a group of individuals should conform. They then instantiate various forms of surveillance in order to ascertain which individuals conform to this model (the normal) and which ones deviate from it (the abnormal). Finally, they deploy a variety of mechanisms for encouraging and "disciplining" individuals to conform to the norm. The "danger" with such disciplinary practices is not that they wrest political power away from individuals in the way that the state might override certain civil liberties. Rather, the more subtle danger is that people's very identities and behaviors become implicitly structured in such a way as to comply with the designated norms—often without the people's knowledge or awareness. Those who fail to conform to the norm, moreover, may be construed as lesser or otherwise "dysfunctional" individuals and may even become socially stigmatized (Foucault 2007:57).

Despite its emancipatory and progressive intent, the framing of AIDS as a human security threat similarly constitutes such a disciplinary practice of normation, which articulates an international norm to which bodies around the world should conform. This norm consists of a body that is not infected with the human immunodeficiency virus—that is, a body that is "HIV-negative." Arguments about HIV/AIDS and human security thus implicitly instantiate a binary, biomedical division between bodies that are normal and desirable in that they conform to this goal (of being HIV-negative) and those that are in a sense abnormal, since they deviate from it (and are HIV-positive). The securitization of HIV/AIDS is certainly not the only discourse through which this norm is articulated in international relations, but drawing upon the rhetorical power of security language further exalts it to unprecedented levels and adds a greater degree of urgency in realizing it.

Having articulated this norm, the human securitization of HIV/AIDS subsequently generates increased political pressure to subject a growing number of bodies to greater biomedical surveillance by examining their HIV status. The securitization of HIV/AIDS has thus intensified the drive toward more routine forms of testing for HIV among the world's populations. In the past, international institutions that collect data on HIV prevalence, such as the World Health Organization and UNAIDS, have argued strongly in favor of a human rights approach to testing—insisting that people should have access to *voluntary* counseling and testing (VCT). In this model, individuals choose whether or not to undergo an HIV test and, if they wish to do so, present themselves at local medical facilities for a test, often returning on a separate occasion to receive the result of the test. The arguments in favor of the VCT approach are well rehearsed. Testing large numbers of people in the population who are deemed to be of "low risk" is a waste of resources, creates unnecessary stress for those at low risk as they undergo the test, overrides their individual rights to decide whether they should be tested or not, and thus ultimately also over their health care. Maintaining the emphasis on human rights is deemed to be particularly important in countries where the illness remains highly stigmatized and where exposing one's HIV status can lead to a variety of discriminatory practices. Faced with demands that HIV/AIDS should be treated like other illnesses for which tests are routinely carried out, these international institutions have consistently argued in favor of the exceptional nature of HIV/AIDS and have resisted such calls for compulsory or mandatory testing.

Yet recently the critics of VCT have become louder and increasingly counter that knowing one's HIV status is a necessary first step in seeking treatment. In many developing countries the vast majority of those living with HIV are not even aware of it. Despite years of education campaigns, many still do not seek voluntary testing. Because they do not even know that they are HIV-positive, many people will not seek treatment, nor will they take measures to prevent the spread of HIV to others. Nor, for that matter, will they have the opportunity to benefit from the possibility of early interventions such as anti-retrovirals, addressing other sexually transmitted diseases, vitamins, or selected interventions to prevent mother-to-child transmissions. In a coauthored article published in the influential British medical journal the *Lancet*, Kevin de Cock, who has since become the director of the World Health Organization's Department of HIV/AIDS, thus argues:

> We think that the emphasis on human rights in HIV/AIDS prevention has reduced the importance of public health and social justice, which offer a framework for prevention efforts in Africa that might be more relevant to people's daily lives and more likely to be effective. . . . On the basis of epidemiological data, we think that HIV/AIDS is the greatest threat to life, liberty, and the pursuit of happiness and prosperity in many African countries. Interventions, therefore, must be quantitatively and qualitatively commensurate with the magnitude of the threat posed by the disease. (de Cock, Mbori-Ngacha, and Marum 2002:68)

If the disease had reached a similar magnitude in, say, New York or Geneva, he chided, there would have been an overwhelming emergency response based on regular testing, diagnosis, prevention and treatment, and so on. Here, the imagery of humanitarian crisis and emergency is being invoked precisely in order to call for more robust and detailed surveillance of populations with respect to HIV/AIDS.

For a long time these advocates of routine testing have been mostly held at bay. There were exceptions, of course. In 2004 China introduced a "Four Frees and One Care" policy, which promised free VCT, free anti-retrovirals, free mother-child transmission prevention, and free schooling for the children. Yet despite care centers being set up across China, people remained hesitant to come forward. Eventually the Chinese decided that a more "pro-active" approach was needed and began to introduce mass screening. In Henan province alone, where the blood trade had caused widespread HIV infections, more than 250,000 former plasma donors were tracked down and tested for HIV—whether they liked it or not (Pisani 2008:169–170). On the back of the securitization of HIV/AIDS, this trend toward more systematic testing and surveillance has been increasing in many other parts of the world as well.

Indeed, as it became clear that international initiatives to roll out access to treatment in developing countries were similarly encountering difficulties in meeting their targets, pressure for more testing increased much more universally. In 2003, for example, the World Health Organization set the first global target in its "3 by 5" initiative, which aspired to extend treatment to 3 million people living with HIV/AIDS in developing countries by the end of 2005. Meeting this target would still have meant that only about half of those estimated to be in need of treatment would be receiving it. Yet the initiative did not even manage to meet this target. At the end of December 2005, only 1.3 million people were receiving treatment in low- and middle-income countries, which means that the initiative did not achieve even half of its initial target. In July 2005, the leaders of the Group of Eight (G8) countries (Canada, France, Germany, Italy, Japan, Russia, the United Kingdom, and the United States) then set an even more ambitious target of "universal access" to ARVs by 2010. Universal access was understood here to represent treatment coverage of around 80 percent of those in need—which is a level Western countries themselves rarely exceed. Yet when the G8 met again two years later, in 2007, they decided to restrict their commitment to extending treatment to roughly 5 million people by 2010.

Given these difficulties in meeting targets, political pressure has increased to make testing more widespread in many developing countries. Some countries have already begun to change their testing practices in favor of "routine" testing, whereby all patients within a clinical setting will be informed that they will be tested for HIV as a matter of course, unless they deliberately opt out of doing so. In January 2004, Botswana changed its policy toward a routine "opt-out" testing policy in antenatal clinics and other medical facilities. The president of Botswana, Festus Mogae, has since stated that he is even in favor of a compulsory testing regime and wishes to make HIV testing a precondition for students applying for scholarships (Rennie and Behets 2006:55). In Uganda, too, the parliamentary committee on HIV/AIDS has called for compulsory testing of pregnant women, with others already advocating compulsory testing of the population at large because "one of the impediments to the anti-HIV/AIDS campaign in the country is the defective data collection methodology" (Monitor 2007). In Kigali, Rwanda, hundreds of parents went to the Petite Stadium in March 2007 to have their children tested for HIV/AIDS in a pilot study for introducing a policy of testing all children (with their parents' consent) (Mazimpaka 2007).

Such has been the pressure to shift toward more routine forms of testing that UNAIDS is now left to openly lament how its hard-fought-for and long-standing emphasis on a voluntary approach to testing is coming under growing pressure by the need of various HIV/AIDS initiatives led by the World Health Organization, the Global Fund, the World Bank, the U.S. administration, and so on to meet their ambitious treatment targets:

> The appropriateness of bringing human rights into these efforts is being severely questioned in recent literature and in statements by public health officials. In general, the contention is that HIV/AIDS should be recognized as an emergency and therefore addressed within a "public health approach," the apparent assumption being that human rights are in some way antithetical to this. (UNAIDS 2003a:2)

Although routine treatment may seem like a sensible approach in light of these public health emergencies, UNAIDS warns that there are legitimate concerns about how "voluntary" such "opt-outs" for routine testing actually are, especially in settings where patients have no prior knowledge about HIV tests, where they may be unfamiliar with biomedical categories, and where medical practitioners enjoy a high social standing. The routine *offer* of an HIV test will, in many cases, mean the routine *imposition* of such a test, raising concerns about human rights (UNAIDS 2003a:2). A wider effect of the securitization of HIV/AIDS, and the construal of the pandemic as a severe human security threat, is thus to create a political climate in which it is deemed increasingly necessary to push medical surveillance mechanisms deeper into society, especially in those developing countries where prevalence rates are thought to be high.

Beyond extending such practices of biomedical surveillance, the securitization of HIV/AIDS also fuels international efforts that "produce" the subjects needed to maintain this norm of having populations that are largely free of HIV/AIDS. The ideal subject cultivated through a variety of international HIV/AIDS initiatives is one who actively seeks knowledge of his or her body's HIV status, who adjusts his or her sexual behavior in a way that is conducive to achieving the norm of being HIV-negative, and who, if found to be positive, will seek treatment and prevent further transmission to other people. Producing this "subject" requires much work and investment in terms of shaping the sexual behavior of individuals in a manner that is conducive to maintaining the desired norm.

The prospect of extending influence over the sexual behavior of people around the world has also been one of the principal attractions driving more conservative and religious political groups in the United States to join the global struggle against AIDS. Conservative factions of the Bush administration used the issue of HIV/AIDS to promote their "healthy" norms of sexual behavior, featuring abstinence before marriage and monogamy. Republicans in the House of Representatives were also able to successfully redirect one-third of the AIDS-prevention funding earmarked in the United States Leadership Against HIV/AIDS, Tuberculosis, and Malaria Act of 2003 to AIDS programs urging abstinence before marriage (Burkhalter 2004:12). They also added an important amendment to this act in form of the "loyalty oath":

> LIMITATION.—No funds made available to carry out this Act, or any amendment made by this Act, may be used to provide assistance to any group or organization that does not have a policy explicitly opposing prostitution and sex trafficking. (U.S. Congress 2003)

The effect of this amendment is that any organization working on HIV/AIDS that wants to use funds from the U.S. government now has to sign a statement opposing prostitution—irrespective of whether its program actually addresses sex workers or not. The refusal by the Brazilian government to sign the oath—which is now also being challenged in the U.S. courts on the grounds that it may violate the First Amendment of the Constitution—cost it $40 million in funding (Pisani 2008:220–221).

Republican members of Congress have also attacked efforts by the U.S. Agency for International Development (USAID) to distribute condoms internationally, preferring their strategy of abstinence and "being faithful." The Bush administration even went so far as to instruct the Centers for Disease Control to change the information on its Web site in such a way as to emphasize condom failure rates and praise the virtues of abstinence (UCS 2004:17). Many of these political actors have also pooled their efforts with members of faith-based organizations who share similar political objectives. Some parts of the Catholic Church, for example, have sought to improve their case for abstinence by arguing that condoms have tiny holes in them through which HIV can pass, despite a widespread scientific consensus that condoms are impermeable to HIV (Bradshaw 2003).

At the other end of the political spectrum, more-liberal voices have similarly been eager to encourage other forms of behavior change, including the "condomization" of Africa, which has resulted in hundreds of millions of condoms flowing into Africa each year. Medical professionals and epidemiologists have also begun to advocate more widespread use of male circumcision as an important tool in reducing the spread of HIV/AIDS. In Lusaka, surgeons at the University Teaching Hospital began to offer circumcisions for $3 in 2006 and even then could not meet the demand for four hundred such procedures to be carried out per month. In Swaziland, the government has invested in training sixty doctors in circumcision—with some clinics now offering the procedure for free while in Soweto there are long waiting lists for the surgery. In 2006 randomized control trials were undertaken with nearly eight thousand people in Kenya and Uganda (LaFraniere 2006). The results were compelling enough that the World Health Organization announced in March 2007 that it considers the evidence on male circumcision to be persuasive and is now happy to recommend it as an additional intervention in reducing the spread of HIV infections. This decision paved the way for a large meeting held in Harare in May of the same year for the purpose of exploring how rates of circumcision in eastern and southern Africa could be accelerated by allowing nurses and midwives to undertake the procedure, setting up mobile teams, and so on. Now the AIDS pandemic will be fought not only by encouraging the emergence of subjects who will actively seek knowledge about their individual HIV status, and who will adjust their sexual behavior accordingly, but also by encouraging them to modify their own bodies in a manner conducive to reducing the international circulation of HIV/AIDS.

In all these ways, the securitization of HIV/AIDS emerges as a site in contemporary world politics where the body becomes "directly involved in a political field; [where] power relations have an immediate hold upon it . . . invest it, mark it, train it . . . force it to carry out tasks, to perform ceremonies, to emit signs" (Foucault 1975:25). To the extent that the securitization of HIV/AIDS creates greater political momentum behind such interventions and animates what Foucault once referred to in a different context as a vast international "curing machine" (2000f:103), it also serves to geographically expand and intensify a range of disciplinary practices of normation that cultivate particular types of "normal" bodies and subjects in accordance with the norm of being "HIV-negative." In the end, realizing the dream of human security for people living with HIV/AIDS around the world will definitely require a lot of discipline—literally. This too is an important "danger" inherent in the securitization of HIV/AIDS.

HUMAN SECURITY NOW: DISCIPLINARY POWER
IN THE ERA OF GOVERNMENTALITY

If it is true that the notion of human security effectively marks the disciplining of security, then claims about its inherent novelty must be treated with some circumspection. Although the human security framework is clearly new in the narrow sense that its emergence can be traced back only to the mid-1990s, it is at the same time based on an underlying economy of power that has a much longer history. At the level of the history of ideas, Emma Rothschild (1995) has already shown that many of the ideas behind the concept of human security have much older Enlightenment roots that can be discerned in the eighteenth and nineteenth centuries, if not earlier. Yet it is also possible to find much more practical historical precursors to human security in the form of the police sciences practiced by several states in seventeenth-century Europe (Foucault 2007:313). "Police" in this early sense of the term did not mean an institutional and uniformed police force; rather it referred to a way of increasing the forces of the state by enhancing the welfare of individuals (Foucault 2000d:317). In this sense it is closer to the contemporary meaning of the term "policy." Key mottos of this early form of police included: "Life is the object of police: the indispensable, the useful and the superfluous. That people survive, live, and even do better than just that, is what policy has to ensure" (Gordon 1991:10). Other phrases were "police sees to living"; "police's true object is man"; it "sees to everything pertaining to man's happiness"; and "the sole purpose of police is to lead to the utmost happiness in this life" (Gordon 1991:10). Once some of the outdated language is stripped away, these principles could well serve as the slogans of human security advocates today! Indeed, the working definition of the Commission on Human Security (2003:4) comes strikingly close to these earlier pronouncements when it considers human security to consist of protecting "the vital core of all human lives in ways that enhance human freedoms and human fulfillment."

Like today's human security agenda, moreover, this early practice of police was comprehensive in its approach and design. In eighteenth-century France, Nicolas Delamare published a multivolume collection that contained a wealth of instructions for police and specified a total of thirteen areas with which police must concern itself. Issues of concern included religion, customs, health, subsistence, public order, care of buildings, care of squares and streets, the sciences, the arts, commerce, factories, mechanical arts, servants and artisans, theater and games, and the poor (Foucault 2007:334). This makes human security's emphasis on "only" seven dimensions look rather modest—even meager—in comparison. And just as human security advocates today continue to highlight the importance of health issues such as HIV/ AIDS, police too had an important health dimension, as is evident from the 1779 publication in Germany of the first volume of J. P. Frank's six-volume *System einer vollständigen medicinischen Polizey*, which presented the first systematic public health program for modern states and covered areas from food and housing to medical institutions and health care—explicitly linking the health of individuals with the strength of the state (Foucault 2000e:404). As a wider treatise of disciplinary power, the notion of human security is thus far from novel.

Irrespective of these historical continuities, however, there is one crucial way in which the human security framework does deviate from the older practices of police. The latter were still explicitly tied to the practice of statecraft and marked the use of disciplinary techniques in order to augment the forces of the state from "within." The human security framework, by contrast, is not principally concerned with strengthening the state; rather it pursues a greater range of more humanitarian aspirations in countries where the state has not been willing or able to properly manage such needs of its population. The human security agenda, in other words, is a manifestation of disciplinary power being deployed as part of a broader strategy for managing and improving the welfare of populations. This mobilization of disciplinary power is also exemplary of precisely the crucial shift that disciplinary power undergoes in the era of governmentality. Just like sovereign power, disciplinary power becomes increasingly transformed and redirected toward the goal of managing the welfare of populations.

There are least three ways in which the framework of human security, as a contemporary form of disciplinary power, can contribute to this broader process of managing the welfare of populations. First, human security's disciplinary gesture of focusing on the individual allows a much wider range of issues crucial to the welfare of populations to be placed on the contemporary security agenda. In the case of HIV/AIDS, actors working on the international politics of HIV/AIDS continue to struggle with establishing firm links between HIV/AIDS and national security. Rather than condemning the issue of HIV/AIDS to a fate of lingering on as a matter of "low" politics, however, this gives policymakers the option of articulating HIV/AIDS as a pressing threat within the framework of human security. The latter, as we have seen in chapter 2, is a fairly straightforward task. In terms of better managing the welfare of populations, human security's disciplinary gesture of problematizing the security of each and every individual facilitates a "useful" discursive shift in security away from narrower concerns about the power of the state and toward the larger issues of the welfare of populations. Moreover, it enables such a project to harness the rhetorical power of security language for this purpose.

Second, the disciplinary gesture of human security to study insecurity in all of its minute details enables a much more comprehensive analysis of how the welfare of populations is affected by various phenomena, and this knowledge is crucial for properly managing the welfare of populations. Many human security advocates thus believe that the excessive focus on the military capabilities of states by realist approaches obscures the extent to which individuals in many parts of the world are threatened every day by a growing range of non-military issues. Rather than focusing solely on questions of armed force, advocates of the human security framework aim to achieve wider "safety from constant threats of hunger, disease, crime and repression . . . [and] from sudden and hurtful disruptions in the patterns of our daily lives— whether in our homes, our jobs, in our communities or in our environments" (UNDP 1994:3). Compared to the sovereign framework of national security, the disciplinary gesture of human security thus analyzes a much more extensive range of impacts on the population. In the case of HIV/AIDS, it generates knowledge not only of how HIV/AIDS affects the armed forces and state institutions, but also of how the disease affects household wealth, agricultural production, health care systems, and so on. Here the human security framework allows the challenge of HIV/AIDS to emerge in all of its social complexity as analysts begin to relate HIV/AIDS to its various subcomponents. This broader knowledge is crucial for governing populations in a manner that will reduce the burden of the AIDS pandemic in the years ahead and that will prevent it from spiraling out of control. From the perspective of a governmental economy of power, the analytical breadth of the human security framework is therefore not, as so many traditional security scholars charge, a liability; it is in fact a distinct advantage.

Finally, the positive and emancipatory language of human security enables a much broader political assemblage of state and non-state actors to be mobilized in this endeavor to improve the welfare of populations. Discipline, Foucault argued in this respect, "was never more important or more valued than when the attempt was made to manage the population: managing the population does not mean just managing the collective mass of phenomena or managing them simply at the level of their overall results; managing the population means managing it in depth, in all its fine points and detail" (2007:107). By giving security a more progressive and positive "human" face with the explicit aim of saving lives, human security is capable of mobilizing a much more extensive set of international organization and humanitarian NGOs, charitable organizations, doctors, scholars, and others for the task of improving the welfare of populations. Human security has been promoted by a coalition of governments including Austria, Canada, Chile,

Costa Rica, Greece, Ireland, Jordan, Mali, Norway, Slovenia, South Africa, Switzerland, and Thailand. But beyond such state institutions it has also spawned an entire network of practitioners and scholars working together—be it on the Human Security Report Project now located at Simon Fraser University in Vancouver, for the Canadian Consortium on Human Security, for the Commission on Human Security, or for some other organization. In the case of HIV/AIDS, the human security framework has enabled a much larger political tent of actors studying, politicizing, and urging action on HIV/AIDS to be constructed. This too is useful in terms of responding to the AIDS pandemic, as the success of these initiatives will depend on their ability to penetrate deeply into populations, engaging large elements of civil society—something that is much more difficult to achieve through recourse to the statist and often intimidating language of national security.

In all these ways, the politics of framing HIV/AIDS as a human security threat exemplifies how, in the securitization of AIDS, disciplinary power remains useful and is redirected toward the goal of managing the welfare of populations. It provides further evidence of Foucault's argument that the era of governmentality consists "to a great extent in the *reactivation* and *transformation* of the juridico-legal techniques and the disciplinary techniques I have talked about in previous years [emphasis added]" (2007:9). Respectively, both national security *and* human security arguments about HIV/AIDS show in the end how the older forms of sovereign power (national security) and disciplinary power (human security) become transformed and redirected for the purposes of managing the welfare of populations in the era of governmentality. What remains to be seen in terms of Foucault's characterization of the era of governmentality as a complex triangle of sovereignty, discipline, and governmental management is whether there is also evidence of a governmental economy of power operating in the securitization of HIV/AIDS. If there is, this would further corroborate the thesis that the securitization of HIV/AIDS is indeed a contemporary manifestation of the governmentalization of security.

Government, Military Risk Groups, and Population Triage

The securitization of HIV/AIDS does, finally, also contain newer strategies for governmental management. This can be seen in arguments that portray the armed forces and the United Nations peacekeepers as "risk groups" with respect to HIV/AIDS. The very idea of a "risk group" is a quintessentially governmental notion. It is a category generated by statistically determining the overall distribution of HIV/AIDS within the population. Such a statistical analysis reveals that there are groups within the population who have a higher prevalence of HIV/AIDS compared to the population as a whole—that is, risk groups. Identification of these segments of the population makes it possible to govern the population economically and efficiently and to target available resources specifically where they will have the greatest impact. Governing populations through the identification of risk groups even respects the principle of laissez-faire in the sense that it does not unduly interfere with the workings of the population. It is no longer necessary to intervene in the population as a whole; direct interventions can be restricted largely to the known risk groups. To the extent that the securitization of HIV/AIDS makes extensive use of this risk groups category, it also reveals the operation of a *governmental* economy of power.

Imbuing the practice of security with a governmental logic, and bringing that to bear on the AIDS pandemic, produce further dangers still. These dangers derive mostly from the political effects of seeking to normalize populations through political technologies based on such "risk group" categories. First, identifying risk groups within the population can further stigmatize members of those groups. In past years this has happened with respect to United Nations peacekeepers, who are now widely associated with the spread of HIV/AIDS. Second, given the unique demands that governments place upon the armed forces as opposed to the civilian population, there is also a danger that the language of risk groups will lead to more-intrusive forms of compulsory HIV testing within these subpopulations, such that people living with HIV are subsequently excluded from participating in these occupations. This too has already begun to happen through the introduction of mandatory testing in many armed forces throughout the world. Finally, there is a danger that the identification of these groups of people as "risk groups" will have undesirable material effects in terms of diverting scarce resources from other, politically more marginalized risk groups who are already struggling to gain access to resources (such as sex workers, injecting drug users, men having sex with men, and others) to the security sector—as can be seen in special funds being directed to programs focused on addressing the spread of HIV/AIDS specifically in the armed forces. Applying such a governmental economy of power to the practice of security could, in short, encourage a form of population triage in which the armed forces henceforth receive undue priority in terms of access to treatment and care.

"RISK GROUPS" AS A GOVERNMENTAL RATIONALITY

Whereas examples of sovereign power can be found in feudal times, and of disciplinary power as early as the late seventeenth century, the emergence of governmental management was dated by Michel Foucault closer to the eighteenth century. Like disciplinary power, governmental management is a "positive" economy of power that seeks to empower and enhance life; but unlike discipline with its focus on individual bodies, governmental management is much more concerned with the "mass" or aggregate effects of populations. It is "not a matter of taking the individuals at the level of individuality but, on the contrary, of using overall mechanisms and acting in such a way as to achieve overall states of equilibration or regularity; it is, in a word, a matter of taking control of life and the biological processes of man-as-species and of ensuring that they are not disciplined but regularized" (Foucault 2003:246–247). For this reason, governmental management also deploys different tactics and mechanisms from those of sovereign and disciplinary power. Whereas disciplinary tactics revolve around training and drill because they are focused on improving the capacities of individual bodies, governmental management operates through aggregate technologies; its mechanisms include "forecasts, statistical estimates, and overall measures," which seek to "intervene at the level of their generality. The mortality rate has to be modified or lowered; life expectancy has to be increased; the birth rate has to be stimulated. And their purpose is not to modify a particular phenomenon as such, or to modify a given individual insofar as he is an individual, but essentially, to intervene at the level at which these general phenomena are determined" (Foucault 2003:246–247).

The proliferation of assigning "risk group" categories in assessing social processes is one of the most important legacies of this new type of governmental management. In his governmentality lectures, Foucault explored in more detail the close historical association between the rise of this language of risk and the emergence of the population as a meaningful political category. It was precisely through the application of statistics to the social body that it first became possible for overarching population phenomena to be broken down and compartmentalized according to the constituent elements of the population most involved in, and affected by, a particular phenomenon (Foucault 2007:60–61). Through statistical analysis of the population it became possible, for example, to calculate for any group of individuals within the population their general risk of becoming infected with a particular disease. One could calculate for people according to their age, their location, and their occupation the risk of dying or becoming ill (Foucault 2007:60–61). These risk calculations subsequently showed that the risks of becoming infected with a particular virus are not identical for all individuals within the population, but vary across age groups, locations, and so on (Foucault 2007:61). In other words, there are differential risks within the population, indicating areas or groups that have a heightened chance of becoming infected, as well as groups or areas with a concomitantly lower probability. This analysis, in turn, allowed for the ascription of certain individuals, behaviors, or regions as being—statistically speaking—"dangerous" or, as we now prefer to say, "at risk." In the case of smallpox, for example, risk calculations showed that it was "dangerous" to be a child under the age of three or to live in a town rather in a rural area (Foucault 2007:61).

What also makes risk calculations such a quintessential expression of a governmental economy of power is that they enable various phenomena to be governed directly at the level of population. Contrary to sovereign power, the purpose of risk calculations in relation to the management of disease is no longer to ban or exclude the sick from the healthy members of society. Nor is the objective to prevent contact between those who are infected and those who are not infected, as it was for disciplinary mechanisms. Instead, the use of risk-based categories allows governmental management to accommodate the totality of healthy people and sick people, without any form of discontinuity (Foucault 2007:62). Risk calculations thus provide a more nuanced analysis of which population subgroups deviate from the population norm so that—through a series of targeted interventions within the population—these groups can be realigned with the overall norm or distribution.

If, to remain with the example of smallpox, the data show that children are at particular risk, then techniques can be developed for intervention at this stage without having to remove the children from the population or confine them (Foucault 2007:62). Risk calculations facilitate treatment of a disease by patiently subjecting it to detailed quantitative evaluation in terms of its distribution within the population and assessing which interventions have proved successful and which ones unsuccessful. Authorities can evaluate statistically the natural rate at which a phenomenon such as HIV/AIDS occurs in the population, determine which subpopulations deviate most from the "natural" norm, and then introduce mechanisms that interfere with the population in the least intrusive manner consistent with managing this phenomenon.

Such risk-based approaches to governing populations can even function without the direct surveillance of each and every member of the population. They can rely instead on compiling a list of general risk *factors* as a proxy, which then makes it necessary to extend more detailed examination only to that much smaller proportion of the population who evidence a combination of various such risk factors. As Robert Castel argued in his influential essay "From Dangerousness to Risk," many discourses on risk dissolve the notion of a subject or concrete individual, and put in its place a combinatory of factors, the factors of risk. . . . The essential component of intervention no longer takes the form of the direct face-to-face relationship between the carer and the cared, the helper and the helped, the professional and the client. It comes instead to reside in the establishing of flows of population based on the collation of a range of abstract factors deemed liable to produce risk in general. (1991:281)

Governing a population through risk factors minimizes the required level of direct intervention upon the population to those instances when various risk factors produce a "dangerous" combination in an individual. Castel's specific reference was to the systematic screening of children at a few days, a few months, and two years after birth, introduced in France in 1976. From that point on, specialists collected data on the medical backgrounds and circumstances of the parents, including their age, nationality, social class, and so on. A certain predetermined combination of factors would then trigger an automatic alert, which, in turn, would prompt a visit by a specialist or a social worker "to confirm or disconfirm the real presence of a danger, on the basis of the probabilistic and abstract existence of risks. Here one does not start from a conflictual situation observable in experience, rather one deduces it from a general definition of the dangers one wishes to prevent" (Castel 1991:287–288). This too makes the notion of risk groups a quintessentially governmental technology; it enables populations to be governed not by direct observation but in a more distant and seemingly less intrusive manner. In all these ways risk calculations are indicative of a governmental form of management operating at the level of population; it is a mode of governing that primarily works through statistical analysis of the population and that enables population dynamics to be managed economically by primarily targeting these risk groups (cost-benefit analysis) and thereby not intruding unduly into the day-to-day workings of the population as a whole (laissez-faire).

Such a risk-based form of governmental management can also be found operating in the securitization of HIV/AIDS in the form of the routine identification of armed forces and United Nations peacekeepers as risk groups with respect to HIV/AIDS. In terms of the broader history of the international politics of AIDS, this decision by organizations such as UNAIDS to focus on the uniformed services as a high-risk group is quite unusual. Most international agencies have traditionally avoided recourse to the language of risk groups for fear of further stigmatizing groups that often already occupy a marginalized and vulnerable social position—such as injecting drug users or men having sex with men. Thus it is surprising that international organizations such as UNAIDS should have played such a key role in the debate about the armed forces constituting a high-risk group in relation to HIV/AIDS. Not wishing to stigmatize other known risk groups, these same international organizations have had remarkably little hesitation or compunction about mobilizing the language of risk groups to full effect with regard to the armed forces.

UNAIDS began to claim as early as 1998 that the armed forces constitute an important risk group for HIV/AIDS (UNAIDS 1998), and the organization continues to argue that "among male population groups, military and police report the highest risk behaviour and number of partners. Sexually transmitted infection rates among military personnel are two to five times greater than those in civilian populations in peacetime. These figures increase dramatically during conflict" (UNAIDS 2006a). In the securitization of HIV/AIDS the armed forces and peacekeepers are thus frequently portrayed as "dangerous" risk groups that exacerbate the spread of AIDS between populations. In this process, the political significance of the armed forces and peacekeepers shifts from their being the core institutions defending sovereignty, territory, and the wider international order (sovereign power) to their being a potentially "dangerous" vector of HIV/AIDS that hinders attempts to reduce the spread of HIV/AIDS among populations (governmental management).

Closer attention to how these risk groups have been identified in the debate on HIV/AIDS and security shows that the process has not always unfolded on the basis of sound epidemiological data. Because such data are frequently unavailable as a result of patchy surveillance systems, as well as being politically very sensitive, reliable figures about HIV/AIDS in the armed forces are difficult to obtain for many countries (Barnett and Prins 2006; Garrett 2005; Whiteside, de Waal, and Gebre-Tensae 2006). The armed forces have thus been indirectly constructed as a risk group in that they are seen to combine various more general risk *factors* associated with the transmission of HIV. UNAIDS (1998:3) pointed out the following:

- Military and peacekeeping service often includes lengthy periods spent away from home, with the result that personnel are often looking for ways to relieve loneliness, stress and the building up of sexual tension.
- The military's professional ethos tends to excuse or even encourage risk-taking.
- Most personnel are in the age group at greatest risk for HIV infection — the sexually active 15–24-year age group.
- Personnel sent on peacekeeping missions often have more money in their pockets than local people, giving them the financial means to purchase sex.
- Military personnel and camps, including the installations of peacekeeping forces, attract sex workers and those who deal in illicit drugs.

The identification of these risk groups has therefore occurred not through direct surveillance of the populations but principally through the compilation and association of more general risk factors.

International organizations such as UNAIDS have been politically quite adept in this respect. It is important to bear in mind that as an international institution UNAIDS remains heavily dependent upon the cooperation of legally sovereign member-states. This is true in terms of both the supply of epidemiological data about the prevalence of HIV/AIDS and implementation of the public health interventions that the UN body recommends. UNAIDS cannot actually compel states to do either; therefore, in its attempts to better govern the spread of HIV/AIDS, UNAIDS continually faces the problem that states can invoke their legal sovereignty as a way of warding off pressure to implement HIV/AIDS policies. The language of risk factors enables international institutions such as UNAIDS to employ a more "indirect" form of governing populations that works through compiling general statistical risk factors instead of concretely manifested dangers. As the case of the armed forces shows, UNAIDS cannot compel states to disclose sensitive information about HIV prevalence in the military. Rather than allowing this limitation to completely stifle its public health activities, however, UNAIDS can partially overcome this problem by working on the basis of more general risk factors, and can thus politicize the armed forces as a risk group requiring targeted interventions because it is argued that they combine a host of more general risk factors. In the language of Castel, we might say the armed forces can be politically construed by UNAIDS as exhibiting a potentially "dangerous combination" of risk factors.

The addition of the armed forces to the list of risk groups in the AIDS pandemic is particularly significant because it begins to draw more explicit attention to the role of heterosexual men in the epidemic. Blame for the epidemic has frequently been directed at groups that are already socially stigmatized and that do not conform to established notions of gender and sexuality (Pisani 2008). Moreover, it has also been mostly directed at women, as can be seen in the various interventions targeted at sex workers. The gendered nature of many of these debates is even mirrored in various testing and HIV surveillance practices (many of which again rely on the sampling of pregnant women). Here the novel construction of the armed forces as a risk group, with their mostly male composition and masculine institutional cultures, is significant, since it begins to draw greater attention to the central role that men, masculinities, and other gender relations play in the pandemic—thereby opening up much wider elements of the population that can eventually be made amenable to various forms of governmental management.

THE DANGERS OF GOVERNMENTAL POWER: STIGMA, EXCLUSION, AND TRIAGE

What happens when the practice of security is imbued with such governmental logic and brought to bear on the AIDS pandemic? More dangers begin to emerge, albeit not necessarily dangers revolving around the prospect of excessive state mobilization or the intensification of a set of disciplinary practices. These additional dangers derive from the particular ways in which populations are "normalized" through the identification and modification of risk groups. Unlike disciplinary power, governmental power is not principally a technology of *normation*, but one of *normalization* (Foucault 2007:63). Although Foucault's choice of terminology may seem somewhat confusing and esoteric here (and, indeed, it changed over time), underlying this differentiation is a crucial distinction in terms of how disciplinary and governmental economies of power derive the norms with which they operate. In processes of disciplinary normation, an ideal norm is imposed from the outside, and the distinction between the normal and the abnormal is undertaken according to this "artificial" norm. Put somewhat schematically, disciplinary power ideally functions not unlike a cookie cutter, or an industrial machine that produces identical goods one after another in the way it is engineered or programmed to do. In a governmental economy of power, by contrast, the norm is not so much imposed from above as it is initially derived by determining the actual and already existing distribution of a phenomenon—such as the level of a disease— within the population. The "abnormals," consequently, are not those who deviate from a more abstract norm but those who deviate from the average statistical distribution of a phenomenon within a population. The norm against which risk groups are evaluated, in other words, is very much *internal* to the population as a whole.

This process of governmental management also creates new internal divisions within the population. The primary distinction according to which governmental management operates is not that between the individual and the state (as in a sovereign economy of power) but that between the individual and the population: "Man is [now] to population what the subject of right was to the sovereign" (Foucault 2007:79). Whereas the sovereign model of power gives rise to systems of exclusion by differentiating between those who submit to the social contract and those who violate it (such as "criminals"), a governmental economy of power differentiates between those who behave in accordance with the welfare of the population and "those who conduct themselves in relation to the management of the population . . . as if they were not part of the population . . . as if they put themselves out of it, and consequently the people are those who, refusing to be the population, disrupt the system" (Foucault 2007:43–44). With the rise of governmental management we thus "see a division being made in which the people are generally speaking those who resist the regulation of the population, who try to elude the apparatus by which the population exists, is preserved, subsists, and subsists at an optimal level. This people/population opposition is very important" (Foucault 2007:44). A governmental economy of power thus singles out those groups of individuals who are at odds with managing the greater welfare of the population. Often, it is precisely these groups who are identified as risk groups.

Normalizing populations through the use of these risk-based methods of differentiation can give rise to further dangers. First, and as was the case with processes of disciplinary normation, risk-based categories can generate further social stigma for individuals who are deemed to be members of those risk groups. To be "at risk" is effectively to be at odds with, or even a danger to, the welfare of the population—creating a close connection between the notions of risk and danger (Foucault 2007:61). Such a connection can also be discerned in the early days of the AIDS pandemic, when people in the United States were cautioned against the four "dangerous" H's that were publicly presented as risk groups: homosexuals, hemophiliacs, heroin addicts, and Haitians. Later the list was expanded to include Africans more generally (both domestically in the United States and internationally) and sex workers (Brown 2000:1274). More recently, the armed forces and peacekeepers have been added as risk groups.

Predictably, the identification of the armed forces and peacekeepers as risk groups in relation to HIV/AIDS has begun to stigmatize these groups as well. A number of examples illustrate this point. In Asia, political problems began to emerge in Cambodia after the United Nations arrived between the spring of 1992 and September 1993 in order to implement the peace agreement and organize democratic elections. The arrival of the UN personnel coincided with a dramatic increase in the spread of HIV/AIDS, with the result that officials in Phnom Penh place considerable blame for the spread of the epidemic in Cambodia on the United Nations Transition Authority in Cambodia (UNTAC). In the mid-1990s Canadian peacekeepers deployed in Croatia were reportedly "frequently reminded that the Kenyan contingent was highly stricken with AIDS. They were told that 'if a Kenyan gets in an accident, don't touch him'" (Bratt 2002:75). In Sierra Leone, officials argued that Nigerian troops—who were deployed there as part of the Economic Community of West African States (ECOWAS) mission—exacerbated the spread of HIV/AIDS in the country, with the Nigerian government

countering that rates of HIV prevalence among its troops rose only after their deployment to Sierra Leone (Bratt 2002:75).

Such finger-pointing about the role of peacekeepers in the spread of
HIV/AIDS has extended well into the current decade. In eastern Africa,
Eritrean officials showing similar concern initially wanted a guarantee
that no HIV-positive soldiers would be deployed there. The Eritrean
government wrote to the Security Council in March 2001 asking that
peacekeepers contributing to the United Nations Mission in Ethiopia
and Eritrea (UNMEE) be screened for HIV/AIDS:

> We appeal to troop contributing countries to understand our concern.
> Eritrea is at the moment engaged in a very rigorous campaign to prevent
> the spread of AIDS . . . this is not a discriminatory practice targeted at
> UNMEE, but it is a standard national practice that has been in effect
> since 1993. Routine testing of the Eritrean army is conducted as a matter
> of policy based on the recognition that the army is one of the most sexu-
> ally active segments of the population. (cited in Bazergan 2001:6)

At around the same time, Richard Holbrooke (2000a) also drew attention to the possible role of peacekeepers in spreading HIV in East
Timor, noting how East Timor "never had a reported case of AIDS until the UN got there. I'm not saying there weren't any cases because
it's a remote area but we now have 20 reported cases." In East Timor,
the United Nations had encouraged its staff to be tested voluntarily for
HIV but did not impose compulsory testing despite calls for it by Denis
Burke, the chief minister of the Northern Territory, after it was reported
that a woman from Darwin had become infected by a UN employee
based in East Timor. According to the government of the Northern
Territory, ten cases of HIV were detected among UN personnel visit-
ing Australia from East Timor. More recently, the Sudanese government
has demanded that troops from Nigeria, and from other members of
the African Union, that were to be deployed in Darfur certify that they
are HIV-negative (AFP 2004). Such episodes show how a greater stigma
has now emerged surrounding peacekeepers, even though the publicly
available epidemiological data do not present an accurate picture of
how justified this designation is. It shows, moreover, how the category

of "risk group" assumes that individuals' sexuality and behavior are one-dimensional rather than complex, with the result that some soldiers will be stigmatized simply by virtue of being members of a risk group (Lupton 1995:78–82; Schiller 1992).

Second, the differentiation between risk groups and the general population has also increased political pressure to subject the armed forces to much stricter forms of medical surveillance, as well as to modify their behavior and exclude those who are living with HIV/AIDS from serving in the armed forces at all. Given that governments need to prepare for going to war, they do tend to make unique and strenuous demands on their armed forces. Because of the special nature of these demands, separate rules and regulations govern the armed forces in many countries. Not surprisingly, the armed forces have frequently invoked the demanding nature of the job to justify the exclusion of people living with HIV/AIDS. Historically the armed forces have thus been among the most stringent entities in terms of imposing mandatory testing and excluding people living with HIV/AIDS from their ranks. In the United States those who were HIV-positive were not enlisted and were subjected to a fairly intrusive surveillance regime—including screening, taking measures to prevent transmission, informing partners and caregivers of their status, and even having their sexual contacts traced and tested without their consent (Baldwin 2005:38). In Europe, Italy initially had mandatory testing but later made it voluntary. Spain used test results from blood donors to unofficially exclude those living with HIV from service, whereas the Belgians and French tested much more selectively, in those groups being posted abroad or returning from areas with high prevalence rates (Baldwin 2005:108–109). In Africa, HIV testing is mandatory for recruits in Angola, Burkina Faso, Burundi, Central African Republic, Côte d'Ivoire, Eritrea, Kenya, Malawi, Nigeria, Rwanda, Sierra Leone, and Uganda. The introduction of such measures is also being considered in the Congo, Liberia, Swaziland, and Tanzania (Sagala 2008:302).

In this context it is unsurprising that the decision by the UN Security Council to draw attention to the role of peacekeepers as a potential vector and risk group in relation to HIV/AIDS has similarly generated calls for compulsory testing to be introduced for peacekeepers before deployment. Those in favor of such a policy viewed it as an important element in reducing the spread of HIV/AIDS from peacekeepers to host populations. Some also argued, again from a military point of view, that an HIV-positive peacekeeper may not be as effective in performing his or her duties and also poses a risk to other peacekeepers through blood transfusion. There was further concern that having to care for HIV-positive soldiers would generate higher costs for such operations because of having to provide more elaborate medical care. Even from the medical perspective of an infected peacekeeper, some added, such peacekeeping operations could be detrimental to their health because of the impact of vaccinations on the immune system and the demanding psychological and physical realities of peacekeeping duties (UNAIDS 2001c:4–5). Many of these same reasons have also been invoked by a growing number of armed forces more generally for introducing compulsory HIV screening and testing (Kingma 2003). Here, the designation of the armed forces and peacekeepers as risk groups has generated political pressure to further extend surveillance mechanisms into these subpopulations.

Again UNAIDS had to come out fighting in order to defend its preference for a human rights approach toward peacekeepers, based on voluntary and confidential testing. It did so by convening an expert panel in 2001, which rebuked many of the arguments for excluding HIV-positive soldiers from peacekeeping operations. The panel found that HIV status itself was not grounds for lack of fitness because soldiers could go through many years of normal psychological and physical functional capacity before developing AIDS. "Walking blood banks," it countered, were no longer used by the armed forces because they were unsafe for other reasons as well, so that objection too should be discounted. It further argued that the available medical evidence suggested that most vaccinations were safe even for soldiers who were HIV-positive. In light of the relatively short duration of many peacekeeping operations, the panel concluded that the chances of a soldier's becoming immuno-suppressed during a peacekeeping operation would be very slim, and the cost implications should therefore be negligible. Even in the rare instances where a soldier might become immuno-suppressed while deployed, it would be analogous to his or her sustaining another kind of battlefield or non-battlefield injury (UNAIDS 2001c:9–11). Again, UNAIDS invoked human rights considerations to defend its position, including both

a) the rights that enable people to avoid infection by HIV—the rights related to education, information, privacy, health and health care, non-discrimination, and for women and children particularly, freedom from rape, sexual violence and exploitation [and]
b) the rights that enable people already infected by HIV to live fully and cope with the impact of HIV/AIDS—the rights related to privacy, health and health care, employment, social assistance, and non-discrimination and reasonable accommodation, including in workplaces such as the armed forces and the United Nations. (2001c:9–11)

In light of the latter rights, the panel concluded that it would be discriminatory to exclude a soldier from peacekeeping duties, since there was no medical evidence to suggest that a soldier would be impaired by HIV status alone. The fitness of any soldier to serve could be determined by standard medical checks such as chest X-rays and laboratory tests. Given the stigmatized nature of the illness and the discriminatory practices that it often fuels, the privacy of soldiers should not be easily overridden. For these reasons the panel once again recommended a policy of voluntary counseling and testing.

Critics were of course quick to point out that this policy effectively put the rights of peacekeepers to serve above the rights of host populations to remain free from infection with a lethal virus. Nevertheless, the panel mostly recommended that measures to be introduced by the United Nations Department of Peacekeeping Operations should ensure that male and female condoms were accessible, that other sexually transmitted diseases which soldiers may have were treated, that peer education about HIV/AIDS was implemented, and that HIV advisers were posted to each peacekeeping mission. Even though UNAIDS was able, on this occasion, to defend its approach on the basis of voluntary counseling and testing, these struggles nevertheless indicate how the identification of UN peacekeepers as a risk group has generated increased pressure for wider surveillance of this group in relation to HIV/AIDS. What is more, even in recommending that troop-contributing countries send only HIV-negative soldiers, UNAIDS has effectively managed only to externalize these difficult struggles over testing to the troop-contributing countries themselves, which, if they wish to benefit financially from participating in United Nations peacekeeping operations, will have to test their soldiers before deployment in order to conform to this recommendation.

Short of introducing mandatory testing for peacekeepers, the debate on HIV/AIDS and security has also spurred other interventions aimed at altering the behavior of this risk group. In this respect, too, governmental management gives rise to dangers that are similar to those of disciplinary power. UNAIDS now promotes the "HIV/AIDS Awareness Card," which is routinely distributed during international peacekeeping operations in response to requests by the Security Council to address the problem of peacekeepers spreading HIV/AIDS where and when they are deployed. The card—which has been produced in several different languages ranging from the obligatory English to Kiswahili—recommends to peacekeepers that "condoms should be used for all types of sexual acts" and urges them to "limit your alcohol intake and stay away from drugs." The most striking feature of this card, however, is undoubtedly that it also uses fear to encourage peacekeepers to exercise self-discipline over their bodies by reminding them that "the HIV virus can be present anywhere in the world. You do not know who is infected with HIV" (UNAIDS 2003c:22). This strategy parallels Jeremy Bentham's famous Panopticon prison design from 1791, whereby the impossibility of any prisoner's knowing whether or not he was being observed at any given time continuously induced him to be obedient and to exercise self-discipline with regard to his behavior. Today, the impossibility of knowing whether any sexual partner is HIV-positive should similarly induce desired behavior changes among UN peacekeepers—including their sexual behavior. Here too the language of risk groups is driving the expansion of medical surveillance and the cultivation of subjects who will conduct themselves in a manner consistent with the need to reduce the levels of HIV/AIDS within populations.

Finally, this identification of the armed forces and peacekeepers as a risk group can have undesirable material consequences by acting as a mechanism for channeling scarce resources. The potential danger here is that the identification of the uniformed services as a risk group will—especially in developing countries—direct resources toward those groups at the expense of politically much more marginalized risk groups who have traditionally had great difficulty in getting access to such resources. This is part of a larger problem that has affected the direction of many international HIV/AIDS initiatives.

In their attempt to avoid further stigmatizing other known risk groups, international organizations have tended to focus their campaigns on the populations as a whole ("AIDS is a danger to everybody"). This strategy clearly has political attractions; it is much more palatable to many politicians because it ensures that politically and culturally sensitive issues surrounding drug use, gender, and sexuality do not have to be discussed openly. As Elizabeth Pisani laments,

> There are not many votes in doing nice things for [what are perceived to be] wicked people. Rich countries don't want to pay for it and poor countries don't want to do it. Recognizing this, the AIDS mafia tried to turn HIV into "everyone's problem," a development problem, a security problem. True in 3 percent of the world. Untrue everywhere else. But rich countries will pay for security problems, so poor countries can get money to do nice things for people who are not wicked. There are votes in doing nice things for people who are not wicked. (2008:316)

Many of those working on the international politics of HIV/AIDS thus continually face the problem that politicians would much rather represent HIV/AIDS as a problem for the general population, rather than having to take on these politically sensitive and controversial issues that many people would prefer not to have to talk about openly.

Yet more recently some epidemiologists have begun to openly challenge the wisdom of this strategy, pointing out that it ultimately culminates in wasteful allocation of valuable resources. Large amounts of money are now directed toward the population as a whole (which is deemed to be at low risk epidemiologically, except for a small number of states in sub-Saharan Africa), rather than toward those groups who are at high risk around the world. James Chin argues that

> UNAIDS and most AIDS activists have either intentionally or out of honest ignorance ignored the fact that HIV is very difficult to transmit

sexually. By refusing to accept the fact that HIV is very difficult to trans-
mit sexually without the highest levels of sexual risk behaviors, AIDS
programs have avoided labeling some populations as being more pro-
miscuous than others. It is a much more socially and politically correct
public health message to say that sexual promiscuity exists in all populations and thus the risk of epidemic heterosexual HIV transmission to the
"general" public or to "ordinary people" can be prevented only by ag-
gressive ABC programs directed at the general population, and especially
to youth. (2007:166)

Chin thereby highlights that the channeling of resources in international campaigns to reduce HIV/AIDS to some extent already fails to reflect underlying epidemiological calculations of risk. The public, which
is generally at a much lower risk in most parts of the world, is receiving
a disproportionately high amount of expenditure, whereas the smaller
risk groups, who are at much higher epidemiological risk, are receiving a proportionately much smaller amount of funding (see also Pisani
2008). The history of many national and international responses to the
AIDS pandemic is marked by considerable discrepancies between the
underlying epidemiological calculations of risk and the decisions about
who receives the available resources.

A concomitant danger is that the designation of the armed forces
as yet another risk group could exacerbate this problem. Although doing so does not portray HIV/AIDS as "everybody's problem," and clearly
does not shy away from using the language of risk groups, it could
nevertheless end up again channeling resources away from the other
known and politically more marginalized risk groups if governments
now focus on their armed forces and make them a priority. Especially
in low-income countries, the identification of the armed forces as a risk
group could implicitly encourage a form of population triage in which
funding priority is given to the armed forces. There is certainly evidence that in many countries members of the armed forces routinely
enjoy preferential access to medicines as compared to the civilian population, or that they have at least moved to the front of the line in
terms of receiving access to expensive anti-retroviral medicines (ARVs).
In Zambia, for example, members of the military have begun to argue
that the armed forces should have priority access to more government

funding for ARVs since the military and their families are more at risk because of the nature of their jobs and because this would contribute to world peace ("Allocate More ARVs" 2003). Similarly, in Rwanda in 2004, high-ranking officers increasingly had access to ARVs, but the general population did not (Amnesty International 2004). Radhika Sarin argues that "quite a few African militaries are committed to providing treatment for their soldiers, such as the Ugandan People's Defense Forces and Nigeria's armed forces. These militaries do try and work with military spouses and civilian communities to provide HIV prevention education. However, access to anti-retrovirals is very low in many African nations" (quoted in Conklin 2003). This is part of a wider development in Africa whereby soldiers in many countries tend to have greater or better access to health care and AIDS medicines than the civilian population (Sagala 2008:301). The identification of the armed forces as a risk group thus advantages those who already have the greatest chances of access to medicines rather than helping those who are least likely to have such access. It may ensure that soldiers and elites who play a crucial role in security terms have access to treatment, yet without ensuring that treatment is also provided to those other "risk groups" who need it. Such a situation would be especially unfortunate given that the lack of reliable epidemiological information about the actual extent to which HIV/AIDS in the armed forces remains a problem.

These three dangers associated with the ways in which governmental management seeks to normalize populations through the use of risk group categories must be added to the dangers already identified in the exercise of sovereign and disciplinary power in the securitization of HIV/AIDS. For Foucault the practice of modern medicine has always been deeply suffused with both disciplinary and governmental forms of power. He once even went so far as to characterize the entire enterprise of modern medicine as "a power-knowledge that can be applied to both the body and the population, both the organism and biopolitical processes, and it will therefore have both disciplinary effects and regulatory effects" (Foucault 2003:252). To the extent that the securitization of HIV/AIDS marks the continuation of medicine by other means, it too spreads and intensifies such disciplinary and governmental economies of power—giving rise to a cocktail of new "dangers." These dangers do not resolve the political dilemma surrounding the securitization of

HIV/AIDS; on the contrary, they render it much more complex. Scholars and policymakers are left confronting a difficult set of trade-offs between the progressive ambitions of many of those political actors driving the securitization of HIV/AIDS, and the multiple "dangers" that this process invariably brings into play.

SECURITY, GOVERNMENTALITY, AND THE INTERNATIONAL ORDER

Beyond these dangers, the application of a governmental economy of power to the contemporary practice of security also represents an important development in and of itself. On one of the rare occasions when he conveyed his understanding of the international order, Foucault argued that it was predominantly characterized by the interplay of the two older forms of sovereign and disciplinary power. The Peace of Westphalia (1648) was an important historical turning point for him, since henceforth the dream that all the world's kingdoms would be unified under a single emperor was no longer sustainable (Foucault 2000e:408). The treaties of Westphalia thus technically marked the end of the Roman Empire and sealed the fact that empire was no longer the ultimate horizon for states. From this point on, the European order would consist of "absolute" states that legally recognized no hierarchy between them (Foucault 2007:295). One was now dealing with an international system that was politically diverse, that operated in an infinite and open time horizon, and in which European states were positioned in a new relationship of permanent competition with one another (Foucault 2007:290).

Once states found themselves in this new position of rivalry, they urgently needed to discover alternative ways of limiting the ambition and growth of states, lest some become too powerful and dominate all others. This goal was eventually achieved through the development of a new European order based on the principle of the balance of power. Ideally, the balance of power system would ensure that no state could completely dominate the European order, because smaller states—now unconstrained by religious affiliation—could in principle always pool their forces into an alliance in order to contain the power of larger states (Foucault 2007:299). When necessary, the balance of power was to be maintained through war, but it could also be achieved through the institutions of diplomacy and the building up of standing armies and weapons arsenals (Foucault 2007:300, 302). Foucault referred to this as the diplomatic-military arm of the European balance of power system, which mostly dealt with balancing the *external* forces that were at play between states. It is associated with all the aspects of sovereign power that were discussed in chapter 4, showing that sovereign power was crucial not only for the survival of individual states but also for the operation of the Westphalian order as a whole.

In addition to this military-diplomatic arm, the functioning of the European balance of power historically also relied on the use of disciplinary power. This order always had an important *internal* dimension in the form of the practices of police that were discussed in chapter 5 (Foucault 2007:266). Whereas the military-diplomatic arm regulated the forces *between* states, police had the task of maximizing the forces *within* states. Police would use disciplinary forms of power to give states the internal strength necessary for avoiding attack or subjugation by other states with which they were in competition. Each state thus needed a police force that was effective at disciplining individual members of society in order to ensure that the state would not be overtaken in power by other states—that is, that the balance of power did not turn against one's own state. It was also at this point that states came to the paradoxical conclusion that if the European balance of power was to remain stable and be preserved, effectively *all* states would need to have good police and discipline. If any state, even a state other than one's own, had a bad or ineffective system of police, the balance of power could become unhinged for all (Foucault 2007:315). In this sense, police (disciplinary power) and the military-diplomatic apparatus (sovereign power)—the "inside" and the "outside" of the European balance of power system—were profoundly interdependent, and the international order has long relied on the mutual constitution of both sovereign and disciplinary economies of power (Campbell 1998c; Walker 1993).

Yet the securitization of HIV/AIDS shows that the practice of international security today also includes a third form of governmental management—something that Foucault explored generally regarding Western societies, but not with specific reference to the international order (Campbell 2005; Coward 2006; Dillon 1995; Dillon and Lobo-

Guerrero 2008a; Dillon and Reid 2001; Duffield 2007; Hardt and Negri 2000; Reid 2005, 2006). To make such a claim about the nature of the contemporary international order is not to deny that a range of international institutions have long been involved with governing population issues internationally—from the International Sanitary Conferences in the nineteenth century to the various international activities of the World Health Organization, the United Nations Development Program, and the United Nations Population Division during the twentieth century. Nor is it to deny that medicine has historically played an important role in issues having to do with the exercise of sovereign power. From the development of the institutions of military medicine (Berry and Greenwood 2005; Gabriel and Metz 1992) to the role of tropical medicine in various formations of empire and colonialism, medicine and security have frequently been linked throughout history (Arnold 1988; Curtin 1998; Levine 2003; Macleod and Lewis 1988; Vaughan 1991). Whether it was the Rockefeller Foundation pursuing yellow fever eradication programs in Central America or European powers intervening in Ottoman rule to stop the spread of cholera, disease prevention has long been an important element of geopolitics (Bashford 2006:2).

In this sense it would be tempting to see nothing novel in the international politics of HIV/AIDS and to view the securitization of HIV/AIDS simply as the continuation, and perhaps even intensification, of this much longer history. As Alison Bashford argues:

> While once disease prevention and geopolitics were simply related, more recently the former has become a vehicle for, and even an instrument of, the latter. The intense twenty-first century manifestations of defensive nationalism, disease and security on the one hand, and global flow, supranational surveillance technologies, actual and immanent world pandemics on the other, suggest a need to think about the provenance of these connections, their effects in the past, and to temper assessments of their alleged novelty, while at the same time recognizing a world linked in time and space in ways altogether new. (2006:2)

This view of disease management as a tool of geopolitics is also shared more widely by scholars who have analyzed the securitization of HIV/AIDS (Ingram 2007).

While the scholars are undoubtedly correct to assert that the link between health and security is not novel in and of itself, the rush to conflate the securitization of HIV/AIDS with this much older history of colonialism, imperialism, and geopolitics would miss something that is not as common historically. The securitization of HIV/AIDS is not just another instance of health issues being subsumed within a broader imperial project; as we have seen, it is also a process driven by public health advocates who are now trying to use the language and institutions of security in order to scale up international efforts to reduce the spread of HIV/AIDS (McInnes 2006:326). Medicine is not merely serving as a blind tool for the institutions of security here; the practices and institutions of security are conversely also being asked to serve as a tool for improving the health of populations. This can be seen, for instance, in the attempt by UNAIDS to use the national military service that is required in many countries around the world as a site for educating populations about HIV/AIDS. UNAIDS has argued:

> Large proportions of young adults in many countries spend one or more years in the military. While this may be seen as a potential threat to civil society in terms of HIV transmission after they leave the military, it must also be seen as a unique opportunity since military service provides a disciplined, highly organized environment in which HIV/AIDS prevention and education can be provided to a large "captive audience." In some ways, such efforts fit perfectly with the ethos of a profession that places a high value on loyalty to comrades and the tradition of officers looking out for the well-being of those under their responsibility. From this perspective, HIV prevention and education are every bit as important to life and health as rescuing a wounded colleague on the battlefield or securing a position once taken. (1998:6)

In this view the demographic composition and unique organizational structure of national military institutions make them an ideal "way in" for state-based international institutions such as UNAIDS to spread their AIDS messages to populations around the world.

Speaking before the Security Council in 2000, Peter Piot reiterated the broader contribution that the armed forces and peacekeepers could make to international efforts to reduce the spread of HIV/AIDS, noting how "humanitarian aid workers and military and police forces that are well trained in HIV prevention and behavior change can be a tremendous force for prevention as long as this is made one of their priorities" (quoted in UNSC 2000b:11). By 2005 UNAIDS, together with several cosponsors, was implementing or developing programs for HIV/AIDS awareness in more than 100 uniformed services (military or police) across the world (UNAIDS 2005). Here the debate on HIV/AIDS and security does not simply mark the most recent marshaling of medicine and public health for geopolitical ends; security is also becoming the continuation of medicine and public health by other means. The ways in which this relationship between medicine and security can also work the other way around have historically not received very much theorization and deserve much more attention as a contemporary manifestation of the governmentalization of security.

All of this, however, still leaves one rather crucial question unresolved. If Foucault could trace the emergence of this era of governmentality in the eighteenth century, why has the more specific governmentalization of security unfolded only much more recently? Why has there been such a considerable historical lag between the rise of the era of governmentality in general, and the much later governmentalization of security? It is not actually that uncommon for such historical lags to occur. In his own account of the rise of the era of governmentality in Europe, Foucault already observed that its rise in the eighteenth century was a gradual and uneven development. In fact, it was possible to find historical precursors or antecedents to this era of governmentality in the late sixteenth and early seventeenth centuries, where an autonomous "reason of state" first began to crystallize. Reason of state was understood, then,

> not in its negative and pejorative sense we give to it today (as that which infringes upon the principles of law, equity and humanity in the sole interest of the state), but in a full and positive sense: the state is governed according to rational principles which are intrinsic to it and which cannot be derived solely from natural or divine laws or the principles of wisdom and prudence; the state, like nature, has its own proper form of rationality, albeit of a different sort. Conversely, the art of government, instead of seeking to found itself in transcendental rules, a cosmo-

logical model or a philosophico-moral ideal, must find the principles of its rationality in that which constitutes the specific reality of the state. (Foucault 1991:97)

Although this idea of the "reason of state" is an important historical precursor to the subsequent emergence of the era of governmentality in the West, the latter could not emerge more fully until the eighteenth century because of the historical peculiarities of the seventeenth century—including the Thirty Years' War, the peasant and urban rebellions, and the financial troubles plaguing many Western monarchies (Foucault 2007:101). Moreover, the problem of sovereignty in its theoretical and practical manifestations still dominated the imagination of the seventeenth century in too strong a fashion for this governmental form of rule to emerge in a specific and autonomous manner (Foucault 2007:102). Only in the eighteenth century would this climate gradually begin to change, through a variety of factors that included rapid demographic expansion, an increase in wealth linked to the expansion of agricultural production, and so forth (Foucault 2007:103). The historical rise of the era of governmentality was itself, in short, a protracted and uneven process.

The governmentalization of security that is manifesting itself today in the securitization of HIV/AIDS is no different; it has similarly followed a gradual and uneven trajectory. The Security Council has traditionally been concerned mostly with the survival of territorial states and their sovereign independence, and it too was paralyzed for many decades because of unique historical factors—such as the ideological confrontation of the Cold War in which either superpower had the ability to veto any resolution. Members of the Security Council thus remained similarly tied to the imagery of sovereign power. As Anna Leander and Rens van Munster argue,

the centrality of state-based thinking and the strong affirmation of state control over security has limited the impact of these [governmental] techniques on the security sector itself. During the bipolar Cold War, the security order was closely tied to the . . . paradigm of sovereignty. The focus on nuclear weapons and the great power competition made (international) security appear as a quintessentially public responsibility to be provided through practices as the arms race, diplomacy, alliance-building, containment, border control and policing. With the end of the Cold War this changed. As the binary great power competition ceased to monopolize attention, discourses on globalization and discourses about alternative security threats (failed states, immigration, terrorism, etc.) made their way into the field of security. . . . The governmentalization of the field of security has been quick. (2006:6)

It was the end of the Cold War that finally "unlocked" the possibility of a wider governmentalization of security practices, thereby also enabling institutions such as the Security Council to embark upon a new trajectory and a broader security agenda.

In this process the AIDS pandemic was always intended to represent only the first of many larger issues that would henceforth have to be included for deliberation at the Security Council. As Al Gore argued at the first meeting of the Security Council on HIV/AIDS:

As our world enters the year 2000, it is not the change in our calendar that matters. What matters is that in this symbolic transition from old to new, we find one of those precious few moments in all of human history when we have a chance to become the change we wish to see in the world, by seeking a common agreement to openly recognize a powerful new truth that has been growing just beneath the surface of every human heart. It is time to change the nature of the way we live together on this planet. From this new vantage point, we must forge and follow a new agenda for world security, an agenda that includes the global environmental challenge, which could render all our other progress meaningless unless we deal with it successfully; the global challenge of defeating drugs and corruption, which now spill across our borders; the global challenge of terror, magnified by the availability of new weapons of mass destruction so small they can be concealed in a coat pocket; the new pandemics laying waste to whole societies; and the emergence of new strains of old diseases that are horrifyingly resistant to the antibiotics that protected the past three generations. Our new security agenda should be pursued with determination, adequate resources and creative use of the new tools at the world's disposal that can be used to bring us together in successful common efforts. (quoted in UNSC 2000b:3)

HIV/AIDS was supposed to be only the first of many issues to be discussed by the Security Council in the future, with other issues such as the environment, drugs, and corruption to follow later. Such grand statements need not be taken at face value, of course—especially when they are made by a sitting vice president of the United States in the middle of a presidential campaign who was trying to appeal to a range of domestic constituencies in the country and who was also trying to come out of the shadow of being vice president and gain credentials on the international stage. In the end, of course, Gore did not become president of the United States and so was not allowed that forum from which to subsequently influence the agenda of the Security Council. Nevertheless, placing HIV/AIDS on the agenda of the UN Security Council was an unprecedented gesture, and over the past decade the Security Council has also considered a range of other issues such as domestic conflicts, repression of ethnic groups, and human rights abuses (David 2001:562). As recently as 2007, there has also been considerable pressure by some members, including the United Kingdom, to follow the precedent established by HIV/AIDS and to place the environment on the Security Council agenda for the first time (Pilkington and Adam 2007). Although it is impossible to tell at present, the securitization of HIV/AIDS may nevertheless turn out in retrospect to represent an important turning point in the (eventual) emergence of a much wider governmentalized security agenda.

7 / THE POWER OF AIDS

Responding to the Governmentalization of Security

Tracing the concurrent operation of sovereign, disciplinary, and governmental forms of power in the securitization of HIV/AIDS has unearthed a complex set of political dangers. How should these competing benefits and drawbacks involved in discussing HIV/AIDS as a security issue be evaluated in the end? Moreover, can Michel Foucault's own cursory reflections on the rise of the era of governmentality help us develop an adequate response to this question? There are at least three possible ways of responding to these complexities. The first (and perhaps easiest) position would be to simply reject the securitization of HIV/AIDS altogether. Such a response would satisfy securitization theory's more general preference for "de-securitizing" issues—that is, for shifting them out of emergency mode and into more routine forms of political deliberation and decision making. It would also assuage those AIDS scholars and activists who remain worried about the longer-term political effects of discussing HIV/AIDS in the language of security. Furthermore, it is a response that would appear to be consistent with Foucault's reputation for being an iconoclast and a formidable critic of modern power relations. It would even please those traditional security scholars and policymakers who for a variety of other reasons wish to maintain a more narrow conception of security revolving around the deployment of armed force in the twenty-first century.

A second possible response would be to eschew an overtly normative standpoint about the securitization of HIV/AIDS altogether, to neither endorse nor reject it. This would effectively defer the decision about how to respond to the securitization of HIV/AIDS to individual readers, who would then have to draw their own conclusions. In the past many scholars conducting governmentality studies outside of the field of international relations have adopted this stance. There are good reasons for responding in this manner too. By consciously avowing an overt normative or political standpoint, scholars avoid the risk that they themselves become a normalizing force (Prozorov 2007:31). In the case of the securitization of HIV/AIDS, this would entail restricting this study to tracing the governmentalization of security and highlighting some of the dangers associated with it in the case of HIV/AIDS—but concluding the analysis there.

This chapter develops yet a third response to the securitization of HIV/AIDS by drawing upon some of the writings and interviews that Foucault undertook in the years after his governmentality lectures. Taking into account the distinction that he subsequently developed between "power relations" and "states of domination," in conjunction with his own political engagements and views on resistance, this concluding chapter suggests that the securitization of HIV/AIDS is a practice that is simultaneously a means of social control and a potential site of resistance to some of the vicissitudes of contemporary world politics. Rather than rejecting the securitization of HIV/AIDS, the chapter therefore seeks to delineate some of the tangible ways in which it could be conducted so as to minimize some of the complex dangers identified in the previous three chapters. The chapter argues, in short, neither for the outright rejection of the securitization of HIV/AIDS nor for a stance of normative detachment. Rather, it makes the case for trying to conduct the securitization more reflexively—that is, with awareness of its multiple potential dangers and with an ethos that seeks to minimize those dangers wherever and whenever possible.

HUMANITARIANISM IN THE ERA OF GOVERNMENTALITY

Foucault has developed a reputation as a formidable critic of modern power, but also as a person whose refusal to set out a more programmatic political stance largely culminates in political paralysis. It is not difficult to see how he would have developed such an image. Even though there is arguably a strong ethical and political sensibility contained in his body of work, by his own admission there are no clear ethical or political rules that follow from his writings. In this regard Foucault remained true to his Nietzschean roots, despising all "believers." The point of his genealogies was not to prescribe new ethical rules but rather "to show people that they are much freer than they feel" (Foucault 1988:10). In an interview about his early work on psychiatry, Foucault even went so far as to argue:

> My project is precisely to bring it about that they "no longer know what to do," so that the acts, gestures, discourses that up until then had seemed to go without saying become problematic, difficult, dangerous. . . . Critique doesn't have to be on the premise of a deduction that concludes, "this, then, is what needs to be done." It should be an instrument for those who fight, those who resist and refuse what is. Its use should be in processes of conflict and confrontation, essays in refusal. It doesn't have to lay down the law for the law. It isn't a stage in a programming. It is a challenge directed to what is. (2000g:235–236)

Even in the reflections on ethics found in his later works, such as *The Use of Pleasure*, Foucault still advocated the aesthetic creation of a unique style of life without recourse to universal moral codes. Any such ethics have to be the result of a personal journey rather than being determined by normative theories. "People," Foucault insisted in this regard, "have to build their own ethics, taking as a point of departure the historical analysis, sociological analysis, and so on that one can provide for them" (1997b:132). This is also very much the spirit in which he delivered his governmentality lectures, in which he restricted himself to providing at most "tactical pointers" for those who wish to struggle (2007:3). There is consequently no clear political program that follows from Foucault's reflections on governmentality, nor from his work as a whole, and this must ultimately caution against deriving any firm political conclusions from his writings—including any political stance regarding the securitization of HIV/AIDS. In this respect one can also see the attractions of adopting a position of normative detachment.

This popular view of Foucault as an iconoclast of the first order must be balanced, however, with other elements of his writings and interviews that point to the need to qualify such a perception of his thought. First, it does not necessarily follow from the fact that Foucault reflected critically upon various social institutions and practices, and raised difficult questions about them, that his interventions were always intended as outright dismissals of these practices. Foucault was actually bemused by the frequent—yet erroneous—construal of his positions as being complete rejections of certain practices. Regarding the reception of his work on psychiatry, for example, he complained in one interview that despite not once commenting on current psychiatric practice, his book was immediately and widely construed as taking an "anti-psychiatry" position (1997b:131–132). So the fact that he raised critical questions about practices such as psychiatry does not mean that he dismissed them altogether, or wanted them completely abandoned. It would be just as absurd to suggest that he was against hospitals because they are institutions used in the governmental management of populations. Similarly, it does not follow from the fact that a governmentality study raises critical questions about the securitization of HIV/AIDS that it must necessarily culminate in a rejection of this practice.

There were also other times when Foucault indicated that he did not even find anything wrong or objectionable with telling people what to do, or how to act, within the context of particular truth games. In one of his interviews he argued in relation to pedagogical institutions:

> I see nothing wrong in the practice of a person who, knowing more than others in a specific game of truth, tells those others what to do, teaches them, and transmits knowledge and techniques to them. The problem in such practices where power—which is not in itself a bad thing—must inevitably come into play is subjected to the arbitrary and unnecessary authority of a teacher, or a student put under the thumb of a professor who abuses his authority. (1997a:298–299)

Foucault found it agreeable in certain contexts to engage in public reflections on how best to act or respond to an issue. Not only was it acceptable to do so, but at times he even insisted that it was absolutely necessary to do so. "I think that the ethico-political choice we have to make every day," he said in the same interview, "is to determine which is the *main* danger [emphasis added]" (1997c:256). Although there are no moral codes that derive from his work, there is nevertheless a clear incitement in his works to think ethically and politically.

This ethos of determining "which is the *main* danger" can also serve as an entry point for delineating a response to the securitization of HIV/AIDS. This entry point rests on an implicit recognition that perfect political solutions and policies do not exist. Politics is ultimately a complex engagement with a range of competing dangers, and it may well be impossible to identify ethical or political positions that are completely without dangers. Politically evaluating the securitization of HIV/AIDS cannot concomitantly consist of finding a political stance that is without dangers, but it can begin to identify what the *main* dangers are and can seek to pragmatically choose the path of the lesser ones. Put differently, Foucault's ethos here seems almost like that of a consequentialist, rather than a deontological, approach to the evaluation of political action—as his concern seems to have revolved primarily around the outcomes of certain actions and the levels of danger they produce. In the case of the securitization of HIV/AIDS, it marks an invitation to revisit the dangers identified in the previous three chapters and to generate a broad hierarchy among them. This will not only make it possible to determine which dangers constitute the "main" ones, but it will also facilitate probing whether any of these dangers—either individually or collectively—outweigh the converse dangers of *not* securitizing HIV/AIDS.

This approach, however, leaves two rather crucial questions unanswered. First, in trying to determine which is "the *main* danger," *whose* danger is to be taken into account? The securitization of HIV/AIDS produces different dangers for different groups, so whose "dangers" should be averted as a matter of priority? Second, what types of dangers are to be prioritized when drawing up this hierarchy? We have already seen in the previous three chapters that the different modalities of power exercised in the securitization of HIV/AIDS give rise to very different dangers. Which ones constitute the *main* ones? Should we prioritize the dangers associated with sovereign power, or those with disciplinary power, or indeed those that emerge during the governmental management of populations?

An implicit answer to these questions can perhaps be found in a very short piece titled "Confronting Governments: Human Rights" (1984), which Foucault composed for his participation at a press conference in Geneva denouncing the piracy committed against those fleeing Vietnam.

In this piece, which was published only after his death, Foucault began to develop a broadly humanitarian political position: "There exists
an international citizenship that has its rights and its duties, and that
obliges one to speak out against every abuse of power, whoever its author, whoever its victims. After all, we are all members of the community of the governed, and thereby obliged to show mutual solidarity"
(2000b:474). Despite its brevity and lack of elaboration, this is a remark-
able formulation in that Foucault here effectively attempts to ground a
broadly humanitarian impulse not in the metaphysical language of human rights but in the common experience of being governed, on the
basis of a solidarity of the "governed" (Campbell 1998b). In terms of
analyzing for whom the securitization of HIV/AIDS is the main danger,
such a perspective would be principally concerned with the lived expe-
riences of those who are the subjects of government and who are suffering abuses of power—wherever they are living in the world.

In the same text, Foucault went on to stipulate a further duty that this
international citizenry has: to publicly air the sufferings of those who
are "governed" and for which governments are partially responsible:

> Because they claim to be concerned with the welfare of societies, gov-
> ernments arrogate to themselves the right to pass off as profit or loss
> the human unhappiness that their decisions provoke or their negligence
> permits. It is a duty of this international citizenship to always bring the
> testimony of people's suffering to the eyes and ears of governments, suf-
> ferings for which it's untrue that they are not responsible. The suffering of
> men [sic] must never be a silent residue of policy. It grounds an absolute
> right to stand up and speak to those who hold power. (2000b:474–475)

Foucault's recourse to a language of "duties" and "absolute rights" may
surprise many; yet he did not stop here. He made a third and final stipulation: that "the will of individuals must make a place for itself in a reality of which governments have attempted to reserve a monopoly for
themselves, that monopoly which we need to wrest from them little by
little and day by day" (2000b:475). This right of private individuals to intervene in the sphere of international policy is something that he cred-
ited nongovernmental organizations such as Amnesty International,
Terre des Hommes, and Medicines du Monde with helping to establish.

Despite their brevity, these passages endow Foucault's earlier incitement to identify the "main danger" with further political specificity—albeit without making concrete political prescriptions. Bringing this humanitarian ethos to bear on the international politics of HIV/AIDS entails examining the extent to which the securitization of HIV/AIDS strengthens the ability of this international citizenry to testify to the sufferings of those who are "governed," and to what extent it may also hide or otherwise obscure this suffering. With this more narrow focus, it becomes possible to ask in relation to each of the modalities of power examined in the previous three chapters whether the dangers associated with its exercise outweigh the dangers of not securitizing AIDS.

TO SECURITIZE OR NOT TO SECURITIZE: WHAT IS THE MAIN DANGER?

Chapter 4 showed that the mobilization of *sovereign* power through the language of national security potentially makes it much easier for states to adopt heavy-handed state responses to people with HIV/AIDS and that it tends to animate more of a "panic politics" approach to the pandemic that is insufficient for addressing the underlying causes of the AIDS epidemic. From a perspective based on "solidarity with the governed," these dangers are not to be dismissed lightly. With the benefit of hindsight, however, neither of them appears to constitute the *main* danger in the case of HIV/AIDS. With respect to the potential threats to civil liberties, those policymakers who are securitizing HIV/AIDS are not claiming that "people with HIV/AIDS are a national security threat," but arguing that the *virus* represents such a threat. While the former would be politically exclusionary and would bring into play a host of political concerns already outlined by other scholars in relation to the securitization of migrants in many countries (Huysmans 1995, 2000), the latter can be understood as a more inclusive gesture, arguing that those living with HIV/AIDS should receive enhanced levels of medical treatment and care. None of the main political actors securitizing HIV/AIDS are advocating the removal of people living with HIV/AIDS from the population or subjecting them to discriminatory and draconian practices by the state. This also helps to explain why, despite this issue's having been framed as a security concern for several years now, there is not much evidence that the civil liberties of persons living with HIV/AIDS have been further infringed upon because of the securitization of HIV/AIDS—especially when compared to the many discriminatory measures that were introduced in the early years of HIV/AIDS when governments and societies were rocked by genuine fear of this unknown disease. It is, of course, undeniable that lamentable restrictions remain, including those on travel; but the introduction of many of these restrictions predates the more formal securitization of HIV/AIDS at the level of the Security Council. In some cases, moreover, concerted attempts have even been made to weaken such restrictions since the more recent securitization of HIV/AIDS—for example, in the ongoing efforts to remove travel restrictions to the United States for people living with HIV. Unlike the ways in which the securitization of issues such as terrorism or migration has culminated in a weakening of certain individual rights, and unlike the ways in which states have historically responded through draconian measures to other diseases, the AIDS pandemic has not—so far—suffered this fate in light of the more recent securitization of HIV/AIDS. There is little evidence to date that the latter has been exacerbating these problems usually associated with the mobilization of sovereign power.

As for the risk of fueling a "panic politics" approach to the pandemic, here, too, many would share the view that in an ideal world HIV/AIDS would be treated patiently, according to the principles of normal politics, and with a concomitant degree of democratic deliberation. Compared to that scenario, the securitization of HIV/AIDS does seem inherently problematic. Yet the difficulty with approaching the issue of HIV/AIDS in this manner is that in the past, normal politics has in fact meant that very little was actually done to treat people living with HIV/AIDS in the developing world. "Normal" politics, in other words, meant several million new infections worldwide, close to three million deaths annually, and a very low rate of access to anti-retroviral medicines for people living in developing countries. In this context, perhaps the main danger is not the securitization of HIV/AIDS because it does not deal with the illness according to normal politics, but that normal politics was not yielding a wider response to HIV/AIDS. Although normal politics remains the ideal in the long run, the securitization of HIV/AIDS has been able to provoke a much broader international response to HIV/AIDS. The rush to scale up international AIDS initiatives may occasionally result in the misallocation or misdirection of funds, and may even mean that at times resources will flow too hastily, but compared to the alternative scenario of having insufficient funds for treatment of those living with HIV/AIDS, this must constitute the lesser of the two dangers from the perspective of those who require access to life-prolonging medicines. As of December 2006, and despite all the invocation of security rhetoric and the scaling up of AIDS initiatives, of the estimated 7.1 million people in need of treatment in low- and middle-income countries, still only 2,015,000 have benefited from access to treatment—less than a third of those deemed to be in need (WHO 2007). Although the current levels of treatment are certainly an improvement when compared to earlier years, they are hardly testament to a "panic politics" that has swung too far in the opposite direction. Although the potential dangers associated with the exercise of sovereign power need to be constantly borne in mind, at this stage in the history of the AIDS pandemic they need not lead to a rejection of the securitization of HIV/AIDS in and of themselves.

Do the dangers associated with the simultaneous exercise of *disciplinary* power in the securitization of HIV/AIDS constitute more of a danger in this regard? Again, it is undoubtedly the case that by providing greater resources and urgency for international AIDS initiatives, the securitization of HIV/AIDS intensifies and geographically expands a range of disciplinary practices of surveillance and normation. Yet here too the wider political evaluation of these practices is quickly rendered complicated, not least because the late Foucault himself no longer considered such disciplinary practices to constitute the *main* danger in the way he had still asserted around the time of writing *Discipline and Punish* and when he set out his stark views and warnings about the modern workings of disciplinary power. In a lecture delivered at Berkeley in 1980, Foucault told his audience as much when he conceded that his earlier studies on subject formation had "insisted maybe too much on the techniques of domination" (quoted in Paras 2006:94). In other forums Foucault went on to clarify that he had never meant to suggest in these earlier studies that power is evil in and of itself; *all* political activity inevitably reproduces power relations, and it would be utopian to believe that it would be possible to develop a political position free of such power relations. Foucault would thus go to great lengths to communicate to his readers that his analysis of power was not pejorative. In one of his interviews, he explicitly pointed to a failure of some of his readers to see that power is not something bad in and of itself, something from which one must always try to break free (1997a:298). Indeed, he insisted, "I do not think that a society can exist without power relations, if by that one means the strategies by which individuals try to direct and control the conduct of others" (1997a:298).

Perhaps it is for this reason that Foucault later went on to argue, in a way that undermines the view of him as a thoroughgoing relativist, that certain practices were categorically worse and more objectionable than the existence and exercise of such power relations. Shortly before his death Foucault introduced an important distinction between *power relations* "understood as strategic games between liberties—in which some try to control the conduct of others" and *states of domination* that people ordinarily call "power" (1997a:299). His use of the term "power," Foucault now clarified, had always been a shorthand for "*mobile, reversible, and unstable*" *power relations* (1997a:292), and these power relations in turn always presupposed a certain degree of freedom: "power relations are possible only insofar as the subjects are free. If one of them were completely at the other's disposal and became his thing, an object on which he could wreak boundless and limitless violence, there wouldn't be any relations of power" (1997a:292). In the absence of such freedom, and with no possibility of effective resistance, one has to speak instead of domination: "States of domination do indeed exist. In a great many cases, power relations are fixed in such a way that they are perpetually asymmetrical and allow an extremely limited margin of freedom" (Foucault 1997a:292).

In his late interviews and writings Foucault mentioned several concrete examples of such "states of domination" that he found to be unacceptable. He referred to the status of married women in the eighteenth and nineteenth centuries. In this case women had quite a few options: "They could deceive their husbands, pilfer money from them, refuse them sex. Yet they were still in a state of domination insofar as these options were ultimately only stratagems that never succeeded in reversing the situation" (Foucault 1997a:292). Resistance in a limited form was possible, but mostly futile in light of the highly asymmetric power relations. Elsewhere Foucault also referred to slavery as being "not a power relationship when a man is in chains, only when he has some possible mobility, even a chance of escape. (In this case it is a question of a physical relationship of constraint)" (2000h:342). In yet another instance Foucault noted his objection to rape, insisting that "there are sexual acts like rape which should not be permitted whether they involve a man and a woman or two men. I don't think we should have as our objective some sort of absolute freedom or total liberty of sexual action" (1997e:143). In all these cases, it is not the existence of power relations that constituted the main danger for Foucault, but the existence of more stratified states of domination. Often his goal was consequently not to dispel power as such (which he did not think was possible), but to "acquire the rules of law, the management techniques, and also the morality, the *ethos*, the practice of the self, that will allow us to play these games of power *with as little domination as possible* [emphasis added]" (1997a:298).

Read in conjunction with his insistence that power is not inherently bad, this crucial distinction between states of domination and power relations also affects the way in which we evaluate whether the disciplinary processes of normation fanned by the securitization of HIV/AIDS merit rejecting the latter as a political practice. The key question now effectively becomes which course of action most approximates such a state of domination—to securitize HIV/AIDS or not to securitize it? Taking the cue from Foucault's ethos of showing solidarity with those who are governed, and publicly exposing the suffering produced by the negligence of governments, it is arguably not so much the disciplinary practices accompanying the securitization of HIV/AIDS that most approximate such a state of domination, but the "politics as usual" that allows millions of people to continue to die. Again, there are no easy choices here, but it is hard to think of anything that would constitute a greater act of domination over others than implicitly exposing them to their inevitable death. Although asymmetrical, the disciplinary practices fanned by the securitization of HIV/AIDS are, by contrast, much closer to the kinds of practices that Foucault characterized as relations of power, which are reversible in the long term—whereas death of those without access to medicines is not. This is not to superficially diminish or downplay the individual and social effects of various disciplinary practices associated with the securitization of HIV/AIDS, but it is to suggest that in terms of the international politics of HIV/AIDS, they do not presently constitute the *main* danger.

What, then, of the dangers associated with the exercise of *governmental* management? Here, too, the political complexity rapidly exceeds any move to simply reject the securitization of HIV/AIDS. It is certainly true that the stigmatization of the armed forces and peacekeepers remains an important and unfortunate effect of the securitization of HIV/AIDS. Unlike the case of many other risk groups, however, this designation of the armed forces as a risk group—although stigmatizing—is frequently accompanied by access to life-prolonging treatment and care through military medical establishments. It is also this factor that sets the politics of framing the armed forces as a risk group apart from using the same language for socially more marginalized groups affected by HIV/AIDS. As for the testing and exclusion of recruits who are HIV-positive, this danger is serious as well, but it too is mitigated by the fact that many of these practices were adopted long before the more recent securitization of HIV/AIDS began to unfold. In the United States testing for HIV was introduced as early as 1985, and efforts to expel people living with HIV from the armed forced occurred as early as 1996. A survey carried out by the Civil-Military Alliance to Combat HIV and AIDS in 1995 found that fifty-eight countries of the sixty-two that decided to respond to the questionnaire already carried out HIV testing (UNAIDS 1998:8). What is more, in some countries where militaries have decided to exclude people living with HIV/AIDS from the armed forces, it has also been possible to subsequently reverse the decisions by recourse to the courts. In Namibia, for example, the policy of not allowing HIV-positive soldiers to serve in the armed forces has already been subjected to a lengthy legal and political contest. In South Africa, too, the decision by the South African National Defence Force not to recruit HIV-positive soldiers has been successfully challenged in the courts (BBC 2008). Not only did the introduction of many of these measures predate the more recent securitization of HIV/AIDS, therefore, but it may also be possible to reverse them in the medium term.

The third and final danger associated with the use of governmental management in the securitization of HIV/AIDS—that of granting privileged access to treatment for the armed forces in developing countries—similarly needs to be viewed in a broader context. Even where resources are specifically allocated to the armed forces for treatment, this money can have a greater beneficial impact. In Kenya, for example, the U.S. military HIV/AIDS program extends to soldiers' dependents, with the result that 1,500 Kenyans, half of whom are not soldiers, were receiving treatment through the program—a program that has also helped to train many HIV counselors (Fisher-Thompson 2005). A similar program has been under way in Tanzania, and a further one has been planned for Nigeria. In the United States, moreover, the military also continues to be engaged in vaccine research on HIV in order to protect troops who might contract HIV while deployed abroad. As long as the funding for such efforts does not come at the expense of funding for civilian programs, in other words, the securitization of HIV/AIDS could free up new resources that are crucial for building the health care infrastructure in poor countries and thus for international efforts to mitigate the spread of HIV/AIDS. To date, this spending earmarked for programs specifically addressing HIV/AIDS in the armed forces has, as we have seen, been accompanied by substantial increases in funding available for civilian programs.

Although the armed forces thus have been the recipients of special funds, and although this has done little to ensure that other risk groups that are socially more stigmatized also have access to resources, this direction of funding toward military programs has not necessarily come at the expense of a concomitant increase in the level of funding for civilian programs overall. This can also be seen more recently in the decision on July 16, 2008, of the U.S. Senate in an 80–16 vote (after some considerable political wrangling) in favor of the Tom Lantos–Henry J. Hyde U.S. Global Leadership Against HIV/AIDS, Tuberculosis, and Malaria Reauthorization Act—a bill committing the United States to spending $48 billion on HIV/AIDS, malaria, and tuberculosis programs over the next five years (AP 2008). While important, these governmental dangers so far also do not constitute the *main* danger when compared with the alternative of continuing with politics as usual in dealing with the AIDS pandemic. In the end, following Foucault's incitement to establish a broad hierarchy of dangers in relation to the securitization of HIV/AIDS shows that, although there are certainly many serious dangers accompanying the securitization of HIV/AIDS, these dangers do not necessarily outweigh the inverse danger of *not* securitizing the AIDS pandemic—either individually or collectively.

MINIMIZING THE DANGERS

Awareness of these dangers is nevertheless important because only after they have been identified does it become possible to think about how the securitization of HIV/AIDS might be conducted in a manner that minimizes some of the dangers. Foucault once argued about the nature of resistance that it always

> is part of this strategic relationship of which power consists. Resistance really always relies upon the situation against which it struggles. For instance, in the gay community the medical definition of homosexuality was a very important tool against the oppression of homosexuality in the last part of the nineteenth century and in the early twentieth century. This medicalization, which was a means of oppression, has always been a means of resistance as well—since you could say, "If we are sick, then why do you condemn us, why do you despise us?" And so on. Of course, this discourse now sounds rather naïve to us, but at the time it was very important. (1997d:168)

In the end the securitization of AIDS is a very similar case in point. It is something that—by virtue of the dangers associated with its concurrent exercise of sovereign, disciplinary, and governmental forms of power—is an ambivalent form of social control, but it can be a useful device for resisting some of the inequalities that characterize contemporary world politics. If HIV/AIDS is a security issue, then it is possible to insist that governments do more to help people living with HIV/AIDS. Indeed, it is worth noting in this context that the new five-year U.S. program authorizing the spending of approximately $10 billion per year on HIV/AIDS, malaria, and tuberculosis was justified by the chief negotiators of both parties on the Senate Foreign Affairs Committee—Joseph Biden (D-Del.) and Richard Lugar (R-Ind.)—on the basis that PEPFAR "has helped to prevent instability and societal collapse in a number of at-risk countries" (AP 2008). In this way the securitization of AIDS can remain a useful vehicle for bringing "the testimony of people's suffering to the eyes and ears of governments, sufferings for which it's untrue that they are not responsible." Of course, there is no denying that this path remains a risky gamble on the ability of those presenting HIV/AIDS as a security issue to maintain control over the uses to which this language will be put—albeit a gamble that has perhaps become necessary due to the particular inequities of contemporary world politics.

In this case the most prudent strategy to adopt in response to the securitization of HIV/AIDS would consist not of rejecting it altogether but of exploring how it can be conducted in a manner that would minimize some of the dangers. The dangers associated with sovereign power could be mitigated in at least two ways. First, HIV/AIDS could be framed as an important security *issue*, or as an international issue with a security *dimension*, or indeed even as a security *risk*—rather than as an overwhelming security *threat*. This approach would allow some of the benefits from adopting a security framework to accrue, such as increasing the level of attention and available resources for addressing HIV/AIDS, yet the use of less-threatening language would result in a lower risk that those living with HIV/AIDS would be subjected to harsh measures in the name of security. Second, those securitizing HIV/AIDS could continue to complement the securitization with a human rights framework emphasizing the rights of people living with HIV/AIDS. This may initially seem like a very counterintuitive course of action to recommend, especially from a broadly Foucauldian perspective. Foucault, after all, remains renowned for his anti-humanist stance, and he himself once explicitly counseled against returning to a language of rights:

> When we want to make some objection against disciplines and all the knowledge-effects and power-effects that are bound up with them, what do we do in concrete terms? What do we do in real life? . . . We obviously invoke right, the famous old formal, bourgeois right. And it is in reality the right of sovereignty. And I think that at this point we are in a sort of bottleneck, that we cannot go on working like this forever; having recourse to sovereignty against discipline will not enable us to limit the effects of disciplinary power. . . . If we are to struggle against disciplines, or rather against disciplinary power, in our search for a nondisci-

plinary power, we should not be turning to the old right of sovereignty; we should be looking for a new right that is both antidisciplinary and emancipated from the principle of sovereignty. (2003:39–40)

Yet in this respect too the later Foucault seems to have shifted his position somewhat. Although he could not resist raising very difficult and probing questions about human rights, he did not dispute their political utility, nor did he insist on rejecting them altogether. The limits of conventional human rights discourse do "not mean that we have to get rid of what we call human rights or freedom, but that we can't say that freedom or human rights has to be limited at certain frontiers" (Foucault 1988:15). Foucault did express deep concern about certain universalizing aspects of the human rights regime, but that concern did not translate into an outright rejection of the idea of human rights as such. In fact, Foucault himself occasionally defended such rights explicitly. "To power," he wrote in *Le Monde* in 1979, "one must always oppose unbreakable laws and rights without restriction" (quoted in Paras 2006:77). In his open letter to Mehdi Bazargan from April of the same year, he invoked human rights no fewer than four times, arguing that "one must—and it's imperative—give to the prosecuted as many means of defense and as many rights as possible" (quoted in Paras 2006:97). Minimizing the dangers that the language of security poses to civil liberties by also appealing to a wider humanitarian framework can therefore be compatible with a broadly Foucauldian perspective—especially when one further takes into account his own political engagements with prominent human rights activists such as Bernard Kouchner, who cofounded Doctors Without Borders and, later, Doctors of the World. This strategy would also mitigate against some of the dangers associated with the mobilization of sovereign power in the securitization of HIV/AIDS.

The dangers associated with practices of disciplinary normation could in turn be minimized (although not avoided) by insisting that international AIDS policies do not privilege prevention and the prescription of specific norms of sexual behavior at the expense of treatment. Clearly prevention is important, but diminishing the extent of the AIDS pandemic can be achieved in the long run only by also scaling up and sustaining treatment programs that are less concerned with how people became infected than with helping those who are already infected to survive. Here those who are involved in implementing international and bilateral AIDS initiatives could seek to conduct these efforts in a less prescriptive manner, and to give countries greater flexibility in how resources are allocated between various treatment and prevention programs. These concerns are increasingly acknowledged by policymakers in the United States, where Congress has now agreed to abandon PEPFAR's controversial requirement that one-third of the funding for HIV prevention must be spent on the promotion of abstinence and fidelity.

The governmental dangers of privileged treatment access to the elites and armed forces could, in turn, be minimized if those securitizing HIV/AIDS insist that it is not *exclusively* a security issue, but rather a security issue *in addition* to a health issue, a development issue, an economic issue, a social issue, a political issue, a humanitarian issue, a gender issue, and so on. Highlighting the security implications of HIV/AIDS in this way would not unreflectively reify the privileged status of the security sector and elites in terms of access to treatment, and it would make it more difficult to simply write off the lives of ordinary civilians living with HIV/AIDS. Again, this danger could also be further minimized by working within a broadly humanitarian framework that lays out particular rights in relation to health.

While the adoption of some of these strategies would not altogether avoid the dangers accompanying the securitization of HIV/AIDS, it would at least minimize these dangers without simultaneously sacrificing the potential of this discourse to challenge some of the global health inequalities that exist in the world today. With this approach it would not be necessary to reject the securitization of HIV/AIDS out of hand, as it can still offer some important benefits for people living with HIV/AIDS. Nor would it be necessary to adopt a stance of normative detachment in order to remain compatible with the deeper ethos of Foucault's scholarship and politics. Rather, it would become possible to conduct the securitization of HIV/AIDS more reflexively, in the full awareness of the multiple dangers to which it gives rise, and with an ethos that continuously seeks to minimize these dangers wherever possible.

In either case, all the renewed political activity surrounding the international circulation of viruses such as HIV is deeply reminiscent of a development that occurred much earlier *within* many European societies. Eighteenth-century Europe witnessed the emergence of much more concerted efforts by states to manage the spread of diseases within their populations. Diseases were no longer seen as individual maladies, but as larger economic and political problems that societies needed to address as a matter of overall policy (Foucault 2000f:91). Henceforth politics would no longer be concerned merely with settling questions of war and peace or with organizing society's material enrichment; it would additionally come to bear on people's physical well-being and health. The securitization of AIDS demonstrates that this politics of disease is today gradually becoming intensified and internationalized as states begin to apply similar consideration in their relations with one another. If this effort is successful in the course of the twenty-first century, then we will need to open a new chapter in the "bio-history" of humanity, which historians are slowly beginning to unearth (Cartwright 1972; Crawford 2007; McNeill 1998; Oldstone 2000; Watts 1997; Zinsser 1937). That bio-history consists precisely of the manifold and subtle ways in which humankind has interacted with the world of microbes, and how it has also intervened upon this world through a range of hygienic and other public health measures (Foucault 2000a:135). Who we are and what we may become in the century ahead will, in short, also depend on how we relate to those invisible and barely living microorganisms called viruses.

SECURITY AND GOVERNMENTALITY

The themes raised in this book in relation to the securitization of HIV/ AIDS also resonate across a range of other contemporary security issues and debates. In many ways the securitization of HIV/AIDS is but a single manifestation of the wider governmentalization of security that is unfolding today. The growing orientation of security practices toward the broader welfare of populations, for instance, can be seen in a variety of other contexts, including virtually the entire human security agenda with its concomitant concerns about economic security, health security, food security, and so on. It can similarly be seen in the more extensive merging of security and development concerns that has been unfolding over the past decade. It lurks in less obvious places too, such as the new anxieties surrounding a range of "lifestyle" diseases like smoking, drugs, obesity, and alcohol on which Western societies and international organizations are increasingly declaring comprehensive and urgent "wars." Even our military campaigns are now justified in efforts to improve the welfare of populations, whether to protect them from the attacks of terrorists and weapons of mass destruction or to forcibly bestow the fruits of democracy upon them from abroad.

Beyond HIV/AIDS there are also plenty of other international "crises of circulation" now populating the security agenda. Within the field of health security, similarly stark concerns are being expressed about a range of newly emerging microbes that are traversing the planet, such as the highly pathogenic H5N1 strand of avian influenza. Outside the domain of health, other crises now frequently discussed in the language of security include the international circulation of migrants, of drugs, of criminals, of terrorists and their finances, and even of greenhouse gas emissions. Nor does one have to look very far to find further evidence of the progressive governmentalization of the state. It is evident, for example, in the much wider assemblages of state and non-state actors that have formed in the field of security, whether this manifests itself in the broad human security–based coalitions that have emerged between some states, international organizations, humanitarian NGOs, and scholars or alternatively in the growing alliances between national armed forces and an extensive network of private security companies that increasingly characterize the field of "hard" security. Even the latter is today more often conducted through the techniques of governmental management, as can be seen, finally, in the extensive role that risk-based categories now play in both the formulation and the execution of a wide range of contemporary security policies.

The framework for analyzing the governmentalization of security developed here in relation to the securitization of HIV/AIDS may therefore have a broader purchase for understanding some of the other important transformations that the practice of security is undergoing in contemporary world politics. If this is true, then there is still much work that needs to be done to trace the effects of the complex interplay of sovereign, disciplinary, and governmental economies of power in these other current manifestations of the governmentalization of security. Only then will it be possible to discern whether the response delineated here in relation to the securitization of HIV/AIDS is also an appropriate way of responding to the wider governmentalization of security. Even now, in other words, much work remains to be done in terms of pursuing the spirit of hyper-pessimistic activism exemplified by Michel Foucault, who died in 1984—of AIDS.

Abebe, Yigeremu, Ab Schaap, Girmatchew Mamo, Asheber Negussie, Birke Darimo, Dawit Wolday, and Eduard Sanders. 2003. "HIV Prevalence in 72,000 Urban and Rural Male Army Recruits, Ethiopia." *AIDS* 17, no. 12:1835–1840.

Abraham, Thomas. 2005. *Twenty-first Century Plague: The Story of SARS*. Baltimore: Johns Hopkins University Press.

Abrahamsen, Rita. 2003. "African Studies and the Postcolonial Challenge." *African Affairs* 102, no. 407:189–210.

Adebajo, Sylvia, J. Mafeni, S. Moreland, and N. Murray. 2002. *Knowledge, Attitudes, and Sexual Behavior Among the Nigerian Military Concerning HIV/AIDS and STDs*. Washington, D.C.: Futures Group International.

AFP. 2003. "AIDS Could Lead to Wars in Africa: General." Agence France-Presse, September 8.

——. 2004. "Sudan Threatens HIV/AIDS Tests on Nigerian Troops in Darfur." Agence France-Presse, October 29.

Afrobarometer. 2004. "Public Opinion and HIV/AIDS: Facing Up to the Future?" Briefing Paper No. 12 (April). http://www.afrobarometer.org/papers/AfrobriefNo12.pdf.

——. 2006. "The Public Agenda: Change and Stability in South Africans' Ratings of National Priorities." Briefing Paper No. 45 (June). http://www.afrobarometer.org/papers/AfrobriefNo45.pdf.

Akella, Devi, Arvind Singhal, and Everett M. Rogers. 2003. *Combating AIDS: Communication Strategies in Action*. London: Sage.

"Allocate More ARVs to Military Personnel." 2003. *Times of Zambia*, November 17. http://www.times.co.zm.

Altman, Dennis. 2000. "Understanding HIV/AIDS as a Global Security Issue." In Kelley Lee, ed., *Health Impacts of Globalization: Towards Global Governance*, 33–46. London: Palgrave.

Ambrosio, Thomas. 2005. "The Geopolitics of Demographic Decay: HIV/AIDS and Russia's Great Power Status." Paper presented at the annual convention of the International Studies Association, Honolulu.

Amnesty International. 2004. "'Marked for Death': Rape Survivors Living with HIV/AIDS in Rwanda." Report AFR 47/007/2004. http://web.amnesty .org/library/index/engafr470072004.

Annan, Kofi. 2001. "Review of the Problem of Human Immunodeficiency Virus/ Acquired Immunodeficiency Syndrome in All Its Aspects." Report of the Secretary General to the United Nations General Assembly, New York, February 16. http://www.undemocracy.com/A-55–779.pdf.

——. 2004. "Secretary-General Kofi Annan's address to the XV International AIDS Conference in Bangkok." Bangkok, Thailand, July 11. http://www .un.org/News/ossg/sg/stories/statments_search_full.asp?statID=36.

AP. 2008. "Senate Agrees to Triple Anti-AIDS Funding: U.S. to Spend Up to $48 Billion in Ambitious Foreign Public Health Program." Associated Press, July 16.

Aradau, Claudia. 2001. "Beyond Good and Evil: Ethics and Securitization/ Desecuritization Techniques." *Rubikon: International Forum of Electronic Publications*. December. http://venus.ci.uw.edu.pl/~rubikon/forum/claudia2.htm.

——. 2008. *Rethinking Trafficking in Women: Politics Out of Security*. Basingstoke: Palgrave.

Aradau, Claudia, and Rens van Munster. 2005. *Governing Terrorism and the (Non-)Politics of Risk*. Political Science Publications No. 11. Odense: Faculty of Social Sciences, University of Southern Denmark.

——. 2007. "Governing Terrorism Through Risk: Taking Precautions, (Un)Knowing the Future." *European Journal of International Relations* 13, no. 1:89–115.

Arndt, Channing, and Jeffrey D. Lewis. 2000. "The Macro-Implications of HIV/ AIDS in South Africa: A Preliminary Assessment." World Bank, Washington, D.C. http://www.worldbank.org/afr/wps/wp9.pdf.

Arnold, David, ed. 1988. *Imperial Medicine and Indigenous Societies*. Manchester: Manchester University Press.

AVERT. 2007a. "AIDS Treatment: Targets and Results." http://www.avert.org/ aidstarget.htm.

——. 2007b. "HIV/AIDS Discrimination and Stigma." http://www.avert.org/ aidsstigma.htm.

——. 2008a. "HIV/AIDS in Brazil." http://www.avert.org/aids-brazil.htm.

——. 2008b. "TRIPS, AIDS, and Generic Drugs." http://www.avert.org/generic .htm.

Ba, Oumar, Christopher O'Regan, Jean Nachega, Curtis Cooper, Aranka Anema, Beth Rachlis, and Edward J. Mills. 2008. "HIV/AIDS in African Militaries: An Ecological Analysis." *Medicine, Conflict, and Survival* 24, no. 2:88–100.

Baldwin, David. 2005. *Disease and Democracy: The Industrialized World Faces AIDS*. Berkeley: University of California Press.

Ban, Jonathan. 2001. *Health, Security, and U.S. Global Leadership*. Washington, D.C.: Chemical and Biological Arms Control Institute.

Barnett, Tony. 2006. "A Long-Wave Event. HIV/AIDS, Politics, Governance, and 'Security': Sundering the Intergenerational Bond?" *International Affairs* 82, no. 2:297–313.

Barnett, Tony, and Colette Clement. 2005. "HIV/AIDS Impact: So Where Have We Got To and Where Next?" *Progress in Development Studies* 5, no. 3:237–247.

Barnett, Tony, and Gwyn Prins. 2005. *HIV/AIDS and Security: Fact, Fiction, and Evidence—A Report to UNAIDS*. London: London School of Economics.

———. 2006. "HIV/AIDS and Security: Fact, Fiction, and Evidence—A Report to UNAIDS." *International Affairs* 82, no. 2:359–368.

Barnett, Tony, and Alan Whiteside. 2002. *AIDS in the Twenty-first Century: Disease and Globalization*. Basingstoke: Palgrave.

———. 2006. *AIDS in the Twenty-first Century: Disease and Globalization*. 2nd ed. Basingstoke: Palgrave.

Barry, Andrew. 1993. "The European Community and European Government: Harmonization, Mobility, and Space." *Economy and Society* 22, no. 3:314–326.

Barry, Andrew, Thomas Osborne, and Nikolas Rose, eds. 1996. *Foucault and Political Reason: Liberalism, Neo-liberalism, and Rationalities of Government*. London: Routledge.

Bashford, Alison, ed. 2006. *Medicine at the Border: Disease, Globalization, and Security, 1850 to the Present*. Basingstoke: Palgrave Macmillan.

Bazergan, Roxanne. 2001. "UN Peacekeepers and HIV/AIDS." *World Today* 57, no. 5:6–8.

———. 2002. *HIV/AIDS and Peacekeeping: A Field Study of the Policies of the United Nations Mission in Sierra Leone*. London: International Policy Institute and King's College.

———. 2003. "Intervention and Intercourse: HIV/AIDS and Peacekeepers." *Conflict, Security, and Development* 3, no. 1:27–51.

Bazergan, Roxanne, and Philippa Easterbrook. 2003. "HIV and UN Peacekeeping Operations." *AIDS* 17, no. 2:278–279.

BBC. 2007. "Outcry at Tanzanian HIV Beating." BBC News, November 28. http://news.bbc.co.uk/1/hi/world/africa/7117184.stm.

———. 2008. "Soldiers Sue South Africa Over AIDS." BBC News, May 15. http://news.bbc.co.uk/1/hi/world/africa/7402250.stm.

Beaver, Paul. 2000. Comments on Voice of America, May 3.

Behnke, Andreas. 2000. "The Message or the Messenger? Reflections on the Role of Security Experts and the Securitization of Political Issues." *Cooperation and Conflict* 35, no. 1:89–105.

Bell, Clive, Shantayanan Devarajan, and Hans Gersbach. 2003. "The Long-Run Economic Costs of AIDS: Theory and an Application to South Africa." Policy Research Working Paper No. 3152. World Bank, Washington, D.C.

Berry, F. Clifton, and John Greenwood. 2005. *Medics at War: Military Medicine from Colonial Times to the 21st Century.* Annapolis, Md.: Naval Institute Press.

Bigo, Didier. 1998. "Sécurité et immigration: Vers une gouvernementalité par l'inquiétude." *Cultures et Conflits* 31–32:13–38.

——. 2002. "Security and Immigration: Toward a Critique of the Governmentality of Unease." *Alternatives* 27, no. 1:63–92.

Bloom, David, and Peter Godwin, eds. 1997. *The Economics of HIV and AIDS: The Case of South and South East Asia.* Oxford: Oxford University Press.

Booysen, Frederick, and Max Bachmann. 2002. "HIV/AIDS, Poverty, and Growth: Evidence from a Household Impact Study Conducted in the Free State Province, South Africa." Paper presented at the annual conference of the Centre for the Study of African Economies, Oxford.

Bradshaw, Steve. 2003. "Vatican: Condoms Don't Stop AIDS." *Guardian,* October 9.

Bratt, Duane. 2002. "Blue Condoms: The Use of International Peacekeepers in the Fight Against AIDS." *International Peacekeeping* 9, no. 3:67–86.

Bray, Rachel. 2003. "Predicting the Social Consequences of Orphanhood in South Africa." Working Paper No. 29. Centre for Social Science Research, University of Cape Town.

Brown, Tim. 2000. "AIDS, Risk, and Social Governance." *Social Science and Medicine* 50, no. 9:1273–1284

Brown, Wendy. 2006. *Regulating Aversion: Tolerance in the Age of Identity and Empire.* Princeton, N.J.: Princeton University Press.

Buma, H., R. Veltink, E. van Ameijden, C. Tendeloo, and R. Coutinho. 1995. "Sexual Behaviour and Sexually Transmitted Diseases in Dutch Marines and Naval Personnel on a United Nations Mission in Cambodia." *Genitourin Medicine* 71, no. 3:172–175.

Burchell, Graham, Colin Gordon, and Peter Miller, eds. 1991. *The Foucault Effect: Studies in Governmentality.* Chicago: University of Chicago Press.

Burkhalter, Holly. 2004. "The Politics of AIDS: Engaging Conservative Activists." *Foreign Affairs* 83:8–14.

Butler, Judith. 2004. *Precarious Life: The Powers of Mourning and Violence.* London: Verso.

Buzan, Barry. 1991. *Peoples, States, and Fear: An Agenda for International Security Studies in the Post Cold War Era.* 2nd ed. Boulder, Colo.: Rienner; Hemel Hempstead: Harvester Wheatsheaf.

Buzan, Barry, and Ole Wæver. 1998. "Liberalism and Security: The Contradic-
tions of the Liberal Leviathan." Working Paper No. 23. Copenhagen Peace
Research Institute, Copenhagen.

Buzan, Barry, Ole Wæver, and Jaap de Wilde. 1998. *Security: A New Framework for
Analysis*. Boulder, Colo.: Rienner.

Bwire, G. S., and A. Musingunzi. 2004. "Trends of HIV in the Ugandan Military, 1991–2003." Paper presented at the Fourteenth International AIDS Conference, Bangkok. http://www.aegis.com/conferences/iac/2004/MoPeC3457
.html.

Campbell, David. 1998a. *National Deconstruction: Violence, Identity, and Justice in
Bosnia*. Minneapolis: University of Minnesota Press.

——. 1998b. "Why Fight: Humanitarianism, Principles, and Post-structuralism."
Millennium 27, no. 3:497–522.

——. 1998c. *Writing Security: United States Foreign Policy and the Politics of Identity*. Rev. ed. Minneapolis: University of Minnesota Press; Manchester: Manchester University Press.

——. 2005. "The Biopolitics of Security: Oil, Empire, and the Sports Utility Vehicle." *American Quarterly* 57, no. 3:943–972.

——. 2008. "The Visual Economy of HIV/AIDS." A Report for the AIDS, Security,
and Conflict Initiative.

Campbell, David, and Michael Dillon, eds. 1993. *The Political Subject of Violence*.
Manchester: Manchester University Press.

Carballo, Manuel, Carolyn Mansfield, and Michaela Prokop. 2000. *Demobiliza-
tion and Implications for HIV/AIDS*. Geneva: International Centre for Migration and Health.

Cartwright, Frederick. 1972. *Disease and History*. Stroud: Sutton.

Castel, Robert. 1991. "From Dangerousness to Risk." In Graham Burchell, Colin
Gordon, and Peter Miller, eds., *The Foucault Effect: Studies in Governmentality*,
281–298. Chicago: University of Chicago Press.

CBACI. 2000. *Contagion and Conflict: Health as a Global Security Challenge*. Washington, D.C.: Chemical and Biological Arms Control Institute.

Cerny, Philip. 2003. "The Governmentalization of World Politics." Paper presented at the annual convention of the International Studies Association,
Portland, Ore.

Cheek, Randy. 2001. "Playing God with HIV: Rationing HIV Treatment in
Southern Africa." *African Security Review* 10, no. 4:19–28.

Cheluget, Boaz, Caroline Ngare, Joseph Wahiu, Lawrence Mwikya, Stephen
Kinoti, and Bannet Ndyanabangi. 2003. "Impact of HIV/AIDS on Public
Health Sector Personnel in Kenya." Paper presented at the ECSA Regional
Health Ministers' Conference, Livingstone, Zambia.

Chen, Lincoln. 2004. "Health as a Human Security Priority for the 21st Century." Paper prepared for Helsinki Process, Human Security Track III. http://ochaonline.un.org/OchaLinkClick.aspx?link=ocha&docId=1087411.

Chen, Lincoln, Jennifer Leaning, and Vasant Narasimhan, eds. 2003. *Global Health Challenges for Human Security*. Cambridge, Mass.: Harvard University Press.

Chen, Lincoln, and Vasant Narasimhan. 2003. "A Human Security Agenda for Global Health." In Lincoln Chen, Jennifer Leaning, and Vasant Narasimhan, eds., *Global Health Challenges for Human Security*, 3–12. Cambridge, Mass.: Harvard University Press.

Chin, James. 2007. *The AIDS Pandemic: The Collision of Epidemiology with Political Correctness*. Abingdon: Radcliffe.

Chowka, Peter. 2000. "AIDS Deemed a 'National Security' Threat by U.S. as South African President Challenges Medical Orthodoxy." *Natural Healthline*, May 1. http://www.naturalhealthvillage.com/newsletter/01may00/aids.htm.

Clarke, Alison. 2004. "'Health on the Road': Designing HIV/AIDS Programs for Truck Drivers." Horizons Report. Population Council, Washington, D.C., June. http://www.popcouncil.org/horizons/newsletter/horizons(8)_3.html.

Coker, Christopher. 2002. *Globalization and Insecurity in the Twenty-first Century: NATO and the Management of Risk*. International Institute for Strategic Studies. Adelphi Paper No. 345. Oxford: Oxford University Press.

Coker, Richard. 2003. "Migration, Public Health, and Compulsory Screening for TB and HIV." Asylum and Migration Working Paper 1. Institute for Public Policy Research, London.

Commission on Human Security. 2003. *Human Security Now*. New York: United Nations Commission on Human Security. http://www.humansecurity-chs.org/finalreport/English/FinalReport.pdf.

Conklin, Steve. 2003. "Interview with Radhika Sarin, Author of *The Enemy Within: AIDS in the Military*." World Watch Institute, Washington, D.C., March 28. http://www.worldwatch.org/live/discussion/70/.

Constantinou, Costas. 2004. *States of Political Discourse: Words, Regimes, Seditions*. London: Routledge.

Cook, Daniel. 2007. "India's Cheap Drugs Under Patent Threat." BBC News, February 15. http://news.bbc.co.uk/1/hi/world/south_asia/6358721.stm?ls.

Cooter, Roger, Mark Harrison, and Steve Sturdy, eds. 1998. *War, Medicine, and Modernity*. Stroud: Sutton.

Coward, Martin. 2006. "Securing the Global (Bio)political Economy: Empire, Post-structuralism, and Political Economy." In Marieke de Goede, ed., *International Political Economy and Poststructural Politics*, 60–76. Basingstoke: Palgrave.

Crawford, Dorothy. 2007. *Deadly Companions: How Microbes Shaped Our History*. Oxford: Oxford University Press.

CSIS. 1994. *Global HIV/AIDS: A Strategy for U.S. Leadership*. Washington, D.C.: Center for Strategic and International Studies.

——. 2002. *The Destabilizing Impacts of HIV/AIDS*. Washington, D.C.: Center for Strategic and International Studies.

——. 2004. *India at the Crossroads: Confronting the HIV/AIDS Challenge*. Washington, D.C.: Center for Strategic and International Studies.

——. 2006. *Public Health and International Security: The Case of India*. Washington, D.C.: Center for Strategic and International Studies.

Cullet, Philippe. 2003. "Patents and Medicines: The Relationship Between TRIPS and the Human Right to Health." *International Affairs* 79, no. 1:139–160.

Curtin, Philip. 1998. *Disease and Empire: The Health of European Troops in the Conquest of Africa*. Cambridge: Cambridge University Press.

Curtis, Bruce. 2002. "Foucault on Governmentality and Population: The Impossible Discovery." *Canadian Journal of Sociology* 27, no. 4: 505–533.

David, Marcella. 2001. "Rubber Helmets: The Certain Pitfalls of Marshaling Security Council Resources to Combat AIDS in Africa." *Human Rights Quarterly* 23, no. 3:560–582.

Dean, Mitchell. 1999. *Governmentality: Power and Rule in Modern Society*. London: Sage.

de Cock, Kevin, Dorothy Mbori-Ngacha, and Elizabeth Marum. 2002. "Shadow on the Continent: Public Health and HIV/AIDS in Africa in the 21st Century." *Lancet* 360:67–72.

Deudney, Daniel. 1990. "The Case Against Linking Environmental Degradation and National Security." *Millennium* 19, no. 3:461–476.

de Waal, Alex. 2002. "'New-Variant' Famine: How AIDS Has Changed the Hunger Equation." http://allafrica.com/stories/200211200471.html.

——. 2003a. "HIV/AIDS: The Security Issue of a Lifetime." In Lincoln Chen, Jennifer Leaning, and Vasant Narasimhan, eds., *Global Health Challenges for Human Security*, 125–140. Cambridge, Mass.: Harvard University Press.

——. 2003b. "How Will HIV/AIDS Transform African Governance?" *African Affairs* 102:1–23.

——. 2006. *AIDS and Power: Why There Is No Political Crisis—Yet*. London: Zed Books.

——. 2007. "Expert Meeting on the Police and HIV/AIDS." Draft Chairperson's Summary. Atlantic Hotel, Kijkduin, September 3–4. http://www.justiceafrica.org/wp-content/uploads/2007/09/aids-police-summary-report.doc.

Diamond, Jared. 1997. *Guns, Germs, and Steel: The Fates of Human Societies*. New York: Norton.

Dillon, Michael. 1995. "Sovereignty and Governmentality: From the Problematics of the New World Order to the Ethical Problematic of the World Order." *Alternatives* 20:323–368.

——. 1996. *Politics of Security: Towards a Political Philosophy of Continental Thought.* London: Routledge.

——. 2004. "The Security of Governance." In Wendy Larner and William Walters, eds., *Global Governmentality*, 76–94. London: Routledge.

——. 2008. "Underwriting Security." *Security Dialogue* 39, nos. 2–3:309–332.

Dillon, Michael, and Luis Lobo-Guerrero. 2008a. "Biopolitics of Security in the 21st Century: An Introduction." *Review of International Studies* 34, no. 2:265–292.

——. 2008b. "The Biopolitical Imaginary of Species Being and the Freedom to Underwrite in the Molecular Age." *Theory, Culture, and Society.* Forthcoming.

Dillon, Michael, and Julian Reid. 2000. "Global Governance, Liberal Peace, and Complex Emergency." *Alternatives* 25, no. 4:117–145.

——. 2001. "Global Liberal Governance: Biopolitics, Security, and War." *Millennium* 30, no. 1:41–66.

Dodgson, Richard, and Kelley Lee. 2002. "Global Health Governance: A Conceptual Overview." In Rorden Wilkinson and Steve Hughes, eds., *Global Governance: Critical Perspectives*, 92–110. London: Routledge.

Drimie, Scott. 2003. "HIV/AIDS and Land: Case Studies from Kenya, Lesotho, and South Africa." *Development Southern Africa* 20, no. 5:647–658.

Duffield, Mark. 2001. *Global Governance and the New Wars: The Merging of Development and Security.* London: Zed Books.

——. 2005. "Human Security: Linking Development and Security in an Age of Terror." Paper prepared for the GDI panel "New Interfaces Between Security and Development," at the Eleventh General Conference of the EADI, Bonn. http://eadi.org/gc2005/confweb/papersps/Mark_Duffield.pdf.

——. 2007. *Development, Security, and Unending War: Governing the World of Peoples.* Cambridge: Polity.

Duffield, Mark, and Nicholas Waddell. 2004. "Human Security and Global Danger: Exploring a Governmental Assemblage." Department of Politics and International Relations, University of Lancaster, October. http://www.bond.org.uk/pubs/gsd/duffield.pdf.

Eberstadt, Nicholas. 2002. "The Future of AIDS." *Foreign Affairs* 81, no. 6:22–45.

Eboko, Fred. 2005. "Patterns of Mobilization: Political Culture in the Fight Against AIDS." Translated by Babacar Mbengue. In Amy S. Patterson, ed., *The African State and the AIDS Crisis*, 37–58. Aldershot: Ashgate.

Elbe, Stefan. 2002. "HIV/AIDS and the Changing Landscape of War in Africa." *International Security* 27, no. 2:159–177.

——. 2003. *The Strategic Implications of HIV/AIDS.* International Institute for Strategic Studies. Adelphi Paper No. 357. Oxford: Oxford University Press.

——. 2004. "Aid gegen AIDS: Die Auswirkungen von HIV/AIDS müssen in der Entwicklungspolitik einbezogen werden." *Internationale Politik* 59, nos. 11–12:65–73.

——. 2005a. "AIDS, Security, Biopolitics." *International Relations* 19, no. 4:403–419.

——. 2005b. "The European Security Strategy and the Global Challenge of Disease." In Antonio Missiroli, ed., *A "D" Drive for the EU: Disasters, Diseases, Disruptions*, 51–66. Chaillot Paper No. 83. Paris: European Union Institute for Security Studies.

——. 2005c. "HIV/AIDS: The International Security Dimensions." In Elke Krahmann, ed., *New Threats and New Actors in International Security*, 111–130. New York: Palgrave.

——. 2005d. "Sida, un enjeu global de sécurité." Translated by Dominique David. *Politique étrangère* 1:165–177.

——. 2006a. "HIV/AIDS: A Human Security Challenge for the 21st Century." *Whitehead Journal of Diplomacy and International Relations* 7:101–113.

——. 2006b. "HIV/AIDS and Security." In Alan Collins, ed., *Contemporary Security Studies*, 331–345. Oxford: Oxford University Press.

——. 2006c. "Should HIV/AIDS Be Securitized? The Ethical Dilemmas of Linking HIV/AIDS and Security." *International Studies Quarterly* 50, no. 1:119–144.

Evans, Richard. 1988. "Epidemics and Revolutions: Cholera in Nineteenth-Century Europe." *Past and Present* 120:123–146.

FAO. 2001. "The Impact of HIV/AIDS on Food Security." Report prepared for the twenty-seventh session of the Committee on World Food Security. Food and Agricultural Organization, Rome, May 28–June 1. http://www.fao.org/docrep/meeting/003/y0310e.htm.

——. 2003. *HIV/AIDS and Agriculture: Impacts and Responses—Case Studies from Namibia, Uganda, and Zambia*. Rome: Food and Agricultural Organization.

Farmer, Paul. 2001. *Infections and Inequalities: The Modern Plagues*. Berkeley: University of California Press.

Feshbach, Murray. 2005. "HIV/AIDS in the Russian Military—Update." Report prepared for the meeting of UNAIDS, Copenhagen.

Fidas, George. 2001. "Infectious Disease and Global Security." Paper presented at the conference "International Disease Surveillance and Global Security," Stanford University, Palo Alto, Calif.

Fidler, David. 1998. "Microbialpolitik: Infectious Diseases and International Relations." *American University International Law Review* 14, no. 1:1–11.

——. 1999. *International Law and Infectious Diseases*. Oxford: Clarendon Press.

——. 2003. "Public Health and National Security in the Global Age: Infectious Diseases, Bioterrorism, and Realpolitik." *George Washington International Law Review* 35:787–856.

——. 2004. *SARS: Governance and the Globalization of Disease*. New York: Palgrave.

Fisher-Thompson, Jim. 2005. "Kenya Provides Firm Ground for U.S. Military AIDS Partnership." Department of State Information Service, Washington, D.C., February 18. http://usinfo.state.gov/gi/Archive/2005/Feb/22-541177.html.

Foucault, Michel. 1975. *Discipline and Punish: The Birth of the Prison*. Translated by Alan Sheridan. London: Penguin Books.

——. 1976. *The History of Sexuality: An Introduction*. Translated by Robert Hurley. London: Penguin Books.

——. 1980. *Power/Knowledge: Selected Interviews and Other Writings, 1972–1977*. London: Harvester.

——. 1981. "The Meshes of Power." Translated by Gerald Moore. In Jeremy Crampton and Stuart Elden, eds., *Space, Knowledge, and Power: Foucault and Geography*, 153–162. Aldershot: Ashgate, 2007.

——. 1988. "Truth, Power, Self: An Interview with Michel Foucault." In Luther H. Martin, Huck Gutman, and Patrick H. Hutton, eds., *Technologies of the Self*, 9–15. London: Tavistock.

——. 1991. "Governmentality." In Graham Burchell, Colin Gordon, and Peter Miller, eds., *The Foucault Effect: Studies in Governmentality*, 87–104. Chicago: University of Chicago Press.

——. 1997a. "The Ethics of the Concern for Self as a Practice of Freedom." In *Essential Works of Foucault*. Vol. 1, *Ethics: Subjectivity and Truth*, 281–302. Edited by Paul Rabinow. Translated by Robert Hurley et al. New York: New Press.

——. 1997b. "An Interview by Stephen Riggins." In *Essential Works of Foucault*. Vol. 1, *Ethics: Subjectivity and Truth*, 121–134. Edited by Paul Rabinow. Translated by Robert Hurley et al. New York: New Press.

——. 1997c. "On the Genealogy of Ethics: An Overview of Work in Progress." In *Essential Works of Foucault*. Vol. 1, *Ethics: Subjectivity and Truth*, 253–280. Edited by Paul Rabinow. Translated by Robert Hurley et al. New York: New Press.

——. 1997d. "Sex, Power, and the Politics of Identity." In *Essential Works of Foucault*. Vol. 1, *Ethics: Subjectivity and Truth*, 163–174. Edited by Paul Rabinow. Translated by Robert Hurley et al. New York: New Press.

——. 1997e. "Sexual Choice, Sexual Act." In *Essential Works of Foucault*. Vol. 1, *Ethics: Subjectivity and Truth*, 141–156. Edited by Paul Rabinow. Translated by Robert Hurley et al. New York: New Press.

——. 1997f. "Society Must Be Defended." In *Essential Works of Foucault*. Vol. 1, *Ethics: Subjectivity and Truth*, 59–66. Edited by Paul Rabinow. Translated by Robert Hurley et al. New York: New Press.

——. 2000a. "The Birth of Social Medicine." In *Essential Works of Foucault*. Vol. 3, *Power*, 134–156. Edited by James Faubion. Translated by Robert Hurley et al. New York: New Press.

——. 2000b. "Confronting Governments: Human Rights." In *Essential Works of Foucault*. Vol. 3, *Power*, 474–475. Edited by James Faubion. Translated by Robert Hurley et al. New York: New Press.

——. 2000c. "Interview with Michel Foucault." In *Essential Works of Foucault*. Vol. 3, *Power*, 239–297. Edited by James Faubion. Translated by Robert Hurley et al. New York: New Press.

——. 2000d. "*Omnes et Singulatim*: Towards a Critique of Political Reason." In *Essential Works of Foucault*. Vol. 3, *Power*, 298–325. Edited by James Faubion. Translated by Robert Hurley et al. New York: New Press.

——. 2000e. "The Political Technology of Individuals." In *Essential Works of Foucault*. Vol. 3, *Power*, 403–417. Edited by James Faubion. Translated by Robert Hurley et al. New York: New Press.

——. 2000f. "The Politics of Health in the Eighteenth Century." In *Essential Works of Foucault*. Vol. 3, *Power*, 90–105. Edited by James Faubion. Translated by Robert Hurley et al. New York: New Press.

——. 2000g. "Questions of Method." In *Essential Works of Foucault*. Vol. 3, *Power*, 223–238. Edited by James Faubion. Translated by Robert Hurley et al. New York: New Press.

——. 2000h. "The Subject and Power." In *Essential Works of Foucault*. Vol. 3, *Power*, 326–348. Edited by James Faubion. Translated by Robert Hurley et al. New York: New Press.

——. 2000i. "Truth and Power." In *Essential Works of Foucault*. Vol. 3, *Power*, 111–133. Edited by James Faubion. Translated by Robert Hurley et al. New York: New Press.

——. 2003. *Society Must Be Defended: Lectures at the Collège de France, 1975–1976*. Translated by David Macy. New York: Picador.

——. 2007. *Security, Territory, Population: Lectures at the Collège de France, 1977–1978*. Translated by Graham Burchell. New York: Palgrave.

Fourie, Pieter, and Martin Schönteich. 2001. "Africa's New Security Threat: HIV/AIDS and Human Security in Southern Africa." *African Security Review* 10, no. 4:29–44.

Frolov, Vladimir. 2004. "Annex 2: The National Security Implications of the HIV/AIDS Epidemic in Russia." In *Reversing the Epidemic: HIV/AIDS in Eastern Europe and the Commonwealth of Independent States*, 91–96. Bratislava: United Nations Development Program.

Gabriel, Richard, and Karen Metz, eds. 1992. *A History of Military Medicine*. Vol. 1. Westport, Conn.: Greenwood Press.

GAO. 2001. *U.N. Peacekeeping: United Nations Faces Challenges in Responding to the Impact of HIV/AIDS on Peacekeeping Operations*. Washington, D.C.: General Accounting Office.

Garrett, Laurie. 1994. *The Coming Plague: Newly Emerging Diseases in a World Out of Balance*. New York: Penguin Books.

——. 1996. "The Return of Infectious Disease." *Foreign Affairs*, January–February, 66–79.

——. 2000. *Betrayal of Trust: The Collapse of Global Public Health*. New York: Hyperion.

——. 2005. *HIV and National Security: Where Are the Links?* New York: Council on Foreign Relations.

Gellman, Barton. 2000. "The Belated Global Response to AIDS in Africa: World Shunned Signs of the Coming Plague." *Washington Post*, July 5.

Gillespie, Stuart, ed. 2006. *AIDS, Poverty, and Hunger: Challenges and Responses*. Washington, D.C.: International Food Policy Research Institute.

Godwin, Peter, ed. 1998. *The Looming Epidemic: The Impact of HIV and AIDS in India*. London: Hurst.

Gordon, Collin. 1991. "Governmental Rationality: An Introduction." In Graham Burchell, Colin Gordon, and Peter Miller, eds., *The Foucault Effect: Studies in Governmentality*, 1–52. Chicago: University of Chicago Press.

Gordon, Peter, Ruth Jacobson, and Tom Porteous. 2004. *A Study to Establish the Connections Between HIV/AIDS and Conflict*. London: John Snow International.

Grasso, June, Jay Corrin, and Michael Kort. 2004. *Modernization and Revolution in China: From the Opium Wars to World Power*. 3rd ed. New York: Sharpe.

Grisin, Sarah, and Celeste Wallander. 2002. *Russia's HIV/AIDS Crisis: Confronting the Present and Facing the Future*. Washington, D.C.: Center for Strategic and International Studies.

Grover, Anand. 2004. "Letter from the Affordable Medicines Treatment Campaign to India's National Human Rights Commission." *Human Rights News*. Human Rights Watch, New York, October 11. http://www.hrw.org/english/docs/2004/10/22/india9556.htm.

Halle, Christian. 2002. Presentation at the conference "HIV/AIDS as a Threat to Global Security," Yale University, New Haven, Conn.

Hankins, Catherine A., S. R. Friedman, T. Zafar, and S. A. Strathdee. 2002. "Transmission and Prevention of HIV and Sexually Transmitted Infections in War Settings: Implications for Current and Future Armed Conflicts." *AIDS* 16, no. 17:2245–2252.

Happymon, Jacob. 2005. *HIV/AIDS as a Security Threat to India*. New Delhi: Manohar.

Hardt, Michael, and Antonio Negri. 2000. *Empire*. Cambridge, Mass.: Harvard University Press.

Harker, John. 2001. "HIV/AIDS and the Security Sector in Africa: A Threat to Canada." Canadian Security Intelligence Service, Ottawa. http://www.csis-scrs.gc.ca/eng/comment/com80_e.html.

Healthlink. 2002. *Combat AIDS: HIV and the World's Armed Forces*. London: Healthlink Worldwide.

Heinecken, Lindy. 2001a. "Living in Terror: The Looming Security Threat to Southern Africa." *African Security Review* 10, no. 4:7–17.

——. 2001b. "Strategic Implications of HIV/AIDS in South Africa." *Conflict, Security, and Development* 1, no. 1:109–113.

——. 2003. "Facing a Merciless Enemy: HIV/AIDS and the South African Armed Forces." *Armed Forces and Society* 29, no. 2:281–300.

Heymann, Denis. 2003. "Evolving Infectious Disease Threats to National and Global Security." In Lincoln Chen, Jennifer Leaning, and Vasant Narasimhan, eds., *Global Health Challenges for Human Security*, 105–124. Cambridge, Mass.: Harvard University Press.

Hinsliff, Gaby. 2003. "Britain Slams the Door on Foreign NHS Cheats." *Observer*, February 9.

Hodgson, Martin. 2001. "Rebels Expel HIV Victims from Homes." *Guardian*, October 23.

Holachek, Jeffrey. 2006. *Russia's Shrinking Population and the Russian Military's HIV/AIDS Problem*. Washington, D.C.: Atlantic Council of the United States.

Holbrooke, Richard. 2000a. "UN Doing Too Little About AIDS Among Peacekeepers: Holbrooke." Agence France-Presse, December 22.

——. 2000b. Comments on Voice of America, June 8.

Holden, Sue. 2003. *AIDS on the Agenda: Adapting Development and Humanitarian Programs to Meet the Challenge of HIV/AIDS*. Oxford: Oxfam.

HSR. 2005. *Human Security Report 2005: War and Peace in the 21st Century*. Human Security Centre, University of British Columbia. Oxford: Oxford University Press.

Huang, Yanzhong. 2003. *Mortal Peril: Public Health in China and Its Security Implications*. Washington, D.C.: Chemical and Biological Arms Control Institute.

Human Rights Watch. 2003. *Just Die Quietly: Domestic Violence and Women's Vulnerability to HIV in Uganda*. New York: Human Rights Watch.

Huysmans, Jef. 1995. "Migrants as a Security Problem: Dangers of 'Securitizing' Societal Issues." In Robert Miles and Dietrich Thranhardt, eds., *Migration and European Integration*, 53–72. London: Pinter.

——. 1998. "Revisiting Copenhagen: Or, on the Creative Development of a Security Studies Agenda in Europe." *European Journal of International Relations* 4, no. 4:479–505.

——. 2000. "The European Union and the Securitization of Migration." *Journal of Common Market Studies* 38, no. 5:751–777.

——. 2004. "A Foucaultian View on Spill-Over: Freedom and Security in the EU." *Journal of International Relations and Development* 7, no. 3:294–318.

——. 2006. *The Politics of Insecurity: Fear, Migration, and Asylum in the EU.* London: Routledge.

ICG. 2001. *HIV/AIDS as a Security Issue.* Washington, D.C., and Brussels: International Crisis Group.

——. 2004. *HIV/AIDS as a Security Issue in Africa: Lessons from Uganda.* Kampala, Uganda, and Brussels: International Crisis Group.

Ingram, Alan. 2007. "HIV/AIDS, Security, and the Geopolitics of US-Nigerian Relations." *Review of International Political Economy* 14, no. 3:510–534.

International Conflict Research Group. 2002. "HIV/AIDS as a Threat to Global Security." Proceedings from conference, Yale University, New Haven, Conn., November 8–9.

Kalipeni, Ezekiel, Susan Craddock, Joseph R. Oppong, and Jayati Ghosh, eds. 2004. *HIV and AIDS in Africa: Beyond Epidemiology.* Oxford: Blackwell.

Kasselow, Jordan. 2001. *Why Health Is Important to U.S. Foreign Policy.* New York: Council on Foreign Relations.

Kauffman, Kyle, and David Lindauer, eds. 2004. *AIDS and South Africa: The Social Expression of a Pandemic.* Basingstoke: Palgrave.

Keim, Willard. 2000. *Ethics, Morality, and International Affairs.* Lanham, Md.: University Press of America.

Kempe, Ronald, ed. 1999. *AIDS and Development in Africa: A Social Science Perspective.* New York: Haworth.

Kesby, Mike. 2004. "Participatory Diagramming and the Ethical and Practical Challenges of Helping Themselves to Move HIV Work 'Beyond Epidemiology.'" In Ezekiel Kalipeni, Susan Craddock, Joseph R. Oppong, and Jayati Ghosh, eds., *HIV and AIDS in Africa: Beyond Epidemiology,* 217–228. Oxford: Blackwell.

Kickbusch, Ilona. 2002. "Global Health Governance: Some Theoretical Considerations on the New Political Space." In Kelley Lee, ed., *Health Impacts of Globalization: Towards Global Governance,* 192–203. Basingstoke: Palgrave.

King, Gary, and Christopher J. L. Murray. 2001. "Rethinking Human Security." *Political Science Quarterly* 116, no. 4:585–611.

King, Nicholas. 2002. "Security, Disease, Commerce: Ideologies of Postcolonial Global Health." *Social Studies of Science* 32, nos. 5–6:763–789.

Kingma, Stuart. 2003. "The HIV/AIDS Pandemic and Critical Policy Issues for the Armed Forces." Paper presented at the Woodrow Wilson International Center for Scholars, Washington, D.C., April 22. http://www.wilsoncenter.org/index.cfm?fuseaction=events.event_summary&event_id=28265.

Kober, Katharina, and Wim van Damme. 2006. "Public Sector Nurses in Swaziland: Can the Downturn Be Reversed?" *Human Resources for Health* 4, no. 13:1–11.

Kristoffersson, Ulf. 2000. "HIV/AIDS as a Human Security Issue: A Gender Perspective." Paper presented at the expert group meeting "The HIV/AIDS Pandemic and Its Gender Implications," Windhoek, Namibia.

LaFraniere, Sharon. 2006. "Circumcision Studied in Africa as AIDS Preventive." *New York Times*, April 28.

Larner, Wendy, and William Walters, eds. 2004. *Global Governmentality*. London: Routledge.

Laubscher, P. 2001. "The Macroeconomic Impact of HIV/AIDS in South Africa." Research Note 10. Bureau for Economic Research, University of Stellenbosch.

Leander, Anna, and Rens van Munster. 2006. "Private Security Contractors in Darfur: Reflecting and Reinforcing Neo-liberal Governmentality." Working Paper No. 82. Copenhagen Business School, Copenhagen.

Lederberg, Joshua, Robert E. Shope, and Stanley C. Oaks, Jr., eds. 1992. *Emerging Infections: Microbial Threats to Health in the United States*. Committee on Emerging Microbial Threats to Health. Institute of Medicine. Washington, D.C.: National Academy Press.

Lee, Kelley. 2003. *Globalization and Health: An Introduction*. Basingstoke: Palgrave.

———, ed. 2002. *Health Impacts of Globalization: Towards Global Governance*. London: Palgrave.

Leen, Maura. 2004. *The European Union, HIV/AIDS, and Human Security*. Dublin: Dochas.

Lemke, Thomas. 1997. *Eine Kritik der politischen Vernunft: Foucaults Analyse der modernen Gouvernementalitaet*. Hamburg: Argument Verlag.

Levine, Philippa. 2003. *Prostitution, Race, and Politics: Policing Venereal Disease in the British Empire*. London: Routledge.

Lindahl, Anna, and Vivian Sundset. 2003. "The Grammar of Threat and Security in HIV/AIDS—An Analysis of the South African Government's Discourse on HIV and AIDS Between 1998–2002." Master's thesis, Department of Management and Economics, Linköping University, Linköping, Sweden.

Linge, Godfrey, and Doug Porter, eds. 1997. *No Place for Borders: The HIV/AIDS Epidemic and Development in Asia and the Pacific*. New York: St. Martin's Press.

Lippert, Randy. 1999. "Governing Refugees: The Relevance of Governmentality to Understanding the International Refugee Regime." *Alternatives* 24, no. 3:391–432.

Lipschutz, Ronnie. 2005. "Global Civil Society and Global Governmentality: Resistance, Reform, or Resignation?" In Gideon Baker and David Chandler, eds., *Global Civil Society: Contested Futures*, 171–185. London: Routledge.

Lipschutz, Ronnie, and James Rowe. 2005. *Globalization, Governmentality, and Global Politics: Regulation for the Rest of Us?* London: Routledge.

Lupton, Deborah. 1995. *The Imperative of Health: Public Health of the Regulated Body*. London: Sage.

Lurie, Peter, Percy C. Hintzen, and Robert A. Lowe. 2004. "Socioeconomic Obstacles to HIV Prevention in Developing Countries: The Roles of the International Monetary Fund and the World Bank." In Ezekiel Kalipeni, Susan Craddock, Joseph R. Oppong, and Jayati Ghosh, eds., *HIV and AIDS in Africa: Beyond Epidemiology*, 204–212. Oxford: Blackwell.

Lwanda, John. 2004. "Politics, Culture, and Medicine: An Unholy Trinity." In Ezekiel Kalipeni, Susan Craddock, Joseph R. Oppong, and Jayati Ghosh, eds., *HIV and AIDS in Africa: Beyond Epidemiology*, 15–28. Oxford: Blackwell.

MacFarlane, S. Neil, and Yuen Foong Khong. 2006. *Human Security and the UN: A Critical History*. Bloomington: Indiana University Press.

Macleod, Roy, and Milton Lewis, eds. 1988. *Disease, Medicine, and Empire: Perspectives on Western Medicine and the Experience of European Expansion*. London: Routledge.

Manning, Ryann. 2002. "AIDS and Democracy: What Do We Know? A Literature Review." Paper prepared for the workshop "AIDS and Democracy: Setting the Research Agenda," Cape Town, South Africa.

Mathers, Colin, and Dejan Loncar. 2006. "Projections of Global Mortality and Burden of Disease from 2002 to 2030." *PLoS Medicine* 3, no. 11:2011–2030.

Mattes, Robert. 2003. *Healthy Democracies? The Potential Impact of AIDS on Democracy in Southern Africa*. Pretoria: Institute for Security Studies.

Mazimpaka, Magnus. 2007. "Children Test for HIV." *Kigali New Times*, March 11.

McInnes, Colin. 2006. "HIV/AIDS and Security." *International Affairs* 82, no. 2:315–326.

McInnes, Colin, and Kelley Lee. 2006. "Health, Security, and Foreign Policy." *Review of International Studies* 32, no. 1:5–23.

McNeill, William. 1998. *Plagues and People*. New York: Anchor Books.

Medecins Sans Frontiers. 2005. "A Guide to the Post-2005 World: TRIPS, R&D, and Access to Medicines." http://www.msf.org/msfinternational/content/advocacy/accesstoessentialmedicinescampaign/index.cfm.

Merlingen, Michael. 2006. "Foucault and World Politics: Promises and Challenges of Extending Governmentality Theory to the European and Beyond." *Millennium* 35, no. 1:181–196.

Meyer, Jani. 2004. "SANDF Unveils Shock AIDS Data." *Sunday Independent* (South Africa), August 1.

Mills, Greg. 2000. "AIDS and the South African Military: Timeworn Cliché or Timebomb?" In Michael Lange, ed., *HIV/AIDS: A Threat to the African Renaissance?*, 67–73. Johannesburg: Konrad Adenauer Foundation.

Mock, Nancy. 2002. "HIV/AIDS in Our Ranks." Paper presented at the Woodrow Wilson International Center for Scholars, Washington, D.C. http://www.certi .org/strategy/military/role_of_the_military.htm.

Monitor. 2007. "Compulsory HIV Testing: Right Move." *Kampala Monitor*, March 11.

Morrison, J. Stephen, and Todd Summers. 2003. "United to Fight HIV/AIDS." *Washington Quarterly* 26, no. 4:177–193.

Mulanga, Claire, Samuel Edidi Bazepeo, Jeanne Kasali Mwamba, Christelle Butel, Jean-Willy Tshimpaka, Mulowayi Kashi, François Lepira, Michel Caraël, Martine Peeters, and Eric Delaporte. 2004. "Political and Socioeconomic Instability: How Does It Affect HIV? A Case Study in the Democratic Republic of Congo." *AIDS* 18, no. 5:832–834.

Museveni, Yoweri. 1995. Opening speech at the Ninth International Conference on AIDS and STDs in Africa, Kampala, Uganda. http://www.museveni.co.ug.

Newman, Laurie Marie, Felicidad Miguel, Bente Belo Jemusse, Agosto Cesar Macome, Robert David Newman. 2001. "HIV Seroprevalence Among Military Blood Donors in Manica Province, Mozambique." *International Journal of STD and AIDS* 12, no. 4:278–279.

NIC. 2000a. *The Global Infectious Disease Threat and Its Implications for the United States*. Washington, D.C.: National Intelligence Council. http://www.cia.gov/ cia/reports/nie/report/nie99–17d.html.

——. 2000b. *Global Trends 2015: A Dialogue About the Future with Nongovernment Experts*. Washington, D.C.: National Intelligence Council.

——. 2002. *The Next Wave of HIV/AIDS: Nigeria, Ethiopia, Russia, India, and China*. Washington, D.C.: National Intelligence Council. http://www.cia.gov/nic/ special_nextwaveHIV.html

OAU. 2001. "Abuja Declaration on HIV/AIDS, Tuberculosis, and Other Related Infectious Diseases." Organization of African Unity, Abuja, Nigeria. http:// www.un.org/ga/aids/pdf/abuja_declaration.pdf.

Odysseos, Louiza. 2002. "Dangerous Ontologies: The Ethos of Survival and Ethical Theorizing in International Relations." *Review of International Studies* 28, no. 2:403–418.

——. 2007. *The Subject of Coexistence: Otherness in International Relations*. Minneapolis: University of Minnesota Press.

Oldstone, Michael. 2000. *Viruses, Plagues, and History*. Oxford: Oxford University Press.

Ostergard, Robert L., Jr. 2002. "Politics in the Hot Zone: AIDS and National Security in Africa." *Third World Quarterly* 23, no. 2:333–350.

——, ed. 2005. *HIV, AIDS, and the Threat to National and International Security*. London: Palgrave.

Ostergard, Robert L., Jr., and Crystal Barcelo. 2005. "Personalist Regimes and the Insecurity Dilemma: Prioritizing AIDS as a National Security Threat in Uganda." In Amy S. Patterson, ed., *The African State and the AIDS Crisis*, 155–170. Aldershot: Ashgate.

Oxfam. 2004. "Undermining Access to Medicines: Comparison of Five US FTAs. A Technical Note." http://www.oxfam.org.uk/what_we_do/issues/health/downloads/undermining_access_ftas.pdf.

Paras, Eric. 2006. *Foucault 2.0: Beyond Power and Knowledge*. New York: Other Press.

Patocka, Jan. 1996. "Wars of the Twentieth Century and the Twentieth Century as War." In James Dodd, ed., *Heretical Essays in the Philosophy of History*, 119–138. Translated by Erazim Kohak. Chicago: Open Court.

Patterson, Amy S. 2006. *The Politics of AIDS in Africa*. London: Rienner.

——, ed. 2005. *The African State and the AIDS Crisis*. Aldershot: Ashgate.

Petersen, Alan, and Rubin Bunton, eds. 1997. *Foucault, Health, and Medicine*. London: Routledge.

Peterson, Susan. 2002/2003. "Epidemic Disease and National Security." *Security Studies* 12, no. 2:43–81.

Pharaoh, Robyn, and Martin Schönteich. 2003. *AIDS, Security, and Governance in Southern Africa: Exploring the Impact*. Pretoria: Institute for Security Studies.

Pilkington, Ed, and David Adam. 2007. "British Push on CO_2 at Security Council." BBC News, March 8.

Piot, Peter. 2000. "Global AIDS Pandemic: Time to Turn the Tide." *Science* 288:2176–2178.

——. 2001. "AIDS and Human Security." Speech delivered at the United Nations University, Tokyo. http://www.unaids.org/html/pub/media/speeches01/piot_tokyo_02oct01_en_doc.htm.

——. 2005a. Remarks at the Council on Foreign Relations meeting "HIV and National Security."

——. 2005b. "Why AIDS Is Exceptional." Speech delivered at the London School of Economics, London.

——. 2006. "Interview with Peter Piot." *Frontline: The Age of AIDS*. http://www.pbs.org/wgbh/pages/frontline/aids/interviews/piot.html#4.

Pisani, Elizabeth. 2008. *The Wisdom of Whores: Bureaucrats, Brothels, and the Business of AIDS*. London: Granta Books.

Poku, Nana, and Alan Whiteside. 2004. *The Political Economy of AIDS in Africa*. Aldershot: Ashgate.

Powell, Colin. 2001. Statement of Secretary of State–Designate Colin L. Powell Prepared for the Confirmation Hearing of the U.S. Senate Committee on Foreign Relations.

Price-Smith, Andrew. 1998. "Ghosts of Kigali: Infectious Disease and Global Stability at the Turn of the Century." *International Journal* 54:426–442.

——. 2001a. *The Health of Nations: Infectious Disease, Environmental Change, and Their Effects on National Security and Development.* Cambridge, Mass.: MIT Press.

——. 2001b. *Plagues and Politics: Infectious Disease and International Relations.* London: Palgrave.

——. 2002. *Pretoria's Shadow: The HIV/AIDS Pandemic and National Security in South Africa.* Washington, D.C.: Chemical and Biological Arms Control Institute.

Prins, Gwyn. 2004. "AIDS and Global Security." *International Affairs* 80, no. 5:931–952.

Prozorov, Sergei. 2007. *Foucault, Freedom, and Sovereignty.* Aldershot: Ashgate.

Quatteck, K. 2000. "Economic Impact of AIDS in South Africa: A Dark Cloud on the Horizon." In Michael Lange, ed., *HIV/AIDS: A Threat to the African Renaissance?*, 29–56. Johannesburg: Konrad Adenauer Foundation.

Rehle, Thoma. 2003. "Epidemiological and Demographic HIV/AIDS Projections: South Africa." *African Journal of AIDS Research* 2, no. 1:1–8.

Reid, Julian. 2005. "The Biopolitics of the War on Terror: A Critique of the 'Return of Imperialism' Thesis in International Relations." *Third World Quarterly* 26, no. 2:237–252.

——. 2006. *The Biopolitics of the War on Terror: Life Struggles, Liberal Modernity, and the Defence of Logistical Societies.* Manchester: Manchester University Press.

Rennie, Stuart, and Frieda Behets. 2006. "Desperately Seeking Targets: The Ethics of Routine HIV Testing in Low-Income Countries." *Bulletin of the World Health Organization* 84, no. 1:52–57.

Roffe, Pedro, and Ricardo Meléndez-Ortiz. 2005. *Resource Book on TRIPS and Development: An Authoritative and Practical Guide to the TRIPS Agreement.* Geneva: United Nations Conference on Trade and Development and the International Centre for Trade and Sustainable Development. http://www.iprsonline .org/unctadictsd/ResourceBookIndex.htm.

Rothschild, Emma. 1995. "What Is Security?" *Daedalus* 124, no. 3:53–98.

Sagala, John Kemoli. 2008. "HIV/AIDS Prevention Strategies in the Armed Forces in Sub-Saharan Africa: A Critical Review." *Armed Forces and Society* 34, no. 2:292–313.

Sanger, David. 2000. "Sometimes, National Security Says It All." *New York Times*, May 7.

Sarin, Radhika. 2003. "A New Security Threat: HIV/AIDS in the Military." *World Watch*, March–April, 17–22.

Schiller, Nina. 1992. "What's Wrong with This Picture? The Hegemonic Construction of Culture in AIDS Research in the United States." *Medical Anthropology Quarterly* 6, no. 3:237–254.

Schoepf, Brooke. 2004. "AIDS, History, and Struggles Over Meaning." In Ezekiel Kalipeni, Susan Craddock, Joseph R. Oppong, and Jayati Ghoshh, eds., *HIV and AIDS in Africa: Beyond Epidemiology*, 15–28. Oxford: Blackwell.

Schönteich, Martin. 1999. "Age and AIDS: South Africa's Crime Time Bomb?" *African Security Review* 8, no. 4:34–44.

Schoofs, Mark. 2000. "A New Kind of Crisis: The Security Council Declares AIDS in Africa a Threat to World Stability." *Village Voice*, January 12–18.

Seckinelgin, Hakan. 2008. *International Politics of HIV/AIDS: Global Disease— Local Pain*. London: Routledge.

Select Committee. 2001. *HIV/AIDS: The Impact on Social and Economic Development*. Third Report of the Select Committee on International Development. London: House of Commons.

Sell, Susan K., and Aseem Prakash. 2004. "Using Ideas Strategically: The Contest Between Business and NGO Networks in Intellectual Property Rights." *International Studies Quarterly* 48, no. 1:143–175.

Seña, A., W. Miller, I. Hoffman, H. Chakraborty, M. Cohen, P. Jenkins, and K. McKee Jr. 2000. "Trends of Gonorrhea and Chlamydial Infections During 1985–1996 Among Active Duty Soldiers at a United States Army Installation." *Clinical Infectious Diseases* 30:742–748.

Shaffer, Richard. 2005. "DoD International HIV/AIDS Activities." Paper presented to the Committee for the Evaluation of the President's Emergency Plan for AIDS Relief Implementation, Baltimore.

Shah, M., N. Osborne, T. Mbilizi, and G. Vilili. 2002. *Impact of HIV/AIDS on Agriculture Productivity and Rural Livelihoods in the Central Region of Malawi*. Lilongwe, Malawi: Care International.

Sharma, Kamalesh. 2001. "Statement by Mr. Kamalesh Sharma, Permanent Representative at the Open Meeting of the Security Council on the Responsibility of the Security Council in the Maintenance of International Peace and Security: HIV/AIDS and International Peacekeeping Operations." http://www.un.int/india/ind499.htm.

Sheehan, Carrie. 2002. "Securitizing Global Health Issues: HIV/AIDS in Africa as a U.S. National Security Threat." Paper presented at the annual convention of the International Studies Association, New Orleans, La.

Shisana, O., et al. 2003. *The Impact of HIV/AIDS on the Health Sector: National Survey of Health Personnel, Ambulatory and Hospitalised Patients, and Health Facilities*. Cape Town: HSRC Press.

Singer, Peter. 2002. "AIDS and International Security." *Survival* 44, no. 1:145–158.

Smit, Ben, and Linette Ellis. 2006. "The Macroeconomic Impact of HIV/AIDS Under Alternative Intervention Scenarios (with Specific Reference to ART) on the South African Economy." Bureau for Economic Research, University of Stellenbosch.

Sontag, Susan. 1988. *AIDS and Its Metaphors*. New York: Farrar, Straus and Giroux.

Spiegel, Paul. 2004. "HIV/AIDS Among Conflict-Affected and Displaced Populations: Dispelling Myths and Taking Action." *Disasters* 28, no. 3:322–339.

Sternberg, Steve. 2002. "Former Diplomat Holbrooke Takes on Global AIDS." *USA Today*, June 10.

Stolberg, Sheryl. 2003. "Bush Proposal on AIDS Funds Shows Concern About Security." *New York Times*, January 29.

Suter, Keith. 2003. *Global Order and Global Disorder: Globalization and the Nation-State*. Westport, Conn.: Praeger.

Tenet, George. 2003. Testimony of Director of Central Intelligence George J. Tenet Before the Senate Select Committee on Intelligence, Washington, D.C.

Thomas, Caroline. 2002. "Trade Policy and the Politics of Access to Drugs." *Third World Quarterly* 23, no. 2:251–264.

Thompson, Andrew. 2004. "International Security Challenges Posed by HIV/AIDS: Implications for China." *China: An International Journal* 2, no. 2:287–307.

Toro, Juan. 2001. "Colombian Rebels Forcing AIDS Tests." Associated Press, October 13.

Tripodi, Paolo, and Preeti Patel. 2002. "The Global Impact of HIV/AIDS on Peace Support Operations." *International Peacekeeping* 9, no. 3:51–66.

——. 2004. "HIV/AIDS, Peacekeeping, and Conflict Crises in Africa." *Medicine, Conflict, and Survival* 20, no. 3:195–208.

UCS. 2004. "Scientific Integrity in Policymaking: An Investigation Into the Bush Administration's Misuse of Science." Union of Concerned Scientists.

UNAIDS. 1998. *AIDS and the Military*. Geneva: UNAIDS. http://data.unaids.org/Publications/IRC-pub05/militarypv_en.pdf.

——. 2001a. *AIDS Epidemic Update*. Geneva: UNAIDS. http://www.unaids.org/en/KnowledgeCentre/HIVData/EpiUpdate/EpiUpdArchive/.

——. 2001b. "AIDS Now Core Issue at UN Security Council." Press release, New York.

——. 2001c. "Report of the UNAIDS Expert Panel on HIV Testing in United Nations Peacekeeping Operations." http://data.unaids.org/pub/Report/2001/20011130_peacekeeping_en.pdf.

——. 2003a. "Current Debates on HIV Testing and Counseling." Issue paper for the second meeting of the UNAIDS Global Reference Group on HIV/AIDS and Human Rights. http://data.unaids.org/Topics/Human-Rights/hrissuepaper_currentdebates_en.pdf.

——. 2003b. "HIV/AIDS and Uniformed Services." Fact sheet, Geneva.

——. 2003c. *On the Front Line: A Review of Policies and Programs to Address HIV/AIDS Among Peacekeepers and Uniformed Services*. Geneva: UNAIDS.

——. 2005. *On the Front Line: A Review of Policies and Programs to Address HIV/ AIDS Among Peacekeepers and Uniformed Services*. 3rd rev. Geneva: UNAIDS.

——. 2006a. *AIDS Epidemic Update*. Geneva: UNAIDS. http://www.unaids .org/en/KnowledgeCentre/HIVData/EpiUpdate/EpiUpdArchive/.

——. 2006b. *2006 Report on the Global AIDS Epidemic*. Geneva: UNAIDS. http:// www.unaids.org/en/KnowledgeCentre/HIVData/GlobalReport/2006/.

——. 2007a. *AIDS Epidemic Update*. Geneva: UNAIDS. http://www.unaids .org/en/KnowledgeCentre/HIVData/EpiUpdate/EpiUpdArchive/.

——. 2007b. *Annual Report 2006: Making the Money Work*. Geneva: UNAIDS. http:// data.unaids.org/pub/Report/2007/2006_unaids_annual_report_en.pdf.

UNDP. 1994. *Human Development Report, 1994: New Dimensions of Human Security*. United Nations Development Program. Oxford: Oxford University Press.

UNSC. 2000a. Resolution 1308.

——. 2000b. Transcript of the 4087th Meeting of the United Nations Security Council. S/PV.4087.

U.S. Congress. 2003. United States Leadership Against HIV/AIDS, Tuberculosis, and Malaria Act of 2003. http://www.govtrack.us/congress/billtext.xpd?bill = h108–1298.

U.S. Department of Defense. 2005. Background Information on HIV/AIDS Prevention Program. http://www.nhrc.navy.mil/programs/dhapp/background/ background.html.

U.S. Department of Health and Human Services. 2005. Ryan White Comprehensive AIDS Resources Emergency (CARE) Act. http://hab.hrsa.gov/history .htm.

USIP. 2001. *AIDS and Violent Conflict in Africa*. Washington, D.C.: United States Institute of Peace.

Vaughan, Megan. 1991. *Curing Their Ills: Colonial Power and African Illness*. Cambridge: Polity.

Vieira, Marco. 2007. "The Securitization of the HIV/AIDS Epidemic as a Norm: A Contribution to Constructivist Scholarship on the Emergence and Diffusion of International Norms." *Brazilian Political Science Review* 1, no. 2:137–181.

Wæver, Ole. 1995. "Securitization and Desecuritization." In Ronnie Lipschutz, ed., *On Security*, 46–86. New York: Columbia University Press.

Wæver, Ole, Barry Buzan, and Morten Kelstrup. 1993. *Identity, Migration, and the New Security Agenda in Europe*. New York: St. Martin's Press.

Walker, R. B. J. 1993. *Inside/Outside: International Relations as Political Theory*. Cambridge: Cambridge University Press.

Walters, William, and Jens Haahr. 2005. "Governmentality and Political Studies." *European Political Science* 4:288–300.

Watts, Sheldon. 1997. *Epidemics and History: Disease, Power, and Imperialism*. New Haven, Conn.: Yale University Press.

Whitehead, Paul C., and David Carpenter. 1999. "Explaining Unsafe Sexual Behavior: Cultural Definitions and Health in the Military." *Culture, Health, and Sexuality* 1, no. 4:303–315.

Whiteside, Alan, Alex de Waal, and Tsadkan Gebre-Tensae. 2006. "AIDS, Security, and the Military in Africa: A Sober Appraisal." *African Affairs* 105, no. 419:210–218.

Whiteside, Alan, and Clem Sunter. 2000. *AIDS: The Challenge for South Africa.* Cape Town: Human and Rousseau.

Whiteside, Alan, and Amy Whalley. 2007. *Reviewing "Emergencies" for Swaziland: Shifting the Paradigm in a New Era.* Durban: Health Economics and HIV/AIDS Research Division, University of KwaZulu-Natal.

Whitman, Jim. 2000. "Political Processes and Infectious Diseases." In Jim Whitman, ed., *The Politics of Emerging and Resurgent Infectious Diseases*, 1–14. London: Palgrave.

WHO. 2001. *Macroeconomics and Health: Investing in Health for Economic Development.* Report of the Commission on Macroeconomics and Health. Geneva: World Health Organization.

——. 2004. *World Health Report 2004.* Geneva: World Health Organization.

——. 2007. *Towards Universal Access: Scaling Up Priority HIV/AIDS Interventions in the Health Sector.* Geneva: World Health Organization.

Williams, Michael. 2003. "Words, Images, Enemies: Securitization and International Politics." *International Studies Quarterly* 47, no. 4:511–531.

Wolfenson, James. 2000. Speech delivered to the United Nations Security Council, New York, January 10.

World Trade Organization. 1994. "The Agreement on Trade-Related Aspects of Intellectual Property Rights." http://www.wto.org/english/docs_e/legal_e/27-trips_01_e.htm.

Yeager, Rodger, and Stuart Kingma. 2001. "HIVAIDS: Destabilizing National Security and the Multi-National Response." *International Review of the Armed Forces Medical Services* 74, nos. 1–3:3–12.

Yeager, Rodger, and Donna Ruscavage. 2000. *HIV Prevention and Behavior Change in International Military Populations.* Complex Emergency Response and Transition Initiative (CERTI). Tulane University, New Orleans.

Youde, Jeremy. 2005. "Enter the Fourth Horseman: Health Security and International Relations Theory." *Whitehead Journal of Diplomacy and International Relations* 6, no. 1:193–208.

——. 2007. *AIDS, South Africa, and the Politics of Knowledge.* Aldershot: Ashgate.

Zinsser, Hans. 1937. *Rats, Lice, and History.* Boston: Little, Brown.